MISTRESSES
OF
MAYHEM

MISTRESSES
OF
MAYHEM

The Book of Women Criminals

By Francine Hornberger

ALPHA

A Pearson Education Company

International Standard Book Number: 0-02-864260-0
Library of Congress Catalog Card Number: 2002101639

04   03   02   8   7   6   5   4   3   2   1

Interpretation of the printing code: The rightmost number of the first series of numbers is the year of the book's printing; the rightmost number of the second series of numbers is the number of the book's printing. For example, a printing code of 02-1 shows that the first printing occurred in 2002.

Printed in the United States of America

Note: This publication contains the opinions and ideas of its author. It is intended to provide helpful and informative material on the subject matter covered. It is sold with the understanding that the author and publisher are not engaged in rendering professional services in the book. If the reader requires personal assistance or advice, a competent professional should be consulted.

For my parents, Paul and Francine Hornberger Sr.—
for their perpetual love and encouragement.

Contents

Foreword

> This is a violent country. There is no reason this wouldn't have rubbed off on [women].
>
> —Coramae Ritchey Mann, Ph.D., Professor Emerita of Criminal Justice, Indiana University

Several years ago, when I was still editing and publishing true crime, I read a very interesting proposal by a female criminologist about the growing phenomenon of female serial killers. What struck me as the most informative fact about the female serial killer was that they differed very little from their male counterparts. Usually coming from an abusive background and having experienced multiple violent sexual relationships as adults, the women exploded in violence with the same ferocity as their male counterparts. Many women had a history of torturing small animals. There was even evidence for the controversial theory championed by the late Dr. Joel Norris that these women had sustained head injuries earlier in life and this affected their ability to control their violent urges.

However, the one thing that seems to separate the men from the women is the sexual component to their murders. Male serial killers murder to satisfy a twisted urge that links sexual fulfillment with violence. Richard Ramirez, Ed Gein, Arthur Shawcross, even Jeffrey Dahmer, all killed the object of their personal sexual desires, often achieving orgasm directly before, during, or after the murder. The frequency of the murders often escalated as the need for gratification grew stronger. Cannibalism, necrophilia, and sexual mutilation often played as integral a role as the murder itself for these killers.

Women killers seem to have a different MO. They murder for a reason other than perverted pleasure: revenge, money, hormonal imbalance after pregnancy, power, drug addiction, even as a means of escape from an abusive marriage or parental relationship. The rare exceptions are women who kill to enhance their sexual relationship with their men such as the infamous couple killers Gerald and Charlene Gallego. But aside from these cases, women are practical in their killing, deriving some sort of "objective benefits" for themselves or their loved one by their crimes.

Fascinating stuff. But if you look at the whole range of criminal activity, the story becomes even more interesting. Every year, the prison population of violent women criminals grows much faster than the male population. "Now, with equal rights, the justice system is looking at females differently," says Dr. Coramae Ritchey Mann. "Whereas before they were excused or overlooked, now they are being apprehended." There are no longer crimes that are deemed the exclusive territory for male offenders. From sexual abuse and rape, violent crimes against the elderly and infirm, to hate crimes and the murder of spouses and children, women have risen—or fallen—in the ranks to hold an equal standing with men. So much for stereotypes.

It is for this reason that *Mistresses of Mayhem: The Book of Women Criminals* is such a timely and important reference work. Not only does it span the history of the modern American female criminal from Ma Barker to Sante Kimes, it covers the full range of criminal activity by women from such non-violent crimes as prostitution, forgery, robbery, kidnapping, corruption, and illegal abortions to the higher profile, more violent variety of domestic violence, sexual torture, and murder. No other work of crime reporting is as encyclopedic, authoritative and, yes, entertaining as Ms. Hornberger's book.

Paul Dinas

Paul Dinas is former editor-in-chief of Pinnacle Books, publisher of the true crime best-sellers *Cruel Sacrifice* by Aphrodite Jones, *Monster* by Steve Jackson, *Daddy's Girl* by Clifford Irving, and *Lobster Boy* by Fred Rosen.

Introduction

When the Himalayan peasant meets the he-bear in his pride,
He shouts to scare the monster, who will often turn aside.
But the she-bear thus accosted rends the peasant tooth and nail.
For the female of the species is more deadly than the male.

—From "The Female of the Species" by Rudyard Kipling

Kipling seemed to have understood something that many of his contemporaries somehow missed. Since before Kipling's time, there's always been a misconception that women are the pacifists of the human species, the nurturers, the caregivers—that it's men who go against the morays of society and follow their animal instincts to their own ends. And if women do commit crimes, it's out of passion, jealousy, or to right some horrible wrong. Sociologists tell us that men—not women—commit crimes out of greed, power, revenge, and hate. But history tells another story: For the most part, women from all social backgrounds and all walks of life commit crimes for many of the same reasons as men. And many commit these crimes without any passion or emotion at all.

Mistresses of Mayhem tells the stories of more than 100 of the most notable "fallen" women of all time. Why did they choose the paths they chose? What were the ramifications of their crimes, both for themselves and for their victims? And what is it about these women and their crimes that is so intriguing to us?

Intriguing is certainly the right word. Of course, there's also gruesome; appalling; and let's not forget sickening. Murder, robbery, prostitution, espionage, blackmail, fraud, embezzlement, kidnapping, terrorism: Women commit the gamut of crimes. Some feel remorse for their sins, but many feel no remorse at all. And sometimes the remorse they feel is insanely misdirected.

What makes a good woman go bad? Failed romance is certainly a biggie. Had David Blakely not been such a caddish ass, perhaps he wouldn't have met his fate at the other side of the jilted Ruth Ellis's gun. Would Amy Fisher ever have shot Mary Jo Buttafucco—wife of Fisher's considerably older lover, Joey—if she had not been under his spell and devastated that he wouldn't leave his wife?

But love gone awry is far from the sole reason that women do very bad things.

Some women act alone, while others commit crimes under the influence of the man—or woman—they "love." And bad men certainly have played a significant role for many of the women in this book. Would Martha Beck have killed if she was not so desperately trying to hold on to Raymond Fernandez's, um, love? Would Caril Ann Fugate have sat back callously while her own parents and half-sister were gunned down by Charles Starkweather if she hadn't been so incredibly brainwashed? Might Karla Homolka's sister, as well as countless others, still be alive if she had not felt that she and Paul Bernardo were the "it" couple of the century? But the man isn't always the ringleader, with the woman devotedly following along. Women, too, have been known to shepherd their male consorts through the various circles of Hell. It was, after all, Karla Homolka who drugged her sister and then offered up the 16-year-old's virginity to boyfriend Bernardo—and then later, on videotape, fondly reminisced about the event and decided it was time to get Bernardo another virgin. And it was Judith Ann Neely, not her husband, who went after the victims of her famed foile a deux—and who today sits on death row for committing all the murders.

It's not just love that sweeps women over the threshold of the dark side, however. Life circumstances, including alcoholic parents, incest, poverty, and physical and sexual abuse, have also played at least supporting roles. If Aileen Wuornos had had a nurturing childhood, would she have become an infamous serial killer? If her early life hadn't been full of drugs and debauchery, would Karla Faye Tucker have wielded the ax with which she pulverized her victims? Of course, some women, like Bonnie Heady, do come from "good" backgrounds—and they still go bad.

And not all women "go bad"; some are simply born that way. Certainly there was no one influencing Jane Toppan to murder her "patients"; no one forced Mary Ann Cotton or Nannie Doss or Judi Buenoano to kill their spouses and offspring for the insurance money; and nothing but good old fashioned malice and an overinflated sense of vanity made Elizabeth Bathroy, the Blood Countess, torture and slay all 650+ of her victims.

The women profiled in this book who committed crimes other than murder were often very cunning and seized criminal opportunities when they presented themselves. Consider Polly Adler, one of the most famous madams of all time. She came to the United States a poor Russian immigrant who found a way to make a comfortable living by opening her chain of whorehouses. And Heidi Fleiss, who seized the opportunity to live the life of utter wealth she had always craved by turning her business smarts into profits.

For better or worse, society is fascinated with the "evil" woman. She has been immortalized in popular culture for thousands of years. Eve's insolence earned humankind a raw deal; Medea murdered her own children and became the mother-monster of all time; hungry for power and flush with greed, Lady Macbeth pushed her unfortunate husband to kill to satisfy her own ambition—and the list goes on and on.

Mistresses of Mayhem takes a close look at the real-life Eves, Medeas, and Lady Macbeths. Each entry examines the crimes of these women, probing into their minds and motives because, let's face it, bad women are just plain interesting.

But be warned: This book is not intended for the faint of heart or the squeamish. Some of the profiles contain horrifyingly graphic information, which is not suitable for children and squeamish adults.

Whatever caused these women to choose lives of crime, the intent here is not to rationalize. Nor is it to explain, condone, or glorify the acts of these women in any way. The job of this book is simply to report. Be prepared to be thoroughly freaked out—but draw your own conclusions.

ACKNOWLEDGMENTS

I must extend my sincerest gratitude to the following people. Without them, this book would not be possible:

First and foremost, thank you to Gary Goldstein, uber-editor, and to how incessant brainstorming can sometimes yield truly brilliant results; and to agent extraordinaire, Linda Konner, for her support and encouragement, and for working out all the messy details. Many thanks to the staff at Alpha Books, especially to developmental editors Mike Thomas and Jennifer Moore, for taking my humble manuscript and making a book of it, and to Charis Santillie for designing such a fabulous cover!

Thanks to Christine Guarino Mayer, whose impeccable research skills helped fill this book with tidbits both gory and juicy (if one is allowed to use those two words in the same sentence, that is); and to Jonathan Ambar for his superb writing assistance. A special thank you goes to Clive Thompson for helping me to relocate my "voice" through hundreds of novel-length e-mail exchanges.

Thanks to my family and friends for enduring my moods and my enforced hermitage during the writing of this book, and to anyone I may have met at any social function or been on line behind at the grocery store or bank over the past six months or so, who politely endured my horrific retellings of murder and mayhem.

And last, but not at all least, many heartfelt thanks to the management and staff of the Omega Diner in Bayside, Queens, New York, for graciously keeping me in french fries and iced tea, and providing me with a perfect haven to work—far, far away from Fluffy, Spike, digital cable, and all the various distractions of working from home.

Polly Adler (1900–1962)

MADAM

Throughout history, various madams have been able to boast high-profile—or at least highly influential—clientele. Sidney Biddle Barrows (page 10) pandered her girls only to the very rich and very powerful. Eva Coo (page 52) blatantly ran a bar and brothel in Oneonta, New York, during the heyday of Prohibition. Heidi Fleiss (page 78) had Hollywood hotshots—married or not—wrapped up in her little black book. So what, or rather, *who,* was Polly Adler's claim to fame? Oddly enough, it was the literati.

Polly Adler was born in 1900 in Yanow, Russia. A teenage immigrant who came to the United States to seek her fortune, Polly got an early taste of "the good life" that was to become hers when she landed a job at a corset factory in Brooklyn in the 1910s. Laboring 12 hours a day in a sweatshop was hardly Polly's vision of the American Dream. By the time she was 24 years old, she had found her calling and opened her first Manhattan-based brothel.

Throughout the 1930s and 1940s, Polly expanded her business and opened brothels all over the Island of Manhattan. She was a quick-thinking entrepreneur and a shrewd businesswoman. And before she knew it, she was a chain like McDonald's or, more

appropriately, Hooters. Adler's bordellos were not like the sleazy, $2-a-jump whorehouses that flourished all over New York City during the Roaring Twenties. Hers were more like gentlemen's clubs, featuring the finest bootleg wines and liquors that money could buy. Sure, there was a full staff of prostitutes on duty at all times, but one didn't have to have sex with them to enjoy an Adler whorehouse. Her establishments were always impeccably decorated, and patrons would sometimes come in simply to read the many volumes that lined the shelves of the library, enjoy a cocktail or two, or even play games, like backgammon, with other customers.

Writers Dorothy Parker and Robert Benchley, regulars of the famed Algonquin Round Table (a group of writers who gathered at the Algonquin Hotel for lunch, gossip, and literary conversation), frequently paid Polly visits. And at the end of their nights out on the town, Benchley often came back for a little more entertainment ... without Parker. Parker and Benchley, who made Adler's acquaintance in the mid-1920s, also brought other members of their literary circle, as well as politicians and other high-profile members of the New York community, to Polly's brothel.

Adler was able to run her business without any real hassles until the 1930s—New York City was still a wide-open town during the Depression, especially if a person knew which palms in city government to grease. Polly also had the help of some of the era's more notorious gangsters in avoiding hassles with the law. In the 1962 biography *The Last Testament of Lucky Luciano,* the mobster spoke warmly of Polly's establishment and of her stable of beautiful women: "Polly ran the best damn house in New York." Of Charlie Lucky, Polly said in return, "He was always a gentleman when he came around," unlike many of the ill-mannered and often uncouth racketeers who dropped in. Polly was arrested a number of times (usually at election time), but never convicted of anything. In 1930, she was called to testify against corrupt judges and police, and instead of being disloyal to her clientele, she fled to Florida. By 1935 she was back in New York and under arrest again, and this time she served a 30-day jail term. She published her autobiography, *A House Is Not a Home,* in 1953. In it she wrote, "I am one of those people who just can't help getting a kick even when it's a kick in the teeth."

Adler retired from the business in the early 1940s and moved to Hollywood, California, where she lived until her death in 1962.

Susan Atkins *(see Manson Women)*

"Sister" Amy Archer-Gilligan *(1873–1962)*

MURDER

Was she a black widow? An angel of death? Or both? Bilking the elderly out of their cash is nothing new by modern standards, but in the early part of the twentieth century, presenting oneself as a nurturer and caregiver, and then administering one's own brand of geriatric genocide to snatch their money, was touted "the biggest crime that ever shocked New England" when "Sister" Amy Archer-Gilligan was found out. Not too shabby considering the last New England crime to cause such a stir was the brutal ax murders of Andrew and Abby Borden 20-some years prior.

An angel of death? Not when you consider that the people she exploited and murdered were all essentially healthy. While old, most were quite a way from being ready for their final exit. And that includes Amy's husbands—both poisoned by their adoring wife.

Little is known about Amy's youth, except that she was born in 1873. In her early 20s, she married James Archer, and in 1898, gave birth to a daughter, and her only child, Mary.

In 1901, Amy opened Sister Amy's Nursing Home for the Elderly in Newington,

Connecticut. Although Amy claimed to be a nurse, there was never any degree earned to substantiate that claim. However, despite her dubious medical background, the self-professed "Sister Amy" was highly regarded by her patients, many of whom were among the wealthy Connecticut elite. Also, in this home, there were no suspicious deaths. Amy had not yet apparently fallen into the pit of madness that would define her next enterprise.

In 1907, the Archers relocated 10 miles north to Windsor, Connecticut, where Amy opened a new, 14-bed facility: the Archer Home for the Elderly and Infirm. This is where things took a turn for the strange.

It was business as usual for several years at the Archer Home. From 1907 to 1910, Amy had lost about 12 patients, which seemed normal for that duration. Attending physician Dr. Howard King, who was also a personal friend of the Archers, attributed the deaths to old age. Howard was himself an elderly chap, and was quite fond of the Archers—especially Amy. That he was but a stone's throw from senility would serve Amy greatly in the coming years.

In 1910, everything changed in Amy's life and the way in which she conducted her business. No one knows for sure what caused her to snap, but it was most likely not the unexpected death of her husband James in 1910. While Amy wore the widow's garb well, it would later be revealed that despite Dr. King's attributing the death to "natural" causes, Amy, in fact, murdered him.

Amy waited a respectable three years to remarry. In 1913, she wed Michael W. Gilligan, himself widowed—and quite wealthy to boot. Gilligan helped Amy run the Archer Home, and even merged his bank account with hers. Meanwhile, the death toll continued to rise at the facility. Amy was able to convince her new husband that the numerous deaths were the inevitable outcome of old age, even though a lot of the patients who died weren't seriously ill at the time.

Barely a year of married bliss had gone by before Michael Gilligan contracted a high fever and passed away. Cause of death? "Natural," according to the certificate signed by Dr. King.

By 1914, the relatives of patients who died at the Archer Home were beginning to get suspicious. Rumors flew around Windsor; it was becoming a well-known fact that a majority of the deceased patients had something in common: They all paid Amy an insurance premium of $1,000, supposedly for lifetime care benefits and other personal needs. As it would be revealed later, Amy took the money. Then, within a matter of weeks, she either poisoned or smothered her victims with their own pillows. And thanks to old Doc King, the cause of death was always listed as "Natural."

In 1916, the surviving relatives of former Archer patient Maude Lynch went to the authorities with their suspicions of foul play. An undercover officer was assigned to pose as a patient and collect evidence. One thing that caught his eye in Amy's records was the high number of inventories for bottled arsenic. Amy explained that it was used to kill rats. The officer was not convinced, and after relating the findings to his colleagues, the police decided to exhume the bodies of five of her former patients and of her late husband Michael Gilligan. Just as they had suspected, high levels of arsenic were found in all the bodies. In May 1916, Amy Archer-Gilligan was arrested and charged with six counts of murder.

Though the naïve Dr. King arduously defended Amy in court, even claiming that the poison must've been planted in the bodies to incriminate her, the facts spoke for themselves: Between 1911 and 1916, there were a total of 48 deaths at the Archer Home for the Elderly and Infirm. According to consulting physicians brought in by the prosecution, the average number in a similarly sized facility for that amount of time would've been eight to ten.

Much like the Lizzie Borden case, Amy's lawyer stood on the defense that the crimes were simply too heinous to have been committed by such a woman. Ultimately, Amy was charged with only one count of murder. On July 1917 she was sentenced to life in prison. The sentence was initially appealed, but when the case went back to court, the verdict was the same.

Amy was jailed until 1923. That year, she was diagnosed as insane and transferred to a state asylum, where she spent the rest of her days. Ironically, considering how many elderly folks she snuffed out before their time, Sister Amy lived to the ripe old age of 89.

Angela Atwood *(see Symbionese Liberation Army Women)*

Gertrude Baniszewski (1929–1990)

MURDER

If ever there was a baby-sitter from hell, it was Gertrude Baniszewski, an Indiana-born and -bred two-time divorcee, who performed menial jobs to substitute the usually delinquent child support payments from her various husbands. Gertrude wasn't much of a mother either, and, as the criminal tortures inflicted on Sylvia Likens in the summer of 1965 were revealed in court, it became clear that Gertrude was not much of a human being. She was a brutally cruel and heartless woman who encouraged some of her own children—as well as a few of the neighborhood children—to perform unspeakable atrocities on the poor young girl entrusted to her care.

Born Gertrude Van Fossan in 1929, Gertrude grew up the third of six children in depression-era Indiana. She enjoyed an exceptionally close relationship with her father; she and her mother, however, never seemed to get along. The great tragedy of Gertrude's young life had to have been watching her father keel over and die of a heart attack when she was 11 years old. The experience, for a child her age, was traumatic enough. But looming in the distance was the knowledge that her life would never be the same again—that she would now be raised solely by a woman whom she barely loved, and who had little love for Gertrude.

When Gertrude was 16 years old, she dropped out of high school to marry 18-year-old John Baniszewski. Fresh out of high school, John decided to become a police officer. But that didn't mean he was a particularly good or upstanding guy. In fact, he was a wife-beater, and later, after he and Gertrude divorced for the first and second time, he also showed himself to be a deadbeat when it came to child support payments.

Whatever their problems, sexual attraction was not one of them. In their first marriage, which lasted 10 years, they had 4 children. Shortly after her divorce, Gertrude married Edward Guthrie, but he hightailed it out of her life after only three months because he realized he wanted no part in raising four kids that weren't his own. In 1956, barely a year after the ink on the divorce papers was dry, Gertrude and John decided to have another go at matrimony. They toughed it out for seven more years and produced two more children. They divorced for the second time in 1963.

When Gertrude was 37, she fell in love with a much younger man: Dennis Lee Wright was only 23. Dennis and Gertrude never married, but they cohabitated, which was practically unheard of, even scandalous by early 1960s Midwestern standards. He wouldn't marry her, but to keep up appearances, she always referred to herself as "Mrs. Wright."

Gertrude had a unique talent for picking losers, and, in Dennis, she found herself the ultimate soul mate. Gertrude became pregnant twice by Dennis. The first pregnancy ended in a miscarriage. The second time, Gertrude gave birth to Dennis Jr., which was just the impetus his young father needed to disappear. So by the summer of 1965, when the Likens sisters entered her life, Gertrude was quite unhappy.

As a single mother of seven children, Gertrude would often work menial jobs to support her family, scraping by through ironing, baby-sitting, selling soft drinks at the Indianapolis Motor Speedway, and the sporadic child support checks from her children's fathers.

That fateful summer, Paula, Gertrude's 17-year-old daughter, befriended Sylvia Likens, a 16-year-old neighborhood girl who also came from a broken home. Lester Likens, Sylvia's father, became acquainted with Gertrude through their children's friendship, and when he got a job traveling with a circus to Florida, Gertrude agreed to look after Sylvia and her 15-year-old sister Jenny for $20 a week.

Sylvia and Jenny, who was physically challenged, made the wrong move of joining the "Wright" household in July. Though the Baniszewskis were already living in near-squalor, life with them at first was fairly normal for the Likens sisters. They went to church, attended the same high school as Gertrude's daughters Paula and Stephanie, and hung out with friends. But things began to change. When Lester Likens was late with his first $20 payment, Gertrude responded by beating Sylvia and Jenny, shouting "I took you bitches in for nothing!" The money arrived the next day. From that point forward, however, the entire Baniszewski household began taking out its frustrations on the Likens sisters—particularly Sylvia—in the most unfathomable ways, with Gertrude acting as sadistic ringleader.

Possibly due to her condition, Jenny was generally left alone by the members of Hell House. Sylvia, on the other hand, was constantly abused, beaten with paddles, belts, and wooden boards, and burned with cigarettes and matches. Paula, who broke her hand from hitting Sylvia too hard once, was persistent, abusing Sylvia with her cast. Pretty soon, neighborhood kids joined in the torture of Sylvia, particularly Coy Hubbard, Stephanie's 15-year-old boyfriend, and 14-year-old Richard "Ricky" Hobbs. By that point, Sylvia was regularly being thrown down the stairs and slammed against walls by the Baniszewski children and their friends and was even used as a punching bag for Coy and Ricky's Judo practice. Eventually, Gertrude tied Sylvia up and forced her to sleep in the basement. Cold, hungry, and terrified to the point of emotional numbness, Sylvia would soil herself, and on occasion, Gertrude forced Sylvia to consume her own waste.

Visitors to the Baniszewskis' would notice the Likens sisters cowering in the background and the bruises on Sylvia. Gertrude convinced them that Sylvia was a problem child and that her disciplinary action on the girl was just. Gertrude began accusing Sylvia of being promiscuous, even making the teenager believe she was pregnant after she admitted to having once permitted a boy to get under the covers with her. Gertrude lashed out at Sylvia by repeatedly kicking her between the legs as her powerless sister, Jenny, watched in horror, as she often had to.

There were other forms of sexual degradation toward Sylvia. On one occasion, Gertrude forced her to strip and shove a soda bottle into her vagina in front of Coy, Ricky, and Gertrude's 12-year-old son John. And although Sylvia was never technically sexually abused, the worse was yet to come.

That October, incensed that Sylvia was "slandering" her daughters at school, Gertrude (with the aid of Ricky) stripped, gagged, and tied Sylvia down while proceeding to carve the words "I am a prostitute and proud of it" on the girl's torso with a heated sewing needle. After another round of senseless beating, Gertrude made Sylvia write her parents a note, in which she was made to confess to having run away with a pack of boys who in turn beat her. After a few more days of torture, Sylvia Likens' body gave out on her, and she died on October 26, 1965, while being bathed fully clothed by Stephanie and Ricky. After placing Sylvia's body on a mattress, Gertrude made Ricky call the police, and when they arrived, Gertrude handed them the letter she forced Sylvia to write, hoping that the fabricated tale would absolve her of any wrongdoing.

But that wouldn't be the case. Before the police officer had a chance to read the note, Jenny Likens stepped up and told him the truth. Gertrude was arrested, while her young accomplices were taken away by juvenile authorities.

The trial of Gertrude Baniszewski became the most notorious and revolting murder case in Indiana's history. Paula, John, Coy, and Ricky were tried for first-degree murder along with Gertrude; it was the largest number of defendants the state had ever tried at once (because of her age, Stephanie was tried separately and acquitted of murder charges). During the trial Gertrude defended herself by claiming that she was too "sick" and too "tired" to be aware of what was happening to the Likens girls, considering all those children running around her house. She also insisted that she had never wanted the Likens sisters to stay with her, but claimed that Sylvia was adamant about it, and that it was she who suggested the payment idea.

But with Jenny Likens as the star witness, and overwhelming evidence against Gertrude, the jury was not convinced. While the other defendants were convicted of manslaughter, Gertrude was convicted of first-degree murder and sentenced to life in

Indiana Women's Prison. Many were surprised that she didn't receive the death penalty.

After 20 years, Gertrude was granted parole, which caused a great deal of controversy among groups such as Protect the Innocent and Society's League Against Molestation (SLAM). But despite their protest, Gertrude, who had been a model prisoner, was released on December 4, 1985. During her parole hearing, she expressed remorse and admitted responsibility for Sylvia's death, but she also claimed amnesia to the actual events, saying that she was on drugs.

Gertrude moved to Iowa, where she changed her name to Nadine Van Fossan. In 1990, she died of lung cancer at the age of 61.

"Ma" Barker *(see Arizona "Kate" Donnie Clark Barker)*

Arizona "Kate" Donnie Clark Barker *(1877–1935)*
a.k.a. "Ma" Barker

MURDER, KIDNAPPING, BANK ROBBERY

Was she simply the doting mother of four out-of-control boys? Or was she a criminal mastermind in her own right? Though it was no secret that Ma Barker enjoyed the spoils of her sons' various criminal exploits, whether she actually took part in any of them is a mystery that for many remains unsolved. While J. Edgar Hoover painted a pretty grim portrait of the infamous madonna of mayhem, many who knew her—in fact, many involved in the criminal exploits of her boys—painted another picture. To them, she was a silly hillbilly who couldn't plan the next meal, let alone orchestrate a robbery. Whatever the case, that Ma Barker went out fighting with her son Freddie in a shower of bullets has perpetuated the legend that she was, indeed, a maternal badass.

As with most of our gals, there was no way Arizona Barker knew she was headed for a life of crime—and to be the vessel through which some of the most ruthless bandits of the golden age of Midwestern gangsters emerged—when she grew up in the Ozarks at the end of the nineteenth century. She was born in 1877, the daughter of ordinary parents, and raised in a Scottish-Irish family in Ash Grove, Missouri. On September 14, 1892, she married George Elias Barker, a man who was 18 years her senior. She was only 15, even though the marriage certificate said she was over 18 at the time. Arizona, generally known as "Arrie," changed her first name to Kate shortly after her marriage.

In 1893, she gave birth to her first son, Herman. Five years later, Lloyd came into their lives, followed just one year later by Arthur, who is generally known as "Doc." Ma's alleged favorite, and the one she would go to the grave with, Frederick, was born in December 1902. In 1904 or 1905, the Barkers moved from Missouri to Tulsa, Oklahoma.

As the Barker boys grew up, they found themselves in more than their share of trouble. It's reputed that Kate had a gentle "boys will be boys" attitude about her sons' shenanigans; their father dodged parental responsibility altogether, replying to complaining neighbors and acquaintances with "You'll have to talk to Mother. She handles the boys." In 1915, a couple of the Barker boys got in trouble for "highway robbery." Kate, or as she was by this time called, Ma, simply laughed the incident off.

Hoover would later say of Ma Barker that she was "probably just an average mother of a family which had no aspirations or evidenced no desire to maintain any high plan socially." He also called her "a monument to the evils of parental indulgence." Whatever her reasons, her less-than-firm parental hand, in tandem with George Barker's neglect and indifference, would mean that the Barker boys would rise through the ranks of Dillinger, Bonnie and Clyde (page 165), and Machine Gun Kelly

and his wife, Kathryn Thorne Kelly (page 124), to become some of the most notorious criminals of the 1930s.

The Barker boys spent most of their young lives in and out of jail. While doing time in the late 1920s, Fred Barker made the acquaintance of one Alvin Karpis, a kindred spirit who had dallied on the wrong side of the law since the tender age of 10. While in the slammer, the two men forged a friendship and decided that on their release, they would bond together and find a way to make some serious money. In 1931, Fred Barker and Karpis were released from prison; when Doc was sprung in 1932, the infamous Barker-Karpis gang began wreaking havoc all over the Midwest. A few members of the gang even had their fingerprints removed, as, at the time, fingerprint identification was the most "high-tech" scientific method crime fighters had to identify perps. Two of the sons were never involved in the gang: Herman swallowed his gun right after he shot a police officer in a botched robbery in 1927; Lloyd was already serving a long-term prison sentence.

The gang specialized in bank robberies. But then they came upon a way to make more than the typical chump's change they were raking in: kidnapping. They successfully pulled off two in a six-month period: One was the abduction of William Hamm in 1933 (ransom $100,000); the second was

Edward Bremer in 1934 (the ransom stakes raised to $200,000).

Again, how much involvement Ma had in all of this is sketchy at best. Aside from harboring her fugitive sons and their fugitive friends, her biggest involvement may just have been feeding them home-cooked meals and tucking them into their beds at night. Ma left George in 1928. She had apparently picked up with another man, but many guess the reason was that she wanted to devote her life to her sons and that George never approved of their activities.

The Barker-Karpis gang enjoyed years of debauchery and derelict behavior, but nothing lasts forever, especially a life of crime. In January 1935, Doc was arrested and locked up. He tried to escape from Alcatraz in 1939, but was killed by guards before he scaled the wall. It was just a matter of time before Karpis and the remaining Barkers fell.

On January 15, 1935, the feds found where Ma and Fred were hiding out on Lake Weir in Florida. A legendary shootout ensued, and in the aftermath, Ma and her beloved Fred were dead. Karpis was taken into custody only days later.

Sidney Biddle Barrows
(1952–) a.k.a. Sheila Devin a.k.a. "The Mayflower Madam"

MADAM

When Sheila Devin's million-dollar-a-year, New York–based prostitution ring was cracked down on in 1984, many were shocked to learn that the true identity of this uber-successful madam. She was really none other than 32-year-old Sidney Biddle Barrows, a descendant of the famous New Jersey Biddles, one of the oldest and most prominent American families, whose heritage could be traced back to ancestors who came over on the *Mayflower*. That was it. The media had its hook: They had their "*Mayflower* Madam."

Barrows was famous for the women she provided through her Cachet escort service. She kept them on strict diet and beauty regimens. Barrows's girls had to be more than just beautiful, however. They had to be intelligent, witty, warm, captivating—they had to be more than just a hot piece of ass. She graded her girls on an A, B, C scale, with C being the babes who brought in the top bucks. The charge for a C-level Cachet girl? How about $400 per hour—or $2,000 per night. And Sidney was a fair madam, only keeping 60 percent of the take for herself. That kind of money was more than corporate lawyers were making in the early to mid-1980s. And considering the roughly 20 or so women in Sidney's stable were, for the majority, students, housewives, and models and actresses who would otherwise be waiting tables to keep themselves alive between gigs, it was an everybody wins endeavor.

Sidney didn't grow up thinking she would one day be a madam. It was something she fell into. She knew she would go into business, however. She graduated first in her class with a business degree from the Fashion Institute of Technology in 1972. After school, she traveled around Europe and then took a job in the executive-training program for the now-defunct A&S department store chain. Within a few years, she moved from the back office to the front lines, so to speak.

When Sidney's operation was busted, she implicated none of her clients and kept a tight hold on her little black book. In fact, she even pled guilty to a lesser charge of "promoting prostitution," so that the case would not go to trial and so the identities of her johns would be protected. She was a class act all the way. Sidney served one year in jail, three years of probation, and was made to pay a $5,000 fine.

In 1985 Sidney Biddle Barrows's name was dropped from the social register, but this mattered not to her. She had already made something of herself without her family connections, and for the following years, would continue to parlay her notoriety into various projects. She served as an "expert commentator" during fellow-madam Heidi Fleiss's trial. And she has published several books. The first, a six-figure deal published in 1986, was a memoir called *Mayflower Madam*. Later, she put out *Mayflower Manners: Etiquette for Consenting Adults* and *Just Between Us Girls: Secrets About Men from the Madam Who Knows*. At the time of this writing, she is working on a fourth book, a consumer's guide to cosmetic surgery and dermatology—and yes, she has had some work done.

Elizabeth (Erzebet) Bathroy (1560–1614) a.k.a. Blood Countess

MURDER

While many believe that Bram Stoker's *Dracula* is based on the legend of Vlad the Impaler, the infamous Romanian warlord, history cannot discount at least one more inspiration for the story: Elizabeth Bathroy, the "Blood Countess." Her wicked crimes, though some feel may have been a wee bit exaggerated over time, have earned her a seat of high distinction in the horror hall of fame among the most heinous of criminals—men and women included.

The Blood Countess was highly revered as the "most beautiful woman in Europe" during her lifetime, but how did she retain her stunning, youthful glow until her death at age 54? Through a daily beauty regimen that consisted of bathing in the blood of virgins, is how. In fact, more than 650 young women met their fate at the hands of the infamous Countess before her ghastly reign was ended in 1610. Her astonishing beauty aside, Bathroy was also remarkably clever—and undeniably cruel. So how did she get away with it for so long? Three reasons: power, station, and genuine fear on the part of anyone who dared cross her.

Born Erzebet Bathroy on August 7, 1560, to Baron George and Baroness Anna Bathroy, Elizabeth lived the privileged life of the Hungarian nobility of the sixteenth century. The family was well connected: Elizabeth's uncle, Stephen Bathroy, was crowned king of Poland in 1575; his brother, Christopher, was prince of Transylvania. There was no rival in Eastern Europe at the time to the utter power the Bathroy name held.

In true noble form, even for a female, Elizabeth was extremely well educated, spoke three languages—Hungarian, German, and Latin—and enjoyed all the pleasures her high station could bestow upon her. But despite the family's wealth and prominence, all was not well in the Bathroy home. Elizabeth was generally known to be more than a little unstable, and it is believed that she showed signs of madness in her childhood. One tale recounts that young Elizabeth was welcome to witness the brutal acts of torture her kinfolk enacted on alleged criminals of the day. One of the most brutal was the torture and killing of a gypsy accused of stealing, who was sewn up in the body of a dying horse with only his head exposed, and left to die. The literature also cites that some of her relatives were known Satan worshippers, and that her aunt, Klara Bathroy, was a famed bisexual who got off torturing servants.

Not unlike other noble families of the day, the Bathroys were not averse to inbreeding: in fact, her parents were both Bathroys by birth. Some say that this inbreeding led to Elizabeth's insanity. She was also prone to seizures as a youth, and many suspect that the blood-closeness of her parents may have also led Elizabeth to suffer from epilepsy. Whatever the factors that created the mindset of the future vampiristic countess, no one can deny that the main catalyst of her crimes was her innate sense of evil.

Early nature and, well, "nurture" arguments aside, there were several more factors that led to Elizabeth's rise or tumble—depending how one looks at it—to the pinnacle of wickedness in the sixteenth century. At age 11, Elizabeth became betrothed to Ferenc Nadasdy, the "Black Hero of Hungary," as a political maneuver orchestrated by the powerful family. They did not marry, however, until Elizabeth was 15 years old.

Nadasdy had a reputation for unrivaled brutality. He was a warlord and it has been widely accepted that it was Nadasdy, in fact, who taught Elizabeth many of the tortures she later inflicted. However, Elizabeth had a wicked side untapped even by her husband. Even he could not have imagined what his wife would be capable of, long after his death and influence on the young Elizabeth.

Some historians cite a specific cause for Elizabeth's descent into the madness that knew no return nor redemption. After her betrothal, Elizabeth was sent to live with her future mother-in-law. Her soon-to-be husband was away at battle, which afforded her the opportunity to have several affairs, most notably one with a common peasant, by whom Elizabeth soon became pregnant. After bearing a daughter, she was forced to give the child away and was not allowed to be in contact with the child again. What Elizabeth Bathroy is not as well known for is the passion she had for each of her children. During their marriage, she bore Nadasdy three daughters and one son. She was well known as a caring and doting mother, which may explain why having to give a child away could have been the drop of blood that caused the bucket to overflow.

What is more widely known, however, is that Elizabeth was a vain woman who was determined to keep her husband interested in her. There was no denying his passion for her, but as she got older, she feared his desire would lapse and that a younger woman might steal him away—if not for the long term (because of his lower station, that would have been unheard of) then at least in the bedroom. It was this desire for eternal youth that led her to believe that the blood of virgins was the only thing that would keep her eternally young and vibrant in the eyes of her husband.

As the legend goes, one day when Elizabeth was preparing for one of her husband's many homecomings, she became violent with a servant girl who pulled the countess's hair while brushing it. Violence was already par for the course in the Bathroy household. Elizabeth was known for her unabashedly wicked temper and had become violent with the staff on several occasions. What was different about this particular occasion, however, was that the girl began to bleed at the hand of her mistress, and the blood trickled onto Elizabeth's face. Call it hallucination, call it madness— but Elizabeth believed that as soon as the blood fell on an area of her face, that area was immediately restored to its youthful vitality.

Elizabeth's husband died in 1604. (Ironically, considering all the trouble the countess had gone through to keep him faithful, he reputedly died of a wound inflicted by a prostitute when he refused to pay for her services.) This means Elizabeth was still a fairly young woman when she maimed the servant girl; the healthy glow of youth she discovered was quite possibly her own. However, her belief that the servant girl's blood restored her sparked a veritable genocide for virgin girls of lower birth.

Once Elizabeth developed her insatiable taste for blood, her palace became a chamber of horrors. In some cases, Elizabeth humiliated young women—sometimes as young as 12—by forcing them to strip nude in front of male servants before torturing them to death. She burned them. She cut them. She sometimes stuck pins into the girls' lips and under their fingernails, or dragged them, naked, out into the cold of winter and poured water on them until they froze to death. The last of these tortures suggests that it wasn't only blood Elizabeth was after—it was sport.

Elizabeth did not act alone in her pursuits. She had a loyal posse of servants who assisted in her grim endeavors. Among these servants were Dorothea Szentes, also called "Dorka," a husky, bulky woman who could not be further away in form or physiognomy than the girls she helped her beloved countess kill. Also in Bathroy's employ was her one and only manservant, known simply as Ficzko ("lad" in Hungarian), and her wet nurse Helena Jo. One of the most significant of all of Elizabeth's accomplices was Anna Darvulia, who thought up some of the most cruel of the tortures and who was also suspected to be Elizabeth's lover. Finally, there was Erzsi Majorova, a local peasant woman, who is credited for planting the idea in the countess's head that led to her downfall.

As the story goes, Elizabeth eventually stopped seeing the desired results she used to enjoy from the blood of servant girls. Perhaps the magical effect had worn off, or her body had become immune to the magic potion, or there never was any effect at all, but in her 40s, the countess began to show the typical signs of aging. Whatever the reason, and with Majorova's encouragement, Elizabeth deduced that the problem was not the blood itself, but the purity of the blood. Virgins' blood was not enough; the blood also needed to be of noble vintage.

And with that, Elizabeth sealed her own doom. While most never batted an eye that the grounds around the Bathroy palace were strewn with the bled-out corpses of ordinary servant girls, because serfs were essentially considered subhuman at the time, and also because Elizabeth's power and position forced lawmakers to look the other way, once the daughters of Elizabeth's peers began to make the hit list, her reign was officially ended.

In 1610 and 1611, the crimes were brought in front of the courts in a case that tried only the accomplices. All of Elizabeth's helpers were sentenced to unspeakable deaths: Helena Jo and Dorothea Szentes had their fingers pulled off with hot pinschers before they were burned alive, Ficzko was decapitated, Erzsi was also executed. Only Anna Darvulia, who had died years before, was spared the humiliation.

The most condemning piece of evidence: a journal that Elizabeth kept, which carefully chronicled the details of each of her 650 crimes.

Elizabeth Bathroy was never convicted of any crime, but was confined in her room for the remainder of her life. She was found there, dead, in 1614.

Martha Beck *(1919–1951)*

MURDER

If ever there was a fitting candidate for a "lonely hearts" club, it was the perennially tubby Martha Beck. A lifetime of unhappiness, of never quite fitting in, of pining for her one true love culminated in quite possibly the worst relationship a gal with little to no self-esteem could ever have: a rela-

tionship rooted in something other than the stuff of true love—swindling, murder—and because of which, ended, for a fully satisfied Martha, in the electric chair.

Born Martha Seabrook in 1919, the Milton, Florida, native had an undeniably horrible childhood. Because of a glandular condition, she weighed in at nearly 250 pounds by age 12. Furthermore, the condition caused her body to develop sexually way before its time, and gave the 12-year-old a libido that could not be rivaled even by the standards of most 17-year-old boys.

Even family members noticed the raw sexuality that emanated from the pitiful child. At age 13, Martha was repeatedly sexually abused by her older brother. Throughout their lives, her mother loved Martha's brother above all, so when young Martha tearfully confessed what her brother had done to her, Mrs. Seabrook's reaction was to tell her daughter that she asked for it—and to leave her brother alone.

The only thing that got Martha through her early years were her dreams of becoming a nurse. After high school, Martha attended nursing school and graduated first in her class. Unfortunately, there was not a lot of work for nurses in Florida at the time, so the only job that Martha could get was bathing female corpses at a local mortuary. Six months proved to be enough time to spend in that grim profession, so Martha moved to California in 1942 and took a job in an army hospital. Her sex drive had not dwindled since her adolescence, and she satisfied her carnal cravings with several of the soldiers. Eventually, she became pregnant and returned to Florida with a story of how her husband was a naval officer abroad. Conveniently, it was wartime, so a few months later, Martha would "fake" his death, reporting to all how he valiantly died in combat.

Martha ended up bearing two children. In 1944, she became pregnant by Alfred Beck, a truck driver who she was briefly married to—until he tried to commit suicide to get away from her and she begrudgingly gave him a divorce.

There are two stories about how Martha became involved in a lonely hearts club. One was that it was a cruel joke—that a cruel cousin had sent in her name in a gesture of spite. The other was that Martha was just plain lonely, and sought out the correspondence on her own. Whatever the method, it was this correspondence that would seal her fate.

Through this club, she met Raymond Martinez Fernandez, a New York–based drifter with a criminal record. As it turned out, Raymond was something of a smooth operator. He had a history of meeting women through the personals. He would subsequently woo them and scam them out

of their savings.

One Friday afternoon in the winter of 1947, Raymond traveled to Florida to meet Martha. Martha fell deeply—obsessively—in love; Raymond left that Sunday more than a little weirded out by a two-day marathon of nonstop lust with a woman he never imagined he could be attracted to. He figured he would just go on with his life and leave the weekend in Florida where it belonged. Martha would not give up as easily.

Shortly after their time together, Martha packed up her kids and moved to the borough of Queens, the three of them showing up unannounced on Raymond's doorstep. Raymond took them in, but when the kids started getting on his nerves, Martha shipped them back to Florida and never saw them again. Raymond explained to Martha what he really did for a living and the lovestruck Martha agreed wholeheartedly to help him in his schemes, as long as his relationships with other women never got physical.

Posing as siblings, Martha and Raymond scoured the lonely hearts clubs looking for potential victims, and ultimately ended up scamming dozens of women out of their money—and ultimately, their lives—throughout the country. One victim was Janet L. Fay from Albany, New York. After convincing her to move to Long Island with them, they depleted her of her $6,000 life savings, and ended up beating her to death with a hammer while strangling her with a scarf. They buried her remains in the cellar of a rented house in Queens.

Soon after, they fled to Grand Rapids, Michigan, where they met Delphine Dowling, a single mother with a two-year-old daughter. Martha and Raymond moved in with Delphine almost immediately, and Raymond started having sex with Delphine soon after. Martha was not too happy about this, but because Raymond continued to satisfy her, she made a weak attempt to look the other way. The pair took money from the unfortunate widow, and attempted to kill her by forcing her to overdose on sleeping pills. When she unexpectedly regained consciousness, Raymond shot her in the head. Delphine's daughter, who had witnessed her mother's brutal murder and would not stop screaming, was "silenced" by Martha, who drowned the child in the bathtub. Both bodies were buried in the basement under two patches of fresh concrete.

Concerned neighbors who hadn't seen Delphine and her daughter in days tipped the police, who searched the house. Raymond and Martha were not there when the police arrived. They were feeling invincible, and decided there was time to blow off the afternoon to catch a flick. Upon their return, the police, who had discovered the bodies under the suspicious mounds of concrete, arrested the pair, who immediately and unashamedly confessed to their crimes. Raymond admitted to killing seventeen women in all, while Martha claimed the reason for the murders was that Raymond would do anything for her. They were feeling cocky because there was no death penalty in Michigan. But the authorities were not about to let the pair get away with it; the couple was extradited to New York for Janet Fay's murder.

The New York press had a field day with Raymond and Martha—especially Martha and her unbelievable heft (she was nearly 300 pounds at this time). They dubbed them the "Lonely Hearts Killers" and documented the trial and ghoulish testimonies that came out of it, which consisted not only of the particulars of the heinous murders, but also the gruesome details of their over-the-top sexual antics. These testimonies in particular knocked away any sympathies a jury member might have been harboring.

On August 18, 1949, Martha and Raymond were convicted of first-degree murder, and four days later, were both sentenced to death. The lovers were to be executed on March 8, 1951.

The ever-suave Raymond refused his final meal, his vanity taking over as he worried he might vomit it out all over himself when he died, and thus not look good "going out"; folklore has it that Martha ordered a double portion of fried chicken and mashed potatoes and finished every bite, gleefully licking her fingers.

Raymond spoke no final words. However, before he was taken to the chair, he wrote a few: "I want to shout it out. I love Martha. What do the public know about love?" Martha was decidedly less dramatic. She had found the love of her life and was satisfied that all her romantic fantasies had been realized. As she was strapped into the death chair and the electrodes placed on her head, she smiled, mouthed the words "So long," and off she went into the big sleep.

Betty Lou Beets
(1937–2000)

MURDER

There was a scandal in Texas in February of 2000. A mother of five, grandmother of nine, and great-grandmother of six, was about to walk down the corridor of death row, be strapped to a gurney, and be administered a lethal injection. That Betty Lou Beets was guilty of the murders that got her in this spot was not in question. She had fully admitted to killing the two husbands investigators dug up in the yard of her mobile home. It was her motive that had folks all stirred up. Betty Lou claimed that she shot the good-for-nothing bastards because they beat her and her children. Supporters of Betty Lou were adamant that she fought back for her own protection, that she suffered from "battered woman's syndrome," and that she should be given special consideration, especially because of her childhood.

And if ever there was a horrible childhood, it was Betty Lou's. Born into a family of poor Texas sharecroppers in 1937, Betty Lou learned about life, sex, and the evils of the world at a very early age. Her mother was mentally ill; her father, a profligate alcoholic. A lethal combination for a happy home. Betty Lou was mentally, emotionally, and physically abused, and reportedly, the little girl was raped at the tender age of five. At age six, she came down with encephalitis, which she barely survived and resulted in permanent diminished hearing. A few years later, Betty was involved in a serious car accident and suffered organic brain damage.

When Betty reached adulthood, or at least age 15, she married her first in a long line of alcoholic, abusive husbands. Her union to Richard Branson spawned two children, Shirley and Robert. By 1965, that marriage was over.

The second husband, Jimmy Lane, married Betty Lou in 1971. It was a tempestuous relationship that ended in divorce in 1972. And then was resuscitated in 1973 for a few years. Why Jimmy remarried Betty Lou is certainly a mystery, especially since in 1972, while they were on a break, she shot him in the back. Twice. He lived, and charges were never pressed.

In the late 1970s, Betty Lou married her third husband, Doyle Barker. The marriage was short-lived. In August of 1981, Doyle simply "disappeared." Betty Lou had the town convinced that he had just up and taken off on his family, and that he was nothing more than a no-good deserter. Doyle Barker reappeared in 1985 as a rotted corpse planted under a tool shed.

Finally, there was James Beets, the poor bastard whose name has been made immortal, linked to the woman who did him in. They married in 1982, and within a year, Betty Lou reported him missing. Apparently, one day James had gone off fishing, but only his boat came back from the trip. It was only a year later, when Betty Lou declared him legally dead so she could collect his pension benefits and life insurance, that suspicion was aroused.

On June 8, 1985, police obtained a warrant to search Betty Lou's property. Their excavation yielded two bodies: Doyle Barker and Jimmy Beets (the latter had been buried under a wishing well). Betty Lou Beets was taken into police custody and charged with the murders of her two husbands.

During her trial, which began October 7, Betty Lou tried to pin the murders on two of her own children, Robbie for Beets and Shirley for Barker. Both kids testified as witnesses for the prosecution, and both admitted the roles they played in the murders: Each had helped their mother dispose of the respective bodies and helped their mother cover her tracks.

If it seems heartbreaking that two children would testify against their own mother, or that she would try to implicate them in her crimes, well, it is. But Betty Lou's children were not known to be the best kids a momma could ever have. Growing up, they were all always in trouble and terrorized the other kids in the trailer park. The search warrant for Betty Lou's home was granted when an anonymous caller tipped the police off that Betty Lou had killed two husbands and buried them in the yard. It would not be at all surprising if that anonymous tipster were someday found out to be one of Betty Lou's very own brood.

Throughout her trial, Betty Lou was depicted as a greedy, heartless woman who killed to collect on her husbands' life insurance. That she had been abused by her parents, her husbands, and lo, quite possibly, her kids, was not given that much attention. Betty Lou had a reputation for being a hard-drinking woman. Neither judge nor jury could be convinced that she was some kind of saint, killing her husbands to protect herself and her children. Of course, this had a lot to do with bad representation.

Perhaps if Betty Lou had chosen a better lawyer, he could have won the jury's sympathies for his client and thus spared her life. But Betty Lou hired E. Ray Andrews, a hard-boiled drinker and slacker who agreed to take on her case in exchange for her signature on a contract for the rights to her story. This did more than a little to jade his performance. In the first place, it was Andrews who made it known to Betty Lou that she was entitled to her second deceased husband's money in the first place, which would have been great for Betty Lou if he would have testified as such on her behalf. Of course, that would mean that he'd have to step down as her attorney and give up his fee. Wasn't happening. So he threw together a slip-shoddy case, completely glossing over any of Betty Lou's abuse and the pathetic events of her past. (Andrews, himself, landed in prison a few

years later when, as a district attorney, he accepted a hefty bribe not to press for the death sentence for a man accused of killing his wife. Ironic.)

On October 11, 1985, Betty Lou Beets was sentenced to death.

Several years and appeals would come and go before Betty Lou's official date of execution was set for 2000. Before her execution, Governor Bush's office received more than 2,000 requests to stop the execution and only 57 that endorsed it. No matter. Bush said that he was comfortable with the decision, and besides, he could not stop the execution on his own. So he didn't. On February 26, a terrified elderly Betty Lou Beets was strapped to a table, and within 10 minutes, at 6:18 P.M., she was gone. At age 62, she was the oldest person to be executed in the state of Texas since the death penalty was reinstated in 1982, and only the second woman.

Mary Bell *(1957–)*

MURDER

Long before Jonesboro. Long before Michael Carneal. Long, long before the Columbine massacre, there were children who killed—and they were even younger than Dylan Klebold and Eric Harris. In Newcastle, England, in 1968, one of these children just happened to be 11 years old. And a girl. Can't blame violent movies or video games for this one.

Today, Mary Bell lives a normal, unpsychotic existence, even raising a child of her own. Psychiatrists believe that Mary must have had a break, and that's why she was only out of her mind as a child. What caused the psychosis? Many believe it was because when Mary was five, she watched her friend get run over by a bus. Therefore, in just this one phase of her life, she happened to be obsessed with murder—especially with the murder of small things, like cats and birds. And toddlers.

Whether or not this can be used as an explanation for her behavior, Mary Bell did not have a normal childhood. Her mother, Betty, was a prostitute who gave birth to Mary out of wedlock when she was all of 17 years old. Although she eventually married, she didn't retire from prostitution. And she forced all her children to call her husband, Billy Bell, "uncle" and not "father" so that she could screw the government out of assistance money.

One of the biggest sorrows in Mary's life was that her mother did not want her. This was not just the melodramatic imaginings of a preteen girl, it was a reality of which all the townspeople were well aware. When Mary was very young, her mother even tried, unsuccessfully, to give the poor girl to a woman standing outside an abortion clinic. Mary was shuffled around from one relative to the next throughout her childhood. In fact, it wasn't until Betty could play the "poor mother of the monster child" role, which she perfected during Mary's trial, that she ever fully claimed the girl as her own.

Mary was an odd child who had few friends. Her closest, and possibly only, friend was Norma Bell, a 13-year-old girl who was not related to her, despite the fact that they shared the same last name. It was always with Norma that Mary would commit her crimes, but Norma was never anything more than a spectator to the murders.

The insanity started on May 11, 1968, when a three-year-old boy that Norma and Mary were playing with "fell" off a roof and injured himself. While the authorities were not suspicious, a few mothers came forward and told police to suspect Mary, as they had each caught her "play" strangling their toddlers. Two weeks later, the body of a four-year-old boy, Martin Brown, was found in an abandoned house. The authorities wrote the cause of death off as ingestion of pills that they located nearby. Even on May 26, when Norma's father found Mary in mid-strangle of one of his other daughters, she was sent home but not reported to police.

The day after Mr. Bell sent Mary home, the local nursery school was vandalized.

The attackers left notes all over the place: "I murder so THAT I may come back"; "fuch [sic] of we murder watch out Fanny and Faggot"; "we did murder Martain [sic] brown Fuckof [sic] you Bastard" among them. Mary and Norma later admitted to ransacking the school "for a giggle." A week later, the girls tried to break in again, but the school had installed an alarm system, and when the police came to answer the call, they found Mary and Norma hanging around outside. Still, no legal action was taken.

That summer, Mary, under Norma's watchful eye, killed her final victim: another male toddler named Brian Howe. This time, the crime was more involved. Not only had the child been strangled, but his tiny body was punctured and slashed by a pair of scissors that was found nearby. His hair was chopped in erratic clumps. And on his belly, an "N" that was changed into an "M," was scratched in with a razor blade. That did it. Mary and Norma—but more so Mary—were brought in as suspects.

Why was Mary more suspect? For one, her behavior in dealing with the deaths of the children was just plain sick. After Martin Brown's death, she jovially went to his house and told his mother she wanted to see him. The shocked mother replied that Martin was dead. Mary said she knew that, and that she just wanted to see him in his

coffin. When Brian's coffin was removed from his house for burial, Mary stood outside, giggling and rubbing her hands together maniacally, as the coffin passed by.

On August 7, 1968, Norma implicated Mary as the killer of both Brian and Martin. She said that she had been present, but that Mary had done the actual killing. She admitted to taking part in the vandalism, but that was the extent of it. When they brought Mary in, she wrote and signed a formal confession that pointed the finger at Norma. The police were not fooled. Both girls were formally arrested and put to trial, even though everyone knew that the guilty party was none other than Mary Bell.

The trial started on December 5, 1968. Norma was acquitted of all charges; Mary was convicted of manslaughter; she avoided a murder conviction because the defense convinced the jury that Mary was not "all there," and due to the "Diminished Responsibility" law passed in Parliament in 1957, someone could not be found guilty of murder if they were not in their right mind. Mary was handed a life sentence.

Mary's mother Betty was a wreck throughout the whole judicial process. It came out during and after the trial that Mary was horribly sexually and physically abused by her mother. She was sometimes brought in to assist Mom with her johns, and Betty regularly administered drug overdoses to her daughter to illicit sympathy from doctors. Was it Munchausen by Proxy Syndrome, or just bad parenting? Probably a little of both. The judge eventually forbade Betty to have any further contact with her daughter.

In prison, Mary was able to prove that she had been successfully reformed, and on May 14, 1980, she was released back into the world, a sane 23-year-old woman.

Lawrencia "Bambi" Bembenek (1958–)

MURDER

How does a Midwestern, middle-class, all-American girl end up not only being sentenced to prison for life for murdering her new husband's ex-wife, but also, more than 10 years later, become a featured segment on *America's Most Wanted* for breaking out of jail, fleeing to Canada, getting captured by the Canadian government, and being released just a couple of years later for good? If that girl happens to be Lawrencia Bembenek, it is all-too-possible. But was she really a killer, or a victim of a highly chauvinistic police department? The truth has never surfaced.

Born on August 15, 1958, Laurie (the nickname she prefers) was an irrepressible youth. Her childhood was fairly normal. She was the youngest of three daughters born to

a former-cop-turned-carpenter and a home-maker in a suburb of Milwaukee, Wisconsin.

In high school, Laurie was always on the go, always involved in something. She was well known as being both outgoing and outspoken, and was generally well liked by her peers. Laurie had several interests, from sports to music—she was a star on her high school track team and a talented flutist. She wasn't the most gifted student, however, so instead of going to school to follow her dream of becoming a veterinarian, she attended a two-year college and received a degree in fashion merchandising. It was a degree she didn't materialize into a career, however.

During her post-collegiate period, Laurie became something of a party girl, experimenting with various drugs, promiscuity, and many of the trappings of shedding one's baby fat and making the transition from girl to woman. She was also very vocally feminist, and because she was such an athletic girl, she loved to challenge men to arm wrestling matches—and beat them. It would be this streak that not only cost her a career, but nearly cost her her life's freedom.

In 1980, Laurie finally found her calling in life: law enforcement. She cleaned up her act and was accepted into the Milwaukee Police Department's training academy. Laurie was so adept and passionate at this choice of career, she managed to graduate sixth in her class.

Her police career would not be so illustrious, however. Remember two vital aspects of Laurie's character: She was a full-fledged fighting feminist and she was extremely outspoken. The men in her department, who had already been reluctant to accept her, made her experience nearly unbearable.

As it turns out, Laurie was soon exposed to activities within the department that unsettled her. She claimed to have discovered that many of the officers in her squad were selling pornography out of their squad cars, receiving oral sex from prostitutes while on patrol, and frequenting well-known drug hangouts. On top of all that, Laurie allegedly endured constant sexual harassment from the male officers, and was appalled at the force's overall treatment of minorities.

On August 25, 1980, less than a month after accepting her badge, Laurie was fired from the Milwaukee police force, allegedly over lying on a police report. She vehemently denied the charge, and promptly filed a lawsuit against the police department, claiming discrimination. In October of 1980, a friend gave her a series of photographs taken of drunken police officers dancing nude at a public picnic. When she turned them over to the press, she had

securely made more than a few enemies for life.

In December of 1980—Laurie was still only 22 years old—she met the man of her dreams, and the relationship she had with him would change her life forever. Elfred "Fred" Schultz was a good-looking, much older (he was 33) police detective who became completely smitten with Laurie, even though he had divorced his wife of several years just a couple of months before. Fred's divorce from his ex-wife, Christine, had been a bitter one. Laurie saw no flaws in her beloved, and they were married on January 30, 1981.

Did Laurie kill Christine Schultz, the crime she was sentenced to life in prison for committing? Some may say that she of course did because she had been overheard on several occasions explaining that her husband was giving too much money to his ex-wife for child support and the like and she wanted it to stop. Others think that Laurie was framed. The animosity her former colleagues felt for her was possibly enough for them to set up the crime scene and the circumstances of the crime, so the jury would have no choice but to accept Laurie's guilt and send her to the klink for life.

How did it happen? On May 28, 1981, at approximately 2 A.M., an intruder dressed in a green jogging suit, with auburn hair, gloved hands, and a ski mask, entered Christine Schultz's home. By the time the intruder left, he or she had managed to wake both of Christine's and Fred's children, Sean and Shannon, and kill Christine by firing a bullet into her back at extremely close range. (In fact, the gun was pressed against Christine's back when it went off, which led to the speculation that only a cop—or an ex-cop—would know how to shoot someone that way.) Christine died almost immediately. Within days, and despite more incriminating evidence pointing to other suspects, including Laurie's husband, Laurie was arrested for the murder. Eventually she would be tried and sentenced to life in prison for the murder, which she swears to this day she did not commit.

What were some of the breadcrumbs on the path that led to Laurie being accused of offing her new husband's ex? For one, shortly after the murder, a reddish-brown wig was found clogging the toilet in the apartment across from Fred and Laurie's unit. That wig matched Christine's son Sean's description of the murderer having had auburn hair, and tests showed that hair from the wig matched hairs found on Christine's body. With that information at hand, the police tested a hairbrush owned by Laurie, and crime lab reports proved that at least one strand from the brush was con-

sistent with hair found on the bandanna that gagged Christine. Plus, Laurie had access to the incriminating gun; it was her husband's off-duty revolver. On June 24, 1981, Laurie Bembenek was arrested for the murder of Christine Schultz. The trial lasted three weeks, and that, along with the remarkable events that occurred afterward, transformed Laurie Bembenek's story into one of the biggest media spectacles of the last two decades.

During the trial, it came out that shortly after being dismissed from the police force, Laurie got a job as a waitress at a local Playboy Club. That and the fact that she was nicknamed "Bambi" during her short-lived career as a police officer gave the media a field day.

The prosecution made Laurie out to be a calculating young woman who greedily detested the monthly $800 child support payments her husband was making to Christine. Also, several witnesses claimed to have seen Laurie in a green jogging suit, like the one Sean described the killer to be wearing. The defense on their part presented a theory: The initial examination of Fred Schultz's off-duty gun showed that it was unused. Yet once it was analyzed at the crime lab, the ballistic reports concluded that it was indeed the crime weapon. Could the gun first looked at and the one later tested have been different guns?

The jury ultimately convicted Laurie of first-degree murder, and she was sentenced to life in prison at the Taycheedah Correctional Institute in Fond du Lac County. Shortly after her conviction, Fred and Laurie divorced. He moved to Florida and became vocal about his belief in Laurie's guilt.

But that was not the end of Laurie Bembenek. While in prison, she met and fell in love with Dominic "Nick" Gugliatto, the brother of a prisoner Laurie befriended. On the night of July 15, 1990, Laurie crawled out of an unsecured window in the prison laundry and escaped; Nick was waiting for her in the woods. The couple crossed the border into Canada, posing as newlyweds. As headlines announced Bambi's escape, Laurie, under the alias Jennifer Gazzana, settled in Thunder Bay, Ontario, with Nick, and found a job as a waitress in a Greek restaurant.

Her freedom lasted only three months, for in October 1990, Thunder Bay authorities arrested Laurie, tipped off by a woman who, watching a segment on Laurie Bembenek on the popular TV show *America's Most Wanted,* recognized her from the Greek restaurant. While Nick was eventually extradited back to the States, Laurie pleaded for refugee status and remained under the custody of Canadian immigration for nearly a year.

Back home, Laurie was gaining many supporters, who believed her claim that she was the victim of a misogynist system. In fact, "Run, Bambi, Run" became a popular mantra during her months as an escapee.

Laurie was ultimately sent back, but not before the Canadian government took a look at her case and discovered a number of legal glitches in her trial. When she returned to Wisconsin, a judicial inquiry was undertaken, and new revelations surfaced that were not a part of the original trial nearly a decade before. For example, a neighbor of Christine Schultz reported that his gun had been stolen the night of the murder. His revolver was a .38, the same as the alleged murder weapon. This brought the whole "switched gun" theory back into light. As for the evidence used against Laurie, Assistant Medical Examiner Elaine Samuels revealed that she felt the hair samples tested might have been tampered with during the investigation, and that the person who was in charge of analyzing those samples lacked solid experience.

Most disturbingly, 22 days before her death, Christine Schultz confessed to her divorce lawyer that Fred had accosted her with the threat of "I'm going to blow your fucking head off." Fred was also given immunity from any possible charges stemming from Christine's murder in exchange for testifying against Laurie. It was also revealed that Judy Zess, a former friend and roommate of Laurie's who testified against her in 1981, was accused of committing perjury in her testimony. A convicted felon claimed to have overheard Judy talking about a deal she worked out with the police—the exchange of favors for her testimony. Some of those favors were sexual, and when her incarcerated boyfriend was paroled, it seemed that Judy's deal had indeed worked to her advantage.

Armed with that information, Laurie was able to plead "no contest" to second-degree murder, and received a reduced sentence. Paroled in 1992, she attended The University of Wisconsin-Parkside, where she graduated with honors with a degree in humanities. She wrote a book, *Woman on Trial,* which later became a TV miniseries, and she also appeared on *Oprah.* Eventually Laurie would slip out of the spotlight. She contracted Hepatitis C and moved to Washington State, hoping to establish a quiet, low-key new life.

Though her innocence has not been firmly established and there are still many unanswered questions surrounding the murder of Christine Schultz, Laurie Bembenek has finally regained the freedom she was yearning for.

Catherine Birnie *(1951–)*

MURDER

The formula for why so many women go bad reads almost like a fractured fairy tale: woman with bad childhood and questionable self-esteem becomes obsessed with maniacal lunatic who gives her the attention she has been craving her whole life and becomes his willing accomplice in a series of sexually perverse crimes that she believes will satisfy her man and herself. And even in the far reaches of Western Australia, the song remains the same, as evidenced in the downfall of one Catherine Birnie.

The hard knocks came a'knocking very early in Catherine's life. She was born on May 31, 1951. Her mother died when she was just 10 months old, and for a while, she was sent to live with her father in South Africa. Before she was toilet trained and speaking full sentences, the toddler was living back in Australia with her grandparents. Growing up, Catherine didn't have any friends. That is until, as a teenager, she befriended her next-door neighbor, David Birnie.

He understood her. He was also abysmally unhappy. The oldest of six children, his childhood wasn't all warmth and smiles either. His parents, Margaret and John Birnie, did what they could to take care of their children, but both were chronic alcoholics, and the kids ended up in foster care regularly while they tried to dry out and get their acts together.

It wasn't long before the two misfits were raising all sorts of hell together. David already had an impressive rap sheet for a kid in his late teens; before she fell in with David, Catherine was squeaky clean. But she would do anything for him, and if it meant going over to his side of the law to better connect with him, she was in. By the summer of 1970, the two had been brought in on numerous charges of breaking and entering, trespassing, burglary, and car theft. Because of his background, David was sent to prison for two and a half years. Catherine got six months. At the time of the sentencing, Catherine was pregnant with David's child. When the baby was born, it was immediately taken from her and never returned.

While David was still behind bars, Catherine met Donald McLaughlan and the two were married on Catherine's twenty-first birthday. This relationship had none of the fire of her David Birnie fling, but Donald was a stable guy who stabilized Catherine—so much so that she bore him six children in devotion and gratitude. But it was not to last.

In 1984, Catherine met up with David again, and before Donald could say "cuckold," Catherine had left her husband and six children far behind. It was quite possibly one of the biggest mistakes she could ever make, but there was no stopping her. Without ever appearing before God or the law, Catherine changed her last name to "Birnie" and became David's wife, for better or for worse.

Whether David and Catherine actually shared true love is debatable; what they did share was incredibly good and wildly adventurous sex. But after a while, even their most outrageous bedroom antics lost their sizzle and it was time to spice up their sex life. David had many ideas about how to do this. He was addicted to pornography and, reportedly, to sex in general. It was rumored that when he lived with his younger brother for a while he repeatedly sodomized him, whether there was a woman in his life or not. He was apparently insatiable, needing sexual release sometimes four or five times a day. Couple that with a propensity for crime, and it's not surprising how the events of the late 1980s unfolded.

Starting in 1986, David and Catherine began picking up young women, sexually torturing them, and murdering them.

The couple's first victim was a 22-year-old student named Mary Neilson. She had responded to an ad the Birnies were running to sell some used tires. When she came to the house, David pulled a knife on her.

The couple tied their victim to the bed, where David raped her repeatedly and Catherine sat back, taking notes, getting pointers about what her man liked and how to best please him. After David had his fill of the poor girl, he strangled her and he and Catherine did away with the body.

The next attacks unfolded in much the same way, except each time, Catherine became less and less a spectator and more and more a willing and eager participant, both in the sex and the murder. They generally chose only strangers for their sex play, but both David and Catherine were particularly entranced by a 31-year-old acquaintance of theirs, Noelene Patterson. Noelene was raped and tortured for three days before Catherine got paranoid, believing that she was going to lose her prize of a man to this other woman. She threatened to kill herself if David didn't do away with Noelene and fast.

It was the last victim that put Catherine over the edge. The brutality of the killing was more than she could handle. Denise Brown went through the rigorous rituals of rape and torture that all of David's victims received, but she didn't die easily. In fact, even as they buried her, Denise clung to life. David cracked her skull open with an ax, and that image remained with Catherine. Catherine got careless with the next victim when David left the house to run an errand; She allowed the girl to escape.

When the near-victim reached the authorities, she was able to take them to the Birnie residence, and the couple was taken into custody. It didn't take long for them to confess, and they even—almost proudly—took the police on a tour of burial sites, showing them where they had buried all their victims. They pleaded guilty on all counts and were sentenced to life in prison, with no hope for parole until at least the year 2007.

Penny Bjorkland *(c. 1940–)*

MURDER

In 1959, the average teenage girl was ponytailed, poodle-skirted, hanging out at the drive-in, and totally boy crazy, dreaming of Elvis and Bobby Darrin and others. Ponytail notwithstanding, the only thing that the young Penny Bjorkland dreamed about was murder.

There were no red flags in young Penny's childhood and family life. Her family was average, as far as families go—no indication of alcoholism, abuse, or even poverty. There was no incest, no divorce, no horrific tales of neglect. Just a quiet family of six living a quiet life in the San Francisco Bay area. So what, on February 2, 1959, compelled Penny Bjorkland to pump August Norry full of bullets, leave his body in a field, and head back to town in the dead man's car?

Twenty-seven-year-old Norry was a landscape gardener. He was married, but had a reputation of being a bit of a tom cat. And having a child on the way didn't slow down his urge to bed other women. Perhaps he should have been more cautious of the urges of women he tried to seduce.

When August Norry saw the blond, perky, freckle-faced Penny one day while emptying his truck of the day's debris, he should have just minded his own business. But she got his attention and his hormones got the better of him. They went out for a late-afternoon date and arranged to meet the following day. Norry thought he would be getting laid; that he would be shot 18 times by this little teen angel never crossed his mind.

When Norry's body was found, it was a big mystery for police who would have so brutally murdered him. While he slept around, Norry was generally well liked in the town and had no known enemies. Luckily, the police hit on a clue that would lead them to his killer.

The type of bullet that killed Norry was a special type typically used in target practice. A police investigation tracked the bullets to a Connecticut distributor, who was able to provide the names of four distributors he sold to in the San Francisco Bay area. They were then able to narrow down the search to customers who bought cartridges that could be filled with more-than-normal the amount of gunpowder. The stores were able to provide police with the names of five men who were known to "hot-load" their guns.

One of the men, Lawrence Schultze, admitted that he had sold a box of these cartridges to a girl he knew, Penny Bjorkland, and took her target shooting. When the police showed up at Penny's house, she was completely unfazed by their being there, and went along with them willingly.

In custody, Penny admitted to killing August Norry. But that was nothing. What the prosecutors and police couldn't seem to wrap their brains around was motive. They tried to blame it on an affair she was having with Norry. No. They guessed that perhaps he had sexually abused her and she was retaliating—or perhaps just defending herself from his advances. No, again.

She then gave them her reason for the murder, pointblank: "For about a year and a half," she calmly explained, "I've had the urge to kill someone. I'll admit the motive sounds crazy," she continued to her baffled audience. "But I wanted to know if a person could commit a crime like this and not worry about the police looking for her or have it on her conscience." And if that wasn't stupefying enough, she finished her statement like so: "I've felt better ever since I killed him."

Griselda Blanco de Trujillo (1944–)

DRUG TRAFFICKING, MURDER

They say you can take the girl out of the neighborhood, but you can't take the neighborhood out of the girl. There couldn't be a truer statement about Griselda Blanco de Trujillo, who was born and bred in Medellín, Colombia, a city known for its drug trafficking and violence and which reportedly sees an average of 10 drug-related murders each day. When Griselda made her way to the States in 1965, she could have left that world behind her. But it was the only world she had ever known. During her career, Griselda went from drug lord's wife to the most feared and reviled name in the drug underworld. All it took was a little planning, a lot of coercion, and, of course, a willingness to blow away anyone who stood in her way.

Whether Griselda had a happy childhood is pretty much a moot point. No matter what her family was like, it's hardly possible that she could have had a good childhood considering the crime-infested environment in which she grew up. Reputedly, before Griselda entered adulthood, she had been a victim of rape and child abuse, lived on the street, supported herself as a pickpocket and a prostitute, and already had four children by the time she moved to Queens, New York, at the age of 21 with her children and husband, Carlos Trujillo. (In all, Griselda would be married four times; one husband would be killed by a rival, the other three by Griselda.)

By 1971, Griselda went from drug moll to drug lord, starting her own cocaine network, which quickly became one of the fiercest and strongest. Griselda was a shrewd woman. A smart woman. A together woman. And yes: Griselda was a psychopath, which, in the dog-eat-dog world of drug trafficking, is an invaluable asset. People who got in Griselda's way, or to whom she owed money, or who simply rubbed her the wrong way, got rubbed out. Sometimes she took them out, and other times, her minions, deathly afraid of her, did her bidding in an effort to spare their own lives.

If there's one thing to be said about Griselda, it's that she was always a devoted mother. She raised her four sons to take care of themselves, and from a very young age, instructed them in the ways of the family business so that they might also someday be successful—even take over the family business should something happen to Mama.

While Griselda's business started in New York, she eventually moved her operation to Miami, where she established one of the most successful networks ever between Colombia and the States.

And Griselda wasn't just a drug peddler; she was a user. Her drug of choice was bazooka, a highly potent, smokable form of cocaine. This developed into an addiction to painkillers and tranquilizers in the mid-1980s. Her drug use made her ever more insane. A known bisexual, Griselda liked her strippers and prostitutes, but in these years, instead of just fooling around with them, she would kill them for kicks. Her drug use got so excessive that her sons ended up running the show from the mid-1980s on—which may have been what led to its downfall.

But during the glory years of Griselda's reign as the undisputed queen of the drug world, others learned quickly not to cross her. Those that did paid the price, and then some.

In 1975, Griselda's trusted lieutenant, Juan Guillermo, stole $2 million from Griselda to start his own network. All of his people were killed. When Griselda's people came for Juan, automatics in hand, Juan threw his own girlfriend in the line of fire and managed to get away. But no sooner had he arrived back in Medellín than his luck was over. Griselda's goons got 'em.

Apparently, Guillermo's murder wasn't lesson enough for all of Griselda's underlings, because in 1978, another one thought he could pull one over on "La Madrina" ("the godmother"), as she liked to be called.

Before she could retaliate on German Panesso, her people gang-raped his wife and abducted and murdered his housemaid. In July 1979, Panesso's luck ran out when he was gunned down in a drive-by, planned by Griselda and carried out by those who feared her.

People continued to cross Griselda, though it happened with less and less frequency as her retaliation methods became ever more ferocious. One of her female rivals was gunned down while riding in a funeral procession! There were no rules. There was no place to be safe. Cross Griselda, and you will pay. Period.

Which is one of the main reasons it was nearly impossible to bring her to justice. Sure, she had been arrested before, but no one would testify against her. Finally, law enforcement got what they needed. They struck a plea bargain with one of Griselda's favorite hit men, a man named Riverito. He could have his sentence reduced to 25 years if he sang. So he sang.

In 1985, Griselda was arrested and handed a 10-year sentence for her drug activities. Her sons were convicted right along with Mama. But when Riverito testified against her in 1993, the charge escalated to numerous counts of murder, and the punishment quickly changed to life imprisonment.

In 1998, however, there was a scandal involving Riverito and a few of the secretaries in the Miami-Dade State Attorney's office, completely shaking his credibility. The DA was forced to work out a plea with Griselda: 20 years only.

Blood Countess *(see Elizabeth Bathroy)*

Anne Bonny *(1698–??)*

PIRACY

Unlike her counterpart, Mary Read (page 174), the pirate Anne Bonny was quite literally born a wild child, and early on showed signs of the wild behavior that would make her one of the most famous and notorious female pirates of all time. But like Read, Anne spent a fair chunk of her childhood disguised as a boy to cover up her father's infidelity to his first wife. But that's where the early similarities end. Mary was filled with wanderlust, but was essentially a calm woman; Anne was anything but calm. In fact, Anne was rumored to have stabbed to death one of the family servants with a butcher knife just because she made the plantation owner's daughter mad one day.

Born in Ireland, in a small town near Cork, Anne Comac was the illegitimate child of a successful lawyer, William Comac, and one of the maids of his estate, Mary Brennan. Comac and the maid had been

lovers for a fair period of time, but their affair was a secret to William's wife—that is, until a flirtatious prank made the secret known.

As the story goes, the maid was being courted by a local tanner. One day when the mistress of the house was on an extended visit with her mother-in-law, the tanner, while paying the ever-popular Mary a visit, swiped three silver spoons from the dining room and snuck them into the maid's bed, thinking she would find them when she turned in for the night. He didn't realize that she didn't always spend the night in her own room; and because the mistress was away, which meant this was one of those nights, the maid didn't realize that the tanner had merely hidden the spoons. She assumed that he had stolen them, and reported him to the police.

When a few days had gone by and she still had not found the spoons, he figured out what must be going on and reported to the mistress of the house upon her return that the maid had stolen the spoons, and showed her where they were hidden in Mary's bed. Because she was suspicious that the maid had not been sleeping in her own bed, she told the maid to find somewhere else to sleep because Mrs. Comac would be sleeping in the maid's room that night. When her own husband entered the room and made more passionate love to her—thinking she was the maid—than he ever had before, she had the maid thrown in jail for the theft and threw her husband to the curb with the day's refuse.

Eventually the case was dismissed, and the maid soon learned she was with child: the soon-to-be-infamous Anne. William remained in contact with Mary and their daughter, and because he was so fond of the infant girl, he decided it was time to claim her as his own. But because he was living off an allowance from his estranged wife, and the wife knew that the maid had borne him a daughter, William decided to dress Anne as a boy and pretend she was the child of a poor relative who he had taken into his home to raise. When the wife found out the truth, she cut him off financially and forced him out of town.

William packed up Brennan and their daughter and headed to the United States, where he became a successful plantation owner in the Carolinas. But Anne's mother did not live to see what hell her daughter would eventually raise. She died when Anne was still quite young.

Despite the sacrifices her father had made for her, Anne never got along with the man. She had a tumultuous childhood, and her behavior did not seem to subside the older she got.

By the time Anne Comac was 16, she had met and married John Bonny, a token bad boy her father had never approved of.

Some accounts of Anne's life state that the entire marriage was a scheme on Bonny's part to steal Comac's plantation from him. The scheme failed miserably, and after this final straw, Comac disowned his daughter and her roguish husband and the young couple moved off to the Bahamas.

Perhaps because she could no longer annoy her father with her choice of spouse, the fun seemed to go out of the marriage and Anne soon lost interest in her husband. When she made the acquaintance of one "Calico" Jack Rackam, she knew it was time to make John Bonny a fixture of the past.

Rackham was just the bit of excitement for which Anne had been chomping. The two enjoyed a torrid affair until Anne's husband got in the way. Bonny could read the writing on the wall, but he still did not want to give up his wife without a fight, so he abducted his wife back and charged her with a felony for desertion. She was Bonny's "property." In a quasi-romantic gesture to win Anne back, Calico Jack made the suggestion that Anne be put up for sale to the highest bidder. A successful pirate, Jack won the auction against his challenger, who had, even since leaving the Carolinas with his wife, never amounted to more than a ne'er-do-well grifter. So Anne dressed herself in men's clothing and joined the crew of the *Revenge* to run away with Calico Jack.

Anne was one of the most successful pirates on the *Revenge*. She was extremely adept with sword and pistol, and fought with a passion and fury unrivaled by most of the men of the crew. And as such a passionate woman, it was hard for Anne to keep herself in check when something—or someone—stirred that passion, which is how she developed her friendship with Mary Read. Mary was a lieutenant on board the *Revenge*, and was also posing as a man. Anne simply had to have "Mark" (Mary's nome-de-male), so she one day finally decided to reveal herself to him. What she learned was that the object of her affection was, in fact, another woman. And while some accounts swear there was a lesbian relationship between the two, the majority depicts them as being "just friends."

When the *Revenge* was overtaken in 1720, the entire crew was taken by surprise. Nearly all members were drunk at the time except for Anne and Mary, who took it upon themselves to fight off the captors. Both Mary and Anne resented their male counterparts, and it was during this siege that Anne perhaps uttered her famous quote: "If there's a man among ye, ye'll come out and fight like the men ye are to be." But Anne and Mary worked alone, planning to fight to the death if need be.

Even the might of these powerful women was not enough to ward off the attackers, so the *Revenge* was overtaken, and the pirates hauled off into custody. All the men on board, including Calico Jack, were sentenced to execution. Anne had never forgiven her calico-clad lover for his drunkenness and cowardice, and as he stood on the gallows awaiting his death, Anne is said to have shouted her last words to him: "Had you fought like a man, you need not have been hanged like a dog!"

What became of Anne Bonny after the capture of the *Revenge* is essentially unknown. In most accounts, she simply falls off the map after her imprisonment, never to be heard from again. However, there are a few reports that Anne's father bought her freedom and that she moved back to the Carolinas, with her son from Calico Jack, where she remarried into a Charleston family in 1721.

Elizabeth "Lizzie" Borden *(1860–1927) a.k.a. Lizbeth Borden*

MURDER

It's a mystery as to what causes a child to kill his or her parents. Sometimes it's a matter of early sexual abuse; once the child grows big enough to retaliate, he or she does. Sometimes it's a crime of passion: perhaps a loaded gun goes off; or in the midst of a heated argument, a mother is pushed just a touch too hard by her angered son or daughter, and falls down the stairs to her death. Or perhaps the child has some other deep-seated psychological problem, and simply snaps in the heat of a sweltering summer day.

All of these conclusions and more were drawn when Andrew Borden, 70 years old, and his second wife, Abby Borden, were found dead in their Fall River, Massachusetts, home on a Thursday morning in August. The prime suspect turned out to be Borden's daughter by his first marriage, Elizabeth—or as she is best known, Lizzie.

At the time of the murders, 32-year-old Lizzie was your typical Victorian-age spinster. A homely, mild-mannered—mousy, even—Sunday school teacher, who lived a comfortable New England life with her father and stepmother. While Andrew had a reputation for being more than a little tight with a dime, he always provided for his family and made sure they never wanted for anything they needed.

Elizabeth Borden was born in 1860, the younger of two daughters delivered by Andrew's first wife, Sarah Borden. Even though she was only three when it happened, Lizzie never fully accepted her mother's sudden death from uterine congestion, and as the last child born to Sarah,

possibly felt—and was made to feel—a certain degree of guilt for the death. Therefore, Lizzie was especially resentful of Sarah's "replacement," Abby Durfree, a 36-year-old spinster her father had married two years after her mother's death, and whom she always and only referred to as "Mrs. Borden."

Lizzie exhibited a dark side only once growing up, in an incident that probably had to do with the resentment she felt for her stepmother. One day, when Abby's cat was annoying Lizzie, Lizzie lashed out at the animal, decapitating it. A case for this being a symbolic attack on the stepmother can be made, as when Lizzie died, she bequeathed her entire fortune to animal rights charities—not the telltale sign of someone who enjoyed being cruel to animals in any way.

For whatever reasons the murders occurred, one thing was certain. After the morning of August 4, 1892, neither the two spinster Borden sisters and family nor the town of Fall River would ever be the same again.

The day began innocently enough at the Borden household, located at 92 Second Street. Andrew, who was one of the town's most successful businessmen, had returned from some morning business in town and retired to his study to relax. Abby was upstairs, dusting and changing the linens in the guest bedroom, cleaning up for John Morse, a visiting uncle. Meanwhile, Irish maid Bridget Sullivan was attending to various other chores around the house. The eldest daughter, Emma, was out of town. Lizzie had come downstairs for a sparse breakfast, exchanged a few words with Bridget, who was also called "Maggie," and then went her own way.

At around 11 A.M., Bridget, who was resting before lunch, heard a terrifying scream. It was Lizzie. She had apparently discovered the bludgeoned body of her father in the study, his eye cut in half and hanging down to his cheek, his nose severed. The complete right side of his face mutilated beyond recognition, seeping blood from the fresh wounds.

And then, another horrific discovery: Abby Borden in the guest bedroom, her head crushed in, struck repeatedly and mercilessly by the same instrument that had killed her husband. The autopsy later revealed that Abby had received 19 blows to the back of her skull; Andrew 11 to his face, head, and neck.

A week later, Lizzie was arrested and charged with three counts of first-degree murder: one count each for her father and stepmother, and one count for the double murder. The ensuing trial became a sensation; gory headlines were blasted across newspapers nationwide as the trial of Lizzie

Borden became the first highly publicized murder case in U.S. history.

From the beginning, there were unanswered questions that left the authorities stumped. Where was Lizzie at the time of the murders? Her own descriptions of her whereabouts were vague, and her demeanor throughout the trial decidedly aloof. Lizzie claimed she was in the barn attic searching for lead fishing weights when the murders were being committed. However, it was a hot summer day, and it had to have been more than 100 degrees inside the barn. Lizzie said she was in there for more than 20 minutes, but considering the heat—not to mention the stifling garments of the era she was wearing—that claim was highly improbable. Deepening the mystery was a lack of apparent motive, and no murder weapon identified, despite the fact that a handleless hatchet found in the Borden basement was submitted as evidence. And it was revealed during the trial that on August 7, three days after the murder, a friend found Lizzie burning a dress in the kitchen stove, a dress that Lizzie claimed was ruined by paint stains.

Despite all evidence pointing to her, Lizzie Borden was acquitted of murdering her father and stepmother. She spoke only once at the trial to say, "I am innocent. I leave it to my counsel to speak for me." The defense stood on one defense: that the crime was so heinous, a good Christian woman from a prominent family simply could not have committed it.

The trial lasted for 12 days, and it took the jury less than an hour to return with their verdict. Many people believe that this was a reflection of Victorian-age standards. The all-male jury couldn't possibly believe that a woman, much less a Christian from such a prominent and well-respected family, could commit such unspeakable acts. Then who was the murderer? Everyone from Bridget to one of Lizzie's Sunday school pupils was whispered about. A theory even developed that the killer was an illegitimate son of Andrew Borden's. But ultimately these were just unfounded rumors, and the murders of Andrew and Abby Borden have forever remained unsolved in the eyes of the law.

Though found not guilty, Lizzie, who was already considered somewhat of an eccentric before the murders, quickly became ostracized from Fall River society. And the trial was such a national event that people everywhere knew who she was. In an attempt to rebuild her life, she changed her name to Lizbeth, sold the infamous house on Second Street, and bought a new home with Emma in a fashionable Fall River district; Lizzie christened it Maplecroft.

Lizzie eventually became a recluse, but in 1904, she took in an actress named

Nance O'Neil, which so perturbed her sister Emma that she moved out of Maplecroft and become estranged from Lizzie for the rest of their lives.

Lizzie Borden died on June 1, 1927, following complications from gall bladder surgery. She was 67 years old. Emma, whom she hadn't spoken to in more than 20 years, died 9 days later after suffering a fall in her Newmarket, New Hampshire, home. They were buried in a family plot in Fall River, next to their birth mother Sarah, and Andrew, and Abby.

Lucretia Borgia
(1480–1519)

MURDER

Along with Lady MacBeth, Lucretia Borgia was one of the most infamous women of the Renaissance. But unlike Shakespeare's character, Lucretia's life was not a work of fiction. And with her fair hair and skin and gray eyes, she, at least physically, probably better resembled Desdemona of *Othello* fame.

A powerful Italian family of Spanish descent, the Borgias were ambitious people who quickly made political gains in Italy during the 1400s and 1500s. Compared to modern times, Lucretia's family more than measures up to the Sopranos or the

Corleones. Like these fictional modern crime families, the Borgias were a powerful brood, and they were feared and respected throughout Italy and beyond. Unlike those families, however, the Borgias were known for their incestuous behavior and numerous orgies, which sometimes simultaneously involved Lucretia, her father, and her half brother.

Lucretia Borgia was born in 1480, the daughter of Cardinal Rodrigo Borgia and his mistress Vannozza de Cattanei. Rodrigo would eventually become Pope Alexander VI, through what many said was bribery. Alexander's reign in the Vatican was beset with rumors of orgies and other not-so-saintly activities.

In an era when Italy was divided into numerous city-states constantly at odds with each other for power and land, the Borgias's alliances through Lucretia's savvy marriages—masterminded by Rodrigo—brought even more clout to an already influential clan. She already had two cancelled engagements behind her when, at the age of 13, she was married to Giovanni Sforza, Count of Pesare. After two years, however, the Borgias had begun to form new alliances, particularly with the powerful Aragon family. At that point, Rodrigo and his son Cesare, Lucretia's brother and one of the most ruthless and ambitious Borgias, decided it was time to get rid of Giovanni

Sforza. This was done by publicly declaring Giovanni impotent, and claiming that his marriage to Lucretia was never consummated; thus an annulment could be granted. Sforza balked, but unable to fight against the Borgias, not to mention the Pope himself, he signed a confession of impotence and his union with Lucretia was quickly terminated.

Lucretia, who was sent to live in a convent during the annulment proceedings, somehow found herself pregnant. Some sources claim the father was a young chamberlain named Perotto. Others say it was Pedro Calderon, a Spanish gentleman. Regardless of who the father was, the story goes that an infuriated Cesare got a hold of Lucretia's lover, and threw him into prison. Six days later, the lifeless body of the lover was found floating on the Tiber River. In March of 1498, Lucretia gave birth to her son Giovanni. Rodrigo announced that he was the son of Cesare and one of his mistresses. However, the mysterious circumstances of Giovanni's birth led to rumors of incest; that the child was a product of Lucretia's liaison with either her father or her brother. These rumors constantly plagued the Borgias, so much so that they became a part of their legacy for centuries to come.

Less than a year after giving birth to Giovanni, 17-year-old Lucretia entered the

House of Aragon by marrying one of its members, Alfonso. Alfonso's uncle was the King of Naples, and Alfonso himself was the Duke of Bisceglie, an important principality, so Rodrigo and Cesare were very pleased with their important new alliance. However, relations between the Borgias and the Aragons soon soured, and rumor had it that Cesare was jealous of Lucretia's affections for her new husband. Cesare sent his henchmen to kill Alfonso, who was brutally attacked and left for dead. He survived, but Cesare, who had gotten the word that Alfonso was still alive, had him strangled while he was recuperating in bed. Lucretia was truly distraught, and mourned her husband.

Before her third marriage was arranged, Rodrigo, acting as Pope Alexander VI, left Lucretia in charge of the Vatican as he went off to survey land he acquired from the short-lived Aragon alliance. At the age of 21 and as a female, no less, Lucretia Borgia became the head of the Holy Roman Empire, albeit for a short while.

Soon after the Pope's return, Cesare selected Lucretia's third husband, Afonso d'Este, heir to Ferrara, a city-state adjacent to Cesare's own principality of Romagna. Afonso was wary at first; he was well aware of the whispers of orgies and incest that surrounded the Borgias. However, he also realized that it would be a powerful alliance,

and the dowry was impressive, so he finally agreed to marry Lucretia.

Lucretia and Afonso's union was enduring, and they had four children together. As she settled into her role as Duchess of Ferrara, she developed a new reputation, that of a woman of charity and a patroness of the arts (so much so that she had affairs with numerous poets, including one, Erocle Strozzi, who was eventually found murdered under mysterious circumstances).

Shortly after giving birth to her fifth child, who died soon after, Lucretia died on June 24, 1519, at the age of 38. Though her life ended with her in a position as a highly respectable noblewoman, tales of incest, murder, and greed are still associated with the Borgia name. Whether she was a conniving vixen in her own right or an innocent pawn of her father and brother's ruthless ambition is still up for debate. Yet there is no denying that Lucretia Borgia has endured as one of the most fascinating figures in history.

Betty Broderick (1947–)

MURDER

Betty Broderick had everything she wanted—or at least everything she had been programmed to believe she wanted: perfect husband, perfect home, perfect children, perfect life. She had always been a person who threw herself wholeheartedly into everything she did. She was a dutiful wife, putting her husband through school and sacrificing every step of the way while he built up his career and his law practice. In the 1970s, she bore her husband four children and peddled Tupperware and cosmetics to make ends meet. And then her husband became successful beyond anyone's wildest dreams. And once Daniel Broderick Jr. had all his ducks in a row, Betty became superfluous. What followed was a downward spiral into madness for Betty; and death for dear old Dan.

Elisabeth Anne Biscelgia was born in 1947 and grew up in a huge Catholic family in Eastchester, New York. The lessons of her childhood taught her that there was no more honorable a place you could attain as a woman than to provide your husband and family with the best life possible. There weren't many professional options open to most women growing up when Betty did. The average woman had three basic choices: secretary, nurse, and teacher—and these, for the most part, were mainly just to occupy a girl until she snared herself a fella. Betty met her husband-to-be when she was only 17, but she still went to a local college and obtained a teaching degree.

Dan Broderick was a college senior when he meet Betty, and was on his way to medical school in the fall. They dated for four years, while Betty finished college and Dan medical school, and on April 12, 1969, they were married. Like clockwork—just like it was "supposed to be"—Betty gave birth to the couple's first daughter, a "honeymoon baby" (do the math), in January 1970. Their next child, also a daughter, came barely a year later. Also in 1971, Dan decided that he would make a better lawyer than doctor, so Betty gracefully raised her children and worked several jobs to put her beloved through school. She was a dutiful wife, everything she believed she was supposed to be.

Finally, by the end of the 1970s, the Brodericks had two additional children, two sons, and Dan's practice was strong enough that Betty no longer had to work. She focused all her attention on her La Jolla, California, home and her children. Dan spent hardly any time at home. These circumstances would spell disaster later. Betty had successfully managed to cut herself off from the outside world. Her life was her family and her family was her life. What she didn't know was that she built everything she had into a "house of cards," and that in just a few short years, when Dan fell in love with a younger woman, that house would tumble to the ground.

Dan Broderick was a successful lawyer, but he had another talent he excelled in equally: ruining women's lives. When he met Linda Kolkena, the woman he would trade in his old-model wife for, she was only 21 years old and a former flight attendant. She and Dan fell in love immediately; before long, he had hired her to become his personal assistant. Linda was young and naïve and thought she had found her prince, not her demise. But that wouldn't be for a few more years.

They say a woman always knows when her man strays, and Betty was suspicious from the very beginning about the true nature of the relationship between Linda and Dan. She confronted him early on, and he vehemently denied it, making her feel like a harpy and a shrew anytime she brought it up. Then one day, when Betty went to her husband's office to surprise him for his birthday with champagne and flowers, the surprise was on her: Both Dan and Linda had left the office for the day, no explanation given.

Dan came home later that night to a bonfire of his best suits blazing away in the backyard. He was calm. He knew why Betty did what she did. But he was completely unapologetic. He told her he was involved with Linda only because he had decided it was time for him and Betty to get a separation, as he intended to marry Linda. It was 1984. Life as Betty had always known it and loved it was over. The supportive and

nurturing wife and mother died that day; in her place was born very bad Betty, a woman with a wicked temper and an uncontrollable, insatiable thirst for revenge. Betty was in pain. She wanted Dan to hurt like her, but she couldn't see that he ever would. The suit bonfire became the tip of the iceberg for the insane acts this scorned woman would commit for the next five years as the divorce proceedings dragged on and on.

Dan was a very high-profile attorney, so Betty's first big problem was to find someone in the area brave enough to go against him and represent her. She ended up having to look in Los Angeles before she found someone who finally would. Soon enough, their roles revealed themselves: Dan was the dastardly villain; Betty, the hapless victim. But Betty wasn't going to play the victim lying down. No sir. She was going to go out kicking and screaming, or at least driving. She drove her car through the front door of the house the couple used to share with their family, and which Dan now shared with Linda.

Betty committed several more of these types of offenses, earning her restraining order after restraining order from her husband, making her look completely unfit for raising the kids, and ultimately discrediting herself and her sanity in court. One of her favorite pastimes was to call Dan and Linda and leave venomous messages on the answering machine. The woman was lonely and desperate, feeling completely betrayed. You bet that those messages would be used against her later!

In January 1989, the divorce was final. And because of a legal loophole, the bazillionaire Dan Broderick was only liable to pay his ex-wife one lump cash sum of less than $30,000.

By November, Betty was a broken, destitute, and desperate woman. It's hard to say what was going through her mind when she woke up at the crack of dawn on November 5, grabbed the .38 she had recently purchased, and drove to the home of her former husband and his new wife. Even she admits that she had no idea things were going to happen the way they ended up happening. She thinks she was there to shoot herself in front of the dastardly Dan and his blushing bride, so no one was more surprised than Betty when the gun went off several times, leaving the newlyweds dead. Betty immediately called the police and turned herself in.

Betty's first criminal trial, in September 1990, was about as bad as her divorce trial, but this time, the courts seemed to be on her side. The jury was hung and the case put off. One of the jurors was so sickened by the mind games Dan played with Betty that he remarked that it was a surprise to many of the jurors that Betty waited so long. Her second trial, in late 1991, did not go so well, however, and she was convicted on two counts of second-degree murder, 30 years to life. She will not be eligible for parole until 2011.

Judias Ann Lou Buenoano (1934–1998) a.k.a. "The Black Widow"

MURDER

Throughout the ages, women have killed for many reasons. Sometimes as crimes of passion; sometimes because of an obsessive passion they have for the wrong man. Some act impulsively; others act with a cool, calculated malice, whereby years pass before anyone suspects them of the numerous deaths that follow them. In the middle of the nineteenth century, Englishwoman Mary Ann Cotton (page 54) poisoned her way through several husbands, lovers, and numerous relatives, including her mother and nearly a dozen of her children for the money she could collect from their insurance policies. About 120 years later, and across the Atlantic, another woman learned of the power of a few bottles of arsenic and how they could figure into a plan for a lifetime of wealth.

The woman who would come to be known as Florida's own Black Widow, Judi Buenoano, was born Judias Wetly, on

43

April 4, 1943. Her childhood was as far from ideal as can be. Growing up in Quanah, Texas, Judi, for the early part of her life, was raised by her father, an itinerant farmer, and her mother, a Mesquite Apache, who died of tuberculosis when Judi was only two. From that point on, the family was ripped apart. Judi and a brother were sent to live with her grandparents, while her older siblings, amazingly, were put up for adoption.

Judi was reunited with her father and his new wife in New Mexico a few years later, but she would most likely have been better off if she had been adopted right out of that family. Judi and her brother were relentlessly abused by both her father and her stepmother, sometimes being forced to work like slaves, sometimes even being burned with cigarettes. It was obvious—at least to Judi—that her father favored his new family, and was only burdened by Judi and her brother's presence.

One day, when Judi was 14, she had had enough. She scalded her stepbrothers with hot grease and attacked both her father and stepmother in a rage. She was thrown in jail for 60 days for her outburst, but chose reform school over going home to her "parents" after she had served out her term.

In 1960, when Judi was working as a nurse's aide under the alias Anna Schultz, she became pregnant, but never disclosed the identity of the father. In 1961, at 26, she gave birth to a son, Michael. Later that year, she met an air force pilot, James Goodyear, and married him in January 1962.

Judi and James seemed to have a good life together. They had two children of their own, James Jr. (1966) and Kimberly (1967), and James adopted Michael as his own son. Goodyear soon moved his family to Orlando, Florida, but then got assigned to combat in Vietnam. He wasn't away very long; within three months he was returned home to his wife and family. On September 15, 1971, James Goodyear was dead—cause unknown.

Within a matter of days, Judi cashed in her husband's life insurance policy. But adding to the Goodyear family's misfortune, within a year, the Goodyears' Orlando home had burned to the ground, and Judi cashed in her $90,000 homeowner's policy and moved herself and her children to Pensacola, Florida.

Judi wasn't alone for long. In 1973, she moved in with her new lover, Bobby Joe Morris. The two were never married, but they were involved enough to compel Morris to invest in a life insurance policy, naming his darling Judi the beneficiary. In 1977, Morris, along with Judi and her brood, moved to Trinidad. Morris would never return.

In January 1978, Morris came down with a sudden illness, and within a month, he was dead. The death certificate cited the cause of death as cardiac arrest. Morris's folks had other suspicions, but they were never able to prove anything.

Almost as soon as she cashed the check from Morris's life insurance settlement, Judi moved her family back to Pensacola, and changed hers and her children's last name to "Buenoano," which means "good year" in Spanish.

Judi's next victim was her own flesh and blood, Michael. Apparently, Michael was always in trouble, providing his mother with endless grief and aggravation. He was so bad, in fact, that he even spent time with a foster family. It's too bad that family didn't adopt him away from his Medea-ish mother. In 1980, Michael, by this time 19, started to become quite ill. His illness had even started to affect his muscular coordination and had caused him to become partially paralyzed. For some reason, on a sunny day in May, Judi took her partially paralyzed son, and her younger son, on a canoe trip. Why no one wondered if it was such a great idea to take Michael in his condition on this trip is a mystery. The canoe tipped. Judi and James swam to safety; Michael perished. And of course, he was fully insured.

Lucky for Judi, she was able to open a beauty parlor with the money she made off

her son's death. Things were really starting to look up. Judi fell in love again, this time with Pensacola businessman John Gentry II. She completely fabricated her past to entice him, naming among her accomplishments various Ph.D.s and an illustrious nursing career. She left out her skill at insurance frauds and getting away with at least three murders.

Early in the relationship, Gentry was so smitten with Judi that he purchased a life insurance policy and named her the beneficiary. Within a couple of months, Gentry began to exhibit the classic signs of illness those under Judi's care typically began to exhibit when they fell out of her favor. He was hospitalized for 12 days and made a complete recovery. This led him to suspect that what had made him ill were the "vitamins" Judi had been giving him on a daily basis. But his love was so blinding, he brushed his suspicions off and continued his relationship with her.

In June 1983, Gentry's car exploded— with him behind the wheel. Miraculously, he survived. And this served as a more-than-adequate wake-up call. He handed over the vitamin pills to the authorities, and they were analyzed. Arsenic was definitely a component of their make-up.

The jig was up. Judi was not only indicted for the attempted murder of Gentry, she was also now blamed for the death of her son and was in huge trouble for her insurance scams. Both Bobby Joe Morris and James Goodyear were exhumed, and traces of arsenic were found in the remains.

Judi was convicted of all crimes and was sentenced to death on November 16, 1985. She managed to win several stays of execution, but in March 1998 she became the first woman to be electrocuted in Florida.

Carol Bundy *(1942–)*

MURDER

In her book, *Letters from Prison: Voices of Women Murderers,* a collection of correspondence between author Jennifer Furio and various female killers, Furio writes of Carol Bundy that, "Of all the women and crimes profiled in these pages, Carol Bundy's story is perhaps the most difficult to understand and is nearly impossible to empathize with." Although many of the inmates Furio corresponded with had committed unspeakable crimes, in their correspondence with the author, she could still find at least a touch of humanity. But Furio found Bundy's utter lack of humanity in the letters she wrote to be so disturbing, that she eventually had to cease corresponding with Bundy altogether.

Carol Bundy came into this world on August 26, 1942, the second of three children born to Charles and Gladys Peters. He

was a movie-theater troubleshooter; she was a hairdresser. Although Carol would always swear differently, her childhood was not a happy one. Charles was a raging alcoholic, and as a result, the already meager living he made in his profession was diminished by the money he spent on booze. Little money made its way home to provide his wife and three children with any of the finer things in life, and in many cases, with many of the bare necessities. But her mother was no better. A vindictive, spiteful, and likely mentally unbalanced woman, Gladys decided Carol was no longer her daughter when the child was eight years old and ignored the child for the rest of her life. Carol and her siblings were all beaten by their parents.

When Carol was a teenager, her mother died. While this was a blessing in a way— for it meant half the beatings and less parental neglect—it initiated an ugly period for her and her younger sister, Vicky. Charles Peters eventually remarried, but until that point, he satisfied his sexual appetites with his daughters. Many surmise that it was the incest that led Carol to have the man trouble of her later years.

One day, Carol came home from school to find the family cat dead. Her father had intended to kill his entire family, and soon confessed this to the police. So for a while, Carol and her siblings were sent to live in foster homes. Somehow, they ended up back in Daddy's, um, care. At 17, Carol married a man just like Dad—who at 56, was possibly older than her father, but who shared his alcoholic and abusive tendencies. Carol left him and took up with a writer, who put her through nursing school, but even as the "healthiest" relationship Carol ever had, this was not meant to last. Carol started having sex with women, but there was one common element in all of her relationships: chronic abuse.

In the late 1960s, Carol married Grant Bundy and bore him two children. During their marriage, Carol began to have several medical problems. Her increasing obesity notwithstanding, she was also afflicted with diabetes and her eyesight was failing. By her early 30s, Carol was nearly legally blind. Not unlike the long string of people whom Carol loved, Grant was an avid woman beater, and by 1979, Carol finally found the strength to leave him. She packed up herself and her two small children and moved to California.

It was here that she would forge the two relationships that changed her life forever. The first was with the Australian manager of the apartment complex in which she and her boys lived. Jack Murray was the first human being who showed Carol unconditional caring and concern, and even though he was married, it wasn't long before their relationship became sexual. Carol begged Jack to leave his wife, and when he wouldn't, she paid Jeanette Murray a visit, offering her $1,500 to leave her husband. The plan backfired and Carol ended up alone. But that didn't stop her from continuing to dote on Jack, even frequenting the country-western bar where Jack sang a couple of nights a week. It was here, at the Little Nashville Club, that Carol would forge the second, and most devastating, relationship of all.

Doug Clark was a Navy brat who had lived all over the world growing up. Although he didn't show any signs of what he would eventually grow into, he was a known braggart, constantly going on about his family's money and his sexual exploits. After school, he enlisted in the Air Force and spent a couple of years decoding Russian messages. Though the circumstances behind it are not known, Doug was honorably discharged from the Air Force before he had fully served out his term. From there, he got married, but was divorced only four years later. In 1980, Doug set fire to his car to collect the insurance money. He was never charged with the crime; it's known that he committed it only because he admitted it to Carol.

Doug had an exceptional talent for making homely women feel beautiful, and thus getting them to do anything he wanted.

Enter Carol Bundy, who was pining after Jack Murray at the Little Nashville Club on that fateful night in 1980 when their paths crossed.

Both Carol and Doug had a fair amount of sexual experience, and neither proved to be all that shy in the bedroom. Doug satisfied Carol; she was hooked. Doug wasn't quite so smitten, but used Carol's devotion as a way to have a place to live. He moved in with Carol and her two sons within a week of their first night together. Doug was not nice to her children, even telling her older son, right in front of his mother, how Doug could easily stab the child to death. So much for playing the motherhood redemption card. After several months with Doug, she finally came to her senses—where her children were concerned at least—and sent her sons to live with their father.

Carol continued her relationship with Doug, even though he would leave sometimes for months at a time—and sometimes take up with other women. One time, Doug even brought one of these women home to live with him and Carol. Carol, in the meantime, appeased herself with the knowledge that she was still in love with Jack, and if he ever came back to her, she would leave Doug in a heartbeat. She even met a man through the personals during this period who was extremely kind to her. But Doug had the stronghold, and when Doug was

ready to be with her again, she always dropped everything.

Carol and Doug had a very rich fantasy life, which eventually morphed into reality. They would play numerous master-and-slave games—with Carol always assuming the role of slave, natch. He would tell her how much he wanted to be with young girls, and how he was intrigued by necrophilia. That she was not repulsed by any of this made him confident and comfortable that he could finally make these fantasies a reality. And thus, the infamous Sunset Strip killer was born.

Doug and Carol began molesting an 11-year-old neighborhood girl, taking many pictures of each other en coitus with the child. Then, Doug would start coming home, bragging about women he had slept with and then killed. Two of the most horrible of these admissions were about a pair of teenage half-sisters, whom he had forced to fellate him, one at a time. When he was brought to orgasm, he shot the girl of the moment in the head. He admitted that after they were dead, he satisfied himself some more with the various orifices of their corpses. As his carnal carnage continued, Carol decided that she was getting jealous of his activities and wanted to be included. Doug was only too pleased. Carol would lure the women to their fates and watch, almost disinterestedly, as Doug did his thing.

Carol was so into her and Doug's killing sprees that she even went so far as to pack him a "kill bag"—a sack filled with all the accoutrements he needed to fulfill his murderous missions. In the bag, Carol had lovingly packed knives, paper towels, liquid cleanser, plastic bags, and rubber gloves.

One day, Doug brought home the head of a prostitute he had decapitated. He kept it in the freezer and took it out once in a while, bringing it into the shower where he would give it a good thaw and then satisfy himself with it. How did Carol react? Not rationally, by any stretch of the imagination. She took the head and made it up, as if she were a beautician-in-training and this was her plastic model.

It was soon time for Carol to commit a murder of her very own—and who better to kill than the man who had jilted her and thus left her free to take up with Doug in the first place? Of course, that's not exactly how it had transpired. As it happened, Carol ended up admitting some of the things she had been up to with Doug to Jack—and then she decided that he knew way too much. So one night, she lured him into his own van, under the guise of a no-strings-sex-fling-thing. She shot Jack in the back of the head, then went on a tear—literally—with a knife all around his body. She stabbed him in the back—after he was dead—several times, then slashed his

buttocks. Thinking the police might be able to trace the bullets in Jack's head back to her, Carol cut it off and absconded with it. Doug was pissed off at Carol and was worried that this murder would be the one that led the police to him. He was almost right.

Carol was about to hit rock bottom. She tried to commit suicide over her brutal murder of the one man she believed had truly loved her. She was becoming increasingly unraveled. On August 21, 1980, she marched into her supervisor's office and admitted the whole thing. Both Doug and Carol were arrested. Doug decided he should defend himself and inadvertently talked the jury right into handing him the death sentence. Carol's lawyers tried to plead insanity, but no one was having it. She decided to plead guilty on two counts of murder, which helped her evade execution. Her combined 25-year sentences ensure she won't be up for parole until 2012, when, if she lives that long, she will already be 72 years old.

Cattle Kate *(see Ella Watson)*

Cynthia Lynn Coffman (1962–)

MURDER

There's no single common denominator that can be found to explain why women do the evil that they do. In some cases, murderous women come from broken homes, from poor and abusive—both physically and sexually—households. But this cannot be said for Cynthia Lynn Coffman, an average Midwestern born-and-bred girl who had a taste for breaking all the rules and a passion for the wrong men. And who became, at 26, the first woman to be handed a death sentence in the state of California since the death penalty was reinstated in 1977, for the crimes she committed with her boyfriend, James Gregory Marlow, and the string of strangled, naked corpses they left in their wake.

Cynthia Coffman was born on January 9, 1962, and raised in a typical, Catholic, middle-class family. Her father was a St. Louis businessman. But Cynthia was something of a wild child, and by the time she was 17, she was pregnant and on the way down the aisle to a loveless marriage. After five years of domestic hell, Cynthia made a break for it. She headed west and within a few weeks shacked up with a guy she met during her stint as a waitress in a Page, Arizona, diner.

For a year, Cynthia carried on with this transition beau. Then, in 1986, after being pulled over for blowing through a stop sign, Cynthia's boyfriend was arrested and sent to jail for six weeks. Even though Cynthia was carrying a goodly supply of methamphetamine and a gun in her bag, she was not detained.

It was during her visits to her jailed lover that Cynthia realized who the true love of her life was—and it wasn't the poor guy who more than likely took the rap for her. James Gregory Marlow was 5 years older than the 24-year-old Cynthia, but had a past that may as well have made him 20 years older. In and out of various detention halls and prisons since he was 10 years old, Marlow was serving out a sentence for stealing his sixth wife's car in the same California jail where Cynthia's boyfriend was being detained. Cynthia forgot who she was originally intending to visit before her boyfriend's six-week term was up in the Barstow jail. By June of 1986, Marlow was released and the two lovebirds took off into the night. They were married in a matter of weeks, and Cynthia had her butt tattooed with "I belong to the Folsom Wolf"—that being Marlow's nickname from time spent in Folsom prison—in celebration.

It was only a matter of weeks before the two began their infamous crime spree. They started out lightly: In July, they robbed a house in Kentucky, where they were able to acquire a shotgun. But by October, their crimes would take quite a sinister turn.

Their first victim was Sandra Neary, who they attacked at an ATM in Costa Mesa, California, on October 26, 1986. They robbed her, strangled her, and disposed of her body in the woods in Riverside County, California. This would become their routine. Within a couple of weeks, they hit their next victim in Bullhead City, Arizona. Paula Simmons's car was found abandoned beside an ATM, and when her body was discovered naked and strangled, the pieces started coming together of a possible connection between the murders.

This would not help Corinna Novis, however, who vanished on November 7 on her final visit to a cash machine. Corinna was abducted by the Folsom Wolf and his, well, bitch, and taken to the apartment that Mr. and Mrs. Marlow were making their residence. According to the California Department of Corrections, Corinna was handcuffed in the bedroom. Marlow sodomized her, while Cynthia reportedly also sexually abused the 20-year-old woman. They strangled her with a necktie and buried her body in a shallow grave in a Fontana vineyard. Once they dumped the body, Cynthia and Marlow headed to Corinna's home, taking her checkbook and forging several checks, and stealing her car.

By November 12, the preying couple was ready for their next kill. This time, they didn't lurk by the ATM in typical fashion. Rather, they were more bold, and came upon 19-year-old Lynel Murray where she worked in a Huntington Beach dry cleaners. They kidnapped Lynel, robbed the registers,

and even helped themselves to some of the customers' clothing. They took the poor girl to a hotel, where they registered under Lynel's name (and used her credit card, so that her next of kin could foot the bill). Marlow raped Lynel while Cynthia was out on an errand, so she decided Lynel would be her kill. Cynthia unsuccessfully tried to strangle their victim, but Marlow had to come in and finish the job. And if that isn't bad enough, it is also reported that after he killed her, he dragged Lynel's body into the bathroom where he urinated on the corpse. Perhaps getting lazy or cocky, they simply left the body in the hotel room and headed for Canada. Perhaps it was a little of both, or perhaps they were simply not working with a whole lot of common sense.

Within a couple of days of their latest crime, Corinna Novis's checkbook was discovered in a fast-food bag that also contained papers with Marlow's and Coffman's names on them. In another motel, the manager found and turned over to authorities sheets of stationery with forged Lynel Murray signatures. When police discovered Lynel's body, they swept the room for fingerprints, and they uncovered ones that matched Marlow's already-on-file prints. It was only a matter of time until the two were in police custody.

On November 14, 1986, Cynthia and Marlow were arrested in Sugarloaf, where they were hitchhiking after dumping

Corinna Novis's car. They were both held without bail. In the three years it took for the case to come to trial, Cynthia and Marlow fell deeply out of love with one another. On August 30, 1989, they were both sentenced to death by the state of California. At the time of this writing, both are still awaiting execution on death row.

Lona Cohen *(see Helen Kroger)*

Eva Coo *(1894–1935)*

MURDER, PROSTITUTION

Eva Coo will forever be known as "the mallet murderess of Milford," but she was more than that. She was a tough broad who ran a thriving business, owned property, and was an entrepreneurial success. All this during the Great Depression, when most people were just barely getting by. But she wasn't convicted for running one of Upstate New York's top brothels. No. Eva's claim to infamy would be the scheme she tried to pull off to make her true fortune. Eva had numerous employees, and had taken out a life insurance policy on each of them, naming herself as the beneficiary. Her plan was for her employees to start disappearing, one by one. Unfortunately for Eva, she didn't get very far.

Eva Coo was a Canadian who moved to Oneonta, New York, to start a new life

when a short-lived marriage ended in 1921. She originally hailed from Haliburton, Ontario, where she was born Eva Currie in 1894. She married William Coo when she was still a teenager, essentially because she had already left home and needed some form of support. But the quick-witted, tall, and outgoing Eva soon learned that she could easily rely on herself.

Eva opened a speakeasy called "Eva's Place" soon after she hit Oneonta. It was one part bar, one part brothel, which in the prohibitive early 1920s was about as illegal a joint as one could run. But she did very well with a steady clientele that consisted mostly of college students and the blue-collar set. Because police, politicians, and various other would-be shutter-downers also enjoyed the pleasures inside Eva's Place, she was never that worried about being, well, shut down. She had more than one law-enforcement official on her client roster, and they knew they were safe enjoying the delights of Eva's Place, as long as they remained on her side. Everyone was happy with the symbiotic sin-fest.

Until Eva devised her scheme, that is. Of course, if Eva had thought it through a little better, she might have gotten away with it. But she didn't. And so she got the chair.

In 1931, a sad and sorry soul named Harry Wright managed to come under Eva's care. Nicknamed "Gimpy," Harry had more than a few problems, not the least of which was his passion for the sauce. He performed some odd jobs for Eva to earn his keep and pay his bar tab, which was jump-started with $2,000 Harry was supposed to inherit when his mother died that instead went directly into Fund Eva. Mrs. Wright had also entrusted the family home to Eva, which she was able to collect on when the house burned down shortly after Mrs. Wright died. As poor Harry was now in her care, Eva took out a few life insurance policy on Harry, with a payout of about $6,000, which would double should Harry meet his demise in an accident.

By mid-1934, Harry had overstayed his welcome, and his death benefits were ripe for the taking; it was time for Eva to collect. But she didn't act alone. She enlisted a young waitress in her employ, Martha Cliff, to help Gimpy have his "accident."

On June 14, 1934, Eva and Martha took the naïve and unsuspecting Harry for a little drive. When they got to what they thought was an isolated enough spot off of Route 7, a highway an inebriated Harry typically stumbled down when on a bender, they pulled off the road. Eva bashed Harry's head in with a mallet; Martha drove over the corpse several times with the car. The women dragged Harry to the side of the road and left him there, hoping it would look like he stumbled in front of the car of a hit-and-run driver.

The next day, Eva reported Harry missing, and just as the police discovered the body, Eva attempted to cash in on Harry's life insurance. Her actions aroused suspicion that Harry's death wasn't an accident, and Eva was investigated. The police did not like what they found. Not only did they learn that Eva and Martha had disappeared from Eva's place for a few hours on the night of Harry's death, they also learned that Eva had taken out life insurance policies on several of her employees and friends, including Martha Cliff. They were only too happy to nip her murderous scheming in the bud.

Eva and Martha were arrested right away, and each woman tried to pin the actual murder on the other. An absurdly gruesome investigation followed, in which poor Gimpy's mangled corpse was exhumed and used as a prop at the crime scene to determine which woman was more responsible for its lifeless state. By August, the case went to trial, and it was determined that Harry was definitely offed by Eva. But just to be sure, and this isn't a joke, they exhumed the poor mangled bastard yet again to check the wounds. Whether this was really necessary or whether there was a morbid fascination to the chronic exhumations is not really known. (In fact, it's almost a surprise that Harry's body isn't still on display in a town-history exhibit somewhere.)

Martha was found guilty of murder in the second degree and sentenced to 20 years in the clink. Eva was not so lucky. In 1934, the death penalty was in full force in New York State, and a first-degree conviction reserved the ill-gone madam a seat in the electric chair. Eva sizzled on June 27, 1935. Her final words: "Good-bye, darlings!" She was the third woman to be executed at Sing Sing in the twentieth century.

Faye Copeland (1921–)

MURDER

She became the oldest female resident of death row when she was sentenced to die in November 1990. At 69, she was grandmother to 14 and great-grandmother to 20. And, as protested vehemently by her defense attorneys, she suffered from battered woman's syndrome. Still, she was going to die for her part in her husband's hustling and murder scheme. In Chillicothe, Missouri, in the late 1980s, farmer Ray Copeland, Faye's husband, concocted a plan to hustle livestock. He hired a few drifters to buy cattle with bad checks and bring them back to the Copelands, who would immediately resell the cattle. A little cattle hustling shouldn't warrant the death penalty, right? It does if you put a bullet in the heads of the poor bastards you hire to steal the cattle. Faye claims not to have had any part in the actual killings; however, when the

Copelands were busted, Faye was diligently at work on a quilt she was stitching together from the dead men's clothes. Additionally, a register produced of the couple's farm workers showed X's drawn, in Faye's handwriting, through the names of the deceased.

The gig was up when a business associate of the Copelands came across some random bones on the Copeland property. Police were summoned, and a dig commenced. They found five bodies in all, each showing the telltale sign of murder in the first degree: a bullet through the back of the head.

Ray Copeland, who was 75 years old when the Copelands got caught, died in prison only 3 years later. Faye's case was repeatedly appealed, until on August 10, 1999, at the age of 78, her sentence was commuted to life in prison.

Mary Ann Cotton (1832–1873)

MURDER, BIGAMY

While the cases have been compared as eerily similar by many crime scholars, there's a huge difference between why Nannie Doss (page 64) killed, and why Mary Ann Cotton seemed to poison everyone standing in her way—and then some. Nannie killed, or so she said, for love. Mary

Ann didn't really understand the concept of "love." She was a cold and calculating woman who made every move in her life, including her numerous murders, for a greater reward: money.

Can this woman be entirely blamed for her obsession with the green stuff? After all, she grew up in abject poverty in mid-nineteenth-century England, where not being financially comfortable meant not that you couldn't afford a new dress, but that you couldn't eat.

Mary Ann Cotton, born Mary Ann Robson to teenage parents in the poor mining town of Low Moorsely in County Durham, England, was the older of two children. Her father was obsessively and oppressively Methodist and terrorized Mary Ann and her little brother, Robert. It might have been lucky that the merciless zealot fell to his death in a mine shaft when Mary Ann was just eight, except that the only means for getting money the small family had had fallen right through that shaft with him. Luckily, her mother soon remarried, but her stepfather got along with Mary Ann even worse than her own father had.

When she was a teenager, Mary Ann left home to work as a servant in the wealthy town of South Hetton. Various sex scandals ensued, possibly because she was reported to be quite a good-looking girl and not because she actually earned her reputation,

but within two years, she cleaned up her act and became Mrs. William Mobray. Mobray, like her father, was a miner. A dutiful wife, Mary Ann bore her husband five children in the first four years of their marriage; unfortunately, only one of these children would survive past infancy. More children were born, but none lived to see a fifth birthday. The cause of death for all: "gastric fever."

The only consolation that William had at the loss of all his progeny was that he had purchased life insurance policies for all his children—and for himself. In 1865, William himself succumbed to the "gastric fever," leaving Mary Ann completely alone, except for her sole living child, Isabella.

After collecting the insurance money from the deaths of her various family members, Mary Ann dumped Isabella off to live with her mother, and moved to Seaham Harbour. There, she met another man, with whom she actually, believe it or not, fell in love. But there was a catch: 28-year-old Joseph Nattrass was already married and not about to leave his wife. So Mary Ann got a job as a nurse to support herself, and there, under her care, she met her second husband, George Ward. A seemingly healthy fellow, George didn't last two years with his new bride. Once he adjusted his will to leave everything to his darling wife, he died suddenly. Cause of death: gastric fever. Luckily, no children came of this marriage.

Before George's body was cold, Mary Ann took a job as a housekeeper for a widower named John Robinson in 1866. Robinson had five children. Within a few months, three of them were dead. Even more gruesome, in early 1867, Mary Ann went home to care for her ailing mother. Within days her mother was dead. By the end of April, Mary Ann's daughter, Isabella, of whom she had just reclaimed custody, was also dead. All the deaths were attributed to the same cause: gastric fever. John married Mary Ann in 1867, after all the deaths, and in the next two years, she bore him two children. Both died shortly after birth—both of gastric fever.

Mary Ann had not given up her passion for money, and even though she was making a small fortune collecting on insurance policies from family members popping off left and right, she could not get enough. She considered the money Robinson gave her a pittance and began to steal from him and even go so far as to pawn valuables sitting around the house for more and more money. When Robinson got wind of his wife's thefts, he promptly kicked her to the curb.

After drifting for a while and taking on odd jobs to get her by, Mary Ann made friends with a woman named Margaret Cotton in Walbottle in 1870. The fatally trusting Margaret introduced her new friend to her widowed brother, Frederick. Mary Ann soon became pregnant with Frederick's child, and Margaret soon succumbed to gastric fever. Mary Ann and Frederick were married within a couple of months, even though Mary Ann had yet to divorce James Robinson.

In 1871, Mary Ann gave birth to a son, adding to the two sons Cotton already had from his first marriage. Frederick soon moved his family to West Auckland to evade rumors that the Cottons had anything to do with the deaths of the livestock of their neighbors. This would prove to be a most fatal move for the poor guy. By coincidence, the Cottons moved to the same street where Joseph Nattrass, no longer married, was making his residence. Mary Ann quickly picked up with Joseph where they had left off, and soon, Frederick Cotton caught gastric fever. Joseph moved in with Mary Ann and her "three" children, and the kids began to pop off, one by one. The only one who survived at this point was Frederick's son by his first marriage, Charles.

Mary Ann took a job as a nurse for a wealthy officer, James Quick-Manning. Mary Ann liked his money, and soon enough, Joseph died suddenly of gastric fever—but not before taking out a life insurance policy to provide for Mary if any harm should ever befall him. There was now only one more obstacle to Mary Ann's wealthier-ever-after plans: her seven-year-old stepson, Charles Cotton.

By this time, Mary Ann had successfully murdered several husbands, a bevy of children, and not to mention her own mother, a sister-in-law, and quite possibly numerous unsuspecting cattle. So she was probably feeling more than a little cocky when she sloppily told a government employee named Tom Reily that she probably could have married again if it weren't for the young Charles. When the child ended up dead, suspicion was finally targeted where it belonged. Charles was exhumed, and the traces of arsenic found in his system confirmed the unthinkable: He was poisoned by his stepmother, Mary Ann Cotton.

Cotton never admitted to any of her crimes and vehemently maintained her innocence. The jury was not convinced. She was sent to the scaffold and hanged on March 24, 1873.

Alice Crimmins (c. 1944–)

MURDER

Was she unfairly convicted of murdering her two young children because the all-male, conservative jury had no tolerance for a woman who was not afraid to embrace and satisfy her sexual appetites? Or did she kill them, which would mean that the manslaughter sentence she received—and then successfully appealed—wasn't nearly enough punishment? Whatever happened that fateful summer night when Alice Crimmins's two children disappeared and later turned up dead remains a mystery to this day.

In a lot of ways, Alice Crimmins wasn't your typical 1960s housewife from Queens. Certainly she paid attention to the little details of her life, providing for her children, Alice (also called "Missy") and Eddie, and trying to make a good home for her husband, Edward. But as satisfying as she tried to make the life for her family, she, herself, was not satisfied—at least sexually. Alice had enjoyed wedded bliss in the early portion of her marriage to Edward, an airline mechanic, but as the years went on, and their children grew, Edward decided he preferred the company of his male friends—and bar buddies—to the company of his wife and children. Neglected, Alice embarked on her own extramarital pursuits.

Eventually, Edward and Alice's problems began to be too much, and the couple separated. Edward remained fixated on his estranged wife, however; after he moved out, he tapped her phone so he could listen in on her conversations with her lovers and bugged her room so he could take a vicarious delight in her exploits.

It was during this period of separation that a tragedy unfolded. On July 14, 1965, according to Mrs. Crimmins's original account of the story, Alice Crimmins fed her children a meal of frozen manicotti at 7:30 P.M. At 9, she took the children for a drive, stopping for gas at 9:30 P.M. She then put her children to bed, and fell asleep herself about midnight. When she woke up at 4 A.M. and went in to check on her children, they were gone.

Missy's body was found the next day in a vacant lot. The tiny, blonde four-year-old was dressed in a T-shirt and a pair of yellow panties and had apparently been strangled by a man's necktie, found around her neck. Her brother's body, that of five-year-old Eddie, was discovered several days later by a neighborhood child.

Alice Crimmins's reaction to learning of the deaths of her children was something beyond stoic: It was almost as if she felt nothing at all, which the police were quick to pick up on. Also, she never cried—even though she had actually been brought to the murder scene to identify her daughter—until she was in front of the cameras, that is. Another factor that pointed the finger of suspicion at Alice Crimmins: Not even a week after the funerals of her two children she was out hitting the bar scene and the singles circuit all over again. Some say that this was just a way for the 26-year-old mother to cope; others say that it proved beyond a

shadow of a doubt that Crimmins was glad to be rid of her kids, possibly because not having that responsibility freed her up to fully experience all the delights of her debaucherous lifestyle.

Whatever the case, there was a general feeling of bias on either side when Alice Crimmins was arrested for the murders of her children on September 11, 1967, and the case finally went to court in May of the following year.

The prosecution portrayed her as a "loose" and uncaring woman. The defense, supported by Alice's wickedly dramatic antics, such as screaming out, weeping profusely, and even fainting, surmised that there was no way this loving mother could destroy her children.

During the initial trial, the evidence was stacked against Crimmins. Not only did the coroner's report show that Alice had been lying about her activities with the children that night, but more than one witness was brought by the prosecution to condemn Alice. The first was a former lover of Alice's, Joseph Rorech. He testified that Alice had not only admitted killing Missy, but had also broken down and confessed that she had had at least something to do with the death of her son.

The second incriminating witness was a neighbor, Sophie Earomirski, who wrote to the police about the night in question. She said she had been looking out her window in the middle of the night because she couldn't sleep. She saw a man and a woman, matching Alice Crimmins's description, holding a small bundle under one arm and holding the hand of a small boy with her other hand, walking to a car parked in the lot.

Crimmins was convicted of first-degree manslaughter for Missy's death and was sentenced to 5 to 20 years. The conviction caused the unbelievably dramatic woman to lapse into a coma for two weeks. However, an appeal was won when it was proved that several of the jurors had not been acting in a nonbiased fashion. In fact, many of them had visited the site of the crime to gather clues and formulate their own opinions. But the appeal was not strong enough: The case was brought to court again, and this time Alice was also charged for the murder of her son. (She hadn't been charged for this in the previous trial because until now, it could not be proven that Eddie had been murdered.)

The new trial began in March 1971. The prosecution stood on their same tenets. The defense sought to disprove the prosecution's evidence, including completely discrediting the sanity of one Sophie Earomirski. This time, Crimmins was defended by a top Manhattan attorney, Herbert Lyon, who had decided to take on the case pro bono because he and his partner, William E.

Erlbaum, fully believed in her innocence. But they lost again: She was guilty of first-degree murder for the death of her son and first-degree manslaughter for the death of her daughter. There were no comas this time. Alice was back to the slammer.

In 1973, Crimmins was released as the Appellate Division of the Supreme Court in Brooklyn ruled that there was insufficient evidence to convict Crimmins for her son's murder. She was free—until 1975, that is, when she was rejailed for her daughter's death.

In 1977, Alice Crimmins was instituted in a work-release program, giving her every weekend free. Having divorced Edward several years back, she was able to marry the boyfriend who stood by her throughout most of her ordeal, to whom, at the time of this writing, she remains married and lives a life of general obscurity as a Long Island housewife.

Moll Cutpurse *(see Mary Frith)*

Iva Toguri D'Aquino *(1916–)*
a.k.a. "Tokyo Rose"

ESPIONAGE

The quiet and diminutive 85-plus-year-old woman who sits behind the counter of a Japanese imports store on the north side of the city of Chicago, Illinois, seems more than a world away from the public-enemy-number-one persona that was slapped on her in the mid-1940s. In fact, even then, it was hard to believe that this seemingly composed spirit was the most hated woman in the United States for the radio broadcasts she delivered that were perceived as an attempt to demoralize American GIs. Was she a ruthless witch? Or just a victim of an odd strain of circumstances?

Iva Ikuko Toguri D'Aquino is as American as they come. Born the daughter of Japanese immigrants, ironically enough, on July 4, 1916, in Los Angeles, California, she grew up in South Central Los Angeles. She was raised a Methodist and enjoyed a fairly normal teenage life. She loved listening to programs on the radio. She played varsity tennis, took piano lessons, even had a crush on Jimmy Stewart. She earned a degree in medical zoology from UCLA. Everything was as normal as could be.

Then, one day, word came from Japan that Iva's aunt, her mother's sister, was ill and needed constant looking after. Iva's mother could not go; she suffered from chronic diabetes. So Iva went in her place. The young Japanese American shipped out for Japan the day after her twentieth birthday in July of 1941, just months before the outbreak of World War II.

From the moment she got to her ancestral home, Iva was met with suspicion, and even hostility, for being an American. She tried to return even before the war broke out, but a misunderstanding with her passport kept her in Japan. Once the war got underway, the situation turned critical. In fact, one night when she returned to her aunt and uncle's home from the job she took as a typist to pay for Japanese lessons, she found all her possessions out in the street.

In 1943, she began working as a typist for Radio Tokyo, where she fell in with POWs who, under strict Japanese supervision, were assigned to create and produce programming aimed at demoralizing U.S. forces. One of the POWs, Australian Army Major Charles Cousens, persuaded Iva to DJ on the popular *Zero Hour* show. The POWs had ulterior motives; their goal was to sabotage the Japanese propaganda emanating through the airwaves. Iva actually operated under the name of "Orphan Ann," and her character was pretty much a tongue-in-cheek parody of a nationalistic Japanese femme fatale. Orphan Ann was created to amuse the listeners who knew better while appeasing the Radio Tokyo supervisors, who had no idea subversive tactics were being used. Iva was one of many who made these broadcasts, but was the only one to take the fall.

Her broadcasts were innocuous enough. The usual format was that Iva, as "Ann," or any of the other women making the broadcasts, would read from a script, usually one of Cousens', but sometimes one of her own. On September 20, 1945, Iva opened one of her last broadcasts thus: "Greetings everybody! This is your Number One Enemy, your favorite playmate, Orphan Ann on Radio Tokyo—the little sunbeam whose throat you'd like to cut! Get ready again for a vicious assault on your morale, 75 minutes of music and news for our friends—I mean, our enemies!—in the South Pacific." And then she played some music.

This was the format of all of her broadcasts. Most everyone knew it was a joke. Even Iva herself was in on the joke from the inside. As an American patriot, she also began smuggling food and medical supplies to the POWs. Around the same time she met and married Portuguese ex-pat Felipe d'Aquino, who was leery of her work at Radio Tokyo.

After the War ended, Iva talked freely about her radio experiences. In fact, she had built a following over the years with American servicemen and she was genuinely proud of the work she had done. However, military investigators were not amused, and thus, the myth of "Tokyo Rose," a Japanese siren who lured American servicemen to their demises over the

Pacific, was born. The truth was, there was no such woman. "Tokyo Rose" was in fact a composite of all the different Japanese women, including Iva, who had hosted radio programs during the war.

Iva, being both Japanese and American, was an easy scapegoat. In October 1945, she was taken from her husband and imprisoned by the American military in Japan without a warrant. Later, she was sent back home to California, only to receive similar treatment, culminating with trial for treason.

At 13 weeks and costing well over half a million dollars, the trial of Tokyo Rose was the most expensive one to date in American history. She was charged with eight counts of treason, and ultimately convicted of one. Iva was fined $10,000 and sentenced to 10 years at Alderson Federal Reformatory in West Virginia. All this with nearly no tangible evidence against her and the defense of former Radio Tokyo POWs, including Charles Cousens.

Iva ended up serving six years, having been released early for being a model prisoner. After winning a two-year battle against being banished to Japan, she attempted to live a relatively normal and quiet life. Unfortunately, that life would not include her husband, Felipe. Her supporter, best friend, and true love signed a document in 1949, during Iva's trial, swearing he would never visit the United States; Iva could never leave the United States again for fear of not being allowed back. The two were divorced. Felipe died in 1996.

Interest in Tokyo Rose resurfaced in 1969, when *60 Minutes* ran a segment on her. In the revisionist eyes of the late 1960s, Iva Toguri's only crime, if it could even be considered that, was being a patriotic American who happened to be of Japanese descent during World War II; a case of good intentions gone awry. Her story became a symbol of the domestic prejudice against the Japanese prevalent during that era. Vindication was finally on its way for Iva, and in 1976, she was pardoned by President Gerald Ford in one of his last acts in office.

The trial has been over for many years, but the jury of the American public is still out on whether Iva was a patriot or a traitor. She has considered writing an autobiography, but at the time of this writing, that project has yet to be undertaken.

Evelyn Dick *(1920-??)*

MURDER

Evelyn Dick was the very picture of glamour. She was a strikingly beautiful and stylish woman who knew how to dress herself and who was exceptionally adept at spending money on just that. She was, as the press playfully coined her during her trial, "the lethal beauty in the mink coat." But underneath that glam exterior beat the heart of a murderess, who was not satisfied merely to murder her husband; she had to chop him to pieces, too, leaving just his torso behind for identification. Not to mention that she killed her infant son as well.

Canadian born and bred, Evelyn MacClean came into the world on October 13, 1920, in Beamsville, near Niagara Falls. When Evelyn was a year old, the MacCleans settled in Hamilton, Ontario. Evelyn's father, Donald, was a streetcar conductor—and a raving drunk. Her mother, Alexandra, had long since forgotten why she married Donald and was a bitter woman with a bad temper, which she usually took out on her only child. To add one more ingredient to the recipe for a disastrous childhood, Evelyn wasn't allowed to play with other children that often because her parents thought she was "too fragile."

Things improved slightly as Evelyn got older, however. Even though her father was a streetcar conductor, and her mother didn't work, the family seemed to always have a lot of cash. Although never substantiated, it has been suspected that Donald was pilfering from the Hamilton Railway System by pocketing much of the fare money he collected. Whatever the reason, the family had enough to live comfortably. Evelyn dressed well, adorning herself in furs and expensive jewelry, and threw extravagant parties in an effort to make some friends—and possibly land herself a husband.

In the friends department, her efforts weren't as effective as she would have liked. Most women felt that Evelyn was a bit of a show-off, overdone and overwrought, trying way too hard. She mostly found herself in the company of older men. Many suspected that it was from these men that her money came: She would grant them various favors, and they would repay her with cash or mink or jewels. Her pregnancy in 1942 only fueled the suspicions.

Evelyn's first daughter, Heather, was born mentally retarded. Evelyn gave Heather the last name "White," trying to pretend that she was, in fact, married, and that her husband was overseas fighting the War. Just two years later, she was pregnant again—and naturally, her "husband" had not been discharged or otherwise available to help sire the child. The baby was stillborn. In 1944, Evelyn gave birth to her third and final child, who she named Peter David—and also gave the mysterious last name "White." By this time, Alexandra MacClean had left her husband, so Alexandra, Evelyn, and the two children lived together in a small apartment in Hamilton. It was quite a shock for Alexandra when she learned that Evelyn

planned to marry a man she had never met—or even heard of before.

More mysterious than where John Dick came from was, in a few months' time, where he went. Barely nine months into his marriage to Evelyn, John Dick disappeared. No one was really surprised that he left her—the marriage wasn't exactly a happy one. In fact, the two didn't even live together for the early weeks of their marriage. Evelyn was closing on a house, and it was her decision to wait until they could move into the house before living together. What's more, Evelyn bought the house entirely by herself—and John Dick's name wasn't even on the deed.

All of this may have seemed innocent enough—had a group of children playing near the Dick property on a late winter afternoon not found a man's torso. On Saturday, March 16, 1946, John Dick's torso was identified by his brother-in-law. Police learned from Alexander Kammerer, John's cousin, that John had been missing since March 6, when John moved out of Kammerer's apartment. He had been staying there for a while to get away from Evelyn, and when he stopped coming back after a while, he assumed John had gone back to his wife.

But the marital problems were not all the police were going on when they brought Evelyn in as a suspect in her husband's murder. When he learned the fate of poor John Dick, Evelyn's neighbor, Bill Landeg, reported that Evelyn had borrowed his Packard earlier that month. She returned it with blood all over the front seat and bloody clothes in the back seat. She had left a note apologizing and saying that her daughter had cut herself and that was why there was blood everywhere. But Landeg wasn't buying any of it.

And that wasn't the worst of it. John Dick wasn't the only male in Evelyn's life who had gone missing. Her infant son, Peter, seemed to have disappeared as well. A search of the Dick house revealed the horrible fate of the son. His tiny body was found encased in cement in a trunk in the attic. Now Evelyn was looking at two murder charges.

Before her case went to trial, enthralled psychologists were compelled to run tests on Evelyn to see what kind of a woman could so brutally murder her husband and child. What they came up with was that Evelyn had an intelligence level bordering on "moron," and the emotional development and metal capacity of a 13-year-old. Whether this was an accurate assessment or not has been disputed for years.

Evelyn tried to pin the murders on everyone, from her lover, Bill Bohuzuk, to her father, Donald MacLean. In fact, all three ended up facing judge and jury for the murders. Bohuzuk was let off; MacLean was sentenced to five years for acting as an accessory. Evelyn was convicted of her husband's murder and set to hang after her first trial. She had a good lawyer; when her sentence was appealed, the conviction was overruled on a technicality: Evelyn's statements had not been submitted into evidence properly and the judge had not properly instructed the jury. Nevertheless, she was sentenced to life imprisonment for the manslaughter of Peter David White. She served just over 10 years of her sentence before she was paroled in 1958.

Once paroled, Evelyn was given a new identity and set up in a new job and new life, compliments of the parole board. No one from her old Hamilton life ever heard from Evelyn again except for Mary Lynch, a member of the parole board who kept in touch with Evelyn for many years. Apparently Evelyn had married an executive and was living a financially comfortable and fashionable life. Everything she always wanted. All it had cost her were a few body parts—and those weren't even her own.

Nannie Doss *(1905–1965)*

MURDER

Much like Mary Ann Cotton (page 54) and Judi Buenoano (page 43), Nancy Hazle Braggs Harrelson Lanning Morton Doss was a big fan of arsenic; unlike these two women, however, Nannie (as she had been called since she was a child because of her infectious good nature) didn't murder just for the insurance bucks. No. Nannie was an incurable romantic. When she killed a husband, it was because he had proven himself to be a grave disappointment to her idea of manly valor, which she invented after reading too many romance novels and magazines. And what of others she killed, such as her mother, her children, and a couple of sisters? Well, if they got in the way of Nannie's finding that one true love, or if they were in general inconveniencing Nannie, they proved to be as expendable as the husbands. Of course, the insurance proceeds didn't hurt.

Nancy was born in 1905 to Loulisa, who was generally called "Lou," and James Hazle, poor farming folk from Alabama. She was the oldest of four children. Her father terrorized the family with his temper; her mother catered to his wishes. Like many poor farming families, the children were not so much the result of parental love as a need for help to work the farm. James treated his children like slaves, and it was a miracle if they could find time to enjoy regular childhood and teenage pursuits—which meant, for Nannie, boys. But the farmer's daughter always found time for a roll in the, um, hay, in her daddy's barn. Between chores, of course.

When Nannie was 16 years old, she went to work at Linen Thread Company. At that job, Mr. Hazle found the ideal husband for his daughter in one Charley Braggs. Nannie hardly knew Braggs, and because of her fantasies of one day being swept away from the family farm by her strong and handsome and adoring young prince, Nannie was none too pleased with her father's choice. It wasn't that Charley wasn't handsome or able, he simply wasn't what she had dreamed of. But she went through with the wedding anyway. After all, what choice did she have?

This, of course, didn't mean that she would give up her romance fantasy. Nannie had several affairs during her marriage to Braggs. Braggs never noticed her indiscretions; he was always either drunk or having his own affairs—or both. The marriage was tumultuous. And even though they had four daughters together, neither Nannie or Charley were happy in the marriage—except for the sex.

Then, in 1927, strange things started to happen in the Braggs' household. That was the year that Nannie and Charley's two middle daughters died one afternoon. Suspected cause: food poisoning. But Braggs was not convinced that this was the real cause. His wife, though usually giggling and full of mirth, had a dark side—and one he did not trust. He asked no questions but packed up himself and their eldest daughter and fled. He was the only husband of Nannie's to come out of his marriage to her alive.

Charley eventually came back, but with another woman and her child. When Nannie realized that the marriage was over, she packed up both her daughters and moved a couple of towns away from her parents. This situation worked out well as Nannie could leave her daughters with her mother during the day while she worked at the local cotton mill. She was content with her domestic life, but she was lonely for a man, so she answered a few personal ads. Through this method, she hooked her second husband, Frank Harrelson, a seemingly dashing gentleman whom she married in 1929. But marriage always brings out the worst in folks, as they say, and it wasn't long before Frank showed his true colors. Not only was he a heavy drinker and a woman-beater, Frankie boy was an ex-con. So much for prince number two.

Nannie endured her marriage to Frank for 16 years, compensating in the same way she had when she was married to Charley. In that time, she watched her surviving daughters get married and have babies, but she worried that those babies would become a burden to her some day when she was able to rid herself of Frank and find her true prince. No problem. It seemed that any child born to either of Nannie's daughters mysteriously died in Grandma's care. Offing

those babies gave Nannie an idea: Instead of waiting for Frank to drink himself to death, why not help the process along? And she did. On September 16, 1945, after a night of rabble-rousing and a subsequent all-night lust marathon with his wife, Frank keeled over and died early the next day. Nannie had put rat poison in his secret stash of liquor that he thought he had kept well hidden in the garden. Nannie had found her secret: Sure, one day her prince would come—but until then, she'd just have to keep picking off the frogs, one by one.

The next frog entered Nannie's life in 1947. A couple of years after Frank's death, Nannie moved to North Carolina in response to a letter she received from Arlie Lanning, who was also a drinker and a philanderer. But Nannie didn't know that right away. Within two days of their meeting, Nannie and Arlie were married. But there was only so long she could pretend she had done the right thing by marrying Arlie: By 1950, he was dead. Shortly after his death, Nannie's house burned to the ground. With nowhere else to turn, Nannie moved in with Arlie's mother. Within a couple of weeks, the hapless mother-in-law died in her sleep, causes cited as "natural." Then Nannie moved in with one of her sisters, who, within a couple of days, also mysteriously died. Everyone felt sorry for Nannie as so much misfortune seemed to follow her around.

In 1952, Nannie fell in love again. Prince number four was a retired Kansas businessman named Richard L. Morton. Because he had such high standing in the community, Nannie thought for sure this must be the one! But he was not what he seemed to be. Not only was he carrying on with another woman the whole time he was married to Nannie, he was also flat broke—and very much in debt. He would have been done away with much sooner had Nannie's mother not come to stay with the couple after Nannie's father died. Richard had to die, but Lou was in the way. In January 1953, Nannie's mother died of mysterious stomach pains. By April, husband number four had joined his mother-in-law in the afterlife.

Nannie married her last husband, Sam Doss, because he seemed solid, steadfast, and stable. Unfortunately, he was a little too stable, and this drove Nannie up a wall. Even at age 48, Nannie had managed once again to marry the wrong man. While he wasn't a drinker, a philanderer, or a beater, old Sam was a penny pincher with no sense of adventure to speak of. He was the type to be in bed every night by 9:30 P.M., and expected his wife to be by his side. He also made the hugest mistake he ever could have made: He forbade Nannie to read her romance magazines or watch the TV shows she had grown to love so dearly. Sam had to go.

Nannie first tried to kill Sam with a poisoned pie, but somehow, during a 23-day stay in the hospital, he was able to fight it off. When he came home, she nursed him dutifully. That night, she made him a delicious roast and served it to her beloved with a cup of coffee, brewed with her extra-special ingredient. If Sam hadn't just been discharged from the hospital, his doctor might not have been suspicious about his death. But the good doctor ordered an autopsy that revealed enough arsenic in Sam's system to kill 20 men. The gig was up.

It was a scandal that this round-faced, loving grandma (her children had finally managed to produce offspring far enough away from Nannie to ensure the continuity of the blood line) could be responsible for such death and devastation. But when one looks at it closely, how could she not have been suspected? Surely no one has *that* much bad luck. Not everyone dies in the same way. Why did no one see past the delightful giggle and put the pieces together?

Nannie finally confessed to all her murders, but only because her interrogators wouldn't let her have her romance magazines back until she did. And when she confessed, she did it in such a lighthearted fashion that she was screened for possible insanity. It was discovered that the woman was indeed not at all insane; she was simply evil.

Nannie was sentenced to life in prison on May 17, 1955, when she finally decided to plead guilty. Her plea, as well as her sex, spared her the electric chair. Nannie died in prison in 1965 of leukemia.

Diane Downs (1955–)

MURDER

When Susan Smith (page 198) let her children ride into the river in her sealed-up car in the name of true love, people thought it was the most deplorable crime ever committed. They were so sickened by it, in fact, that they had all but forgotten that just 10 years prior, Diane Downs committed an even more heinous filicide, and for the very same reason. Downs was obsessed with Lew Lewiston, a married man she had had an affair with and whom she believed was resisting being with her because of her children. She needed to have him in her life. She would do anything it took to make him to hers. Anything. Even if it meant getting rid off any obstacle, perceived or real. And she did. On May 19, 1983, Downs shot all three of her children, point blank, in her car. One died; one ended up paralyzed; one suffered brain damage. And as it turns out, Lew never had any intention of leaving his

wife, nor had he ever given Diane any indication he would.

Elizabeth Diane Frederickson was born on August 7, 1955. Her parents, Willadene and Wes, weren't the worst parents—although Diane claimed that her father had molested her when she was 11—but they weren't the best, either. They were just kids themselves when they had Diane, and essentially did what they could for their daughter, when it occurred to them, which wasn't very often.

When she was a kid, Diane didn't stand out either academically or in popularity. She was chubby, dumpy, and a bit tomboyish. But when she was 14, her parents sent her to charm school, which changed her life. At charm school she learned how to wear her hair, flirt, and, well, be charming. In her teens, she used her new-found skills to catch any boy she wanted. And later in life, when she stood trial for the murder of one daughter and the attempted murder of her two other children, it was her charm that caused the media to compare her to Great Britain's Lady Diana. Of course, in an effort not to sully the prominence of the pure one, they would refer to Downs as "Lady Die."

Diane met her husband while she was swishing her hips through the halls of her high school. For Steven Downs, it was love at first sight. After graduation, though they each pursued separate post-high-school aspirations for a couple of years, they stayed together. On November 13, 1973, they married. Unfortunately, this proved to be a big mistake. It was only after they tied the knot that Diane realized she wasn't "in love" with Steve—not the way she dreamed it should be. Both partners felt the gap between them widen by the day. And then a miracle happened: Diane became pregnant.

Christie Downs was born in October of 1974. During her pregnancy and into the first couple of months of Christie's life, the couple was once again happy. When the relationship started to fall apart again, Diane got pregnant with her second child. Cheryl Lynn was born in January 1976. But the kids weren't strong enough glue to hold the marriage together. Over the next couple of years, Diane packed up the kids and left Steve several times, but she kept returning to him.

In late December 1979, Diane gave birth to her third and last child, Danny, who was not, in fact, sired by Steve. Oops. This nugget of information wasn't kept from Steve; and Steve accepted it and agreed to raise Danny as his own flesh-and-blood son. All the children in the world were not going to help this marriage, however. Within a year of Danny's birth, the couple had filed for divorce.

Diane took a job at the post office, and it was here that she met the love of her life, or so she believed: Lew Lewiston. He was happily married, but the perky blonde Diane intrigued him. He began sleeping with her, thinking it was just sex. After all, it was common knowledge that Diane had bedded several of the other post office employees. He didn't realize that he was "special." When he realized the depth of Diane's obsession, when it was no longer just about the sex, as it had been always for him, he cut bait. A devastated Diane packed up her kids and moved from Arizona to Oregon.

She never forgot Lew, however, and would call his house constantly, even going so far as to threaten his wife. She scribed to him a mountain of pornographic letters. Lew had come clean to his wife about the affair, and she had forgiven him by this point. There was no way Diane was going to tear that marriage apart. But why didn't he want *her*, Diane wondered. Certainly, *she* was a much better catch than Lew's wife. What was it about her that Lew didn't want to have anything to do with? And then it hit her. Of course. It was her kids. If she didn't have her kids anymore, then she could have Lew—or so she thought.

What happened next is vile and heart-wrenching. On the night of May 19, 1983, Diane Downs packed up her children in the car and took them for a drive. When she came to a secluded area, she pulled out a gun, shot her daughter Christie, who was sitting in the front seat, whipped around and sliced a bullet through Danny, and then got Cheryl Ann. To make it look like she was attacked as well, Diane shot herself a nice flesh wound in her arm. Then she drove her blood-filled car to the emergency room.

When the Downs family arrived, Christie was already gone and Danny and Cheryl Ann were holding on by a thread. Diane told emergency room workers that a man had stopped them to ask for directions, and then began randomly shooting at the children. Diane was able to just get away with her life as the bad man had already managed to get her in the arm. Police were called in, and there was immediate suspicion for several reasons: Diane didn't cry; when they told her that her son would probably live, she replied, "Do you mean the bullet missed his heart? Gee whiz!"; when she visited her daughter, the child greeted her with utter fear, and the child's heart rate shot up, as several were able to witness on her heart monitor. But these were only a few indications that would point the blame squarely on Diane. She was arrested on February 28, 1984.

Assistant district attorney Fred Hugi was assigned to prosecute Diane, and he knew right away that she had to go down. His first priority was the children. He didn't trust Diane to visit them, and ordered around-the-clock surveillance for the tots. If Cheryl Ann was ever able to speak again, she would be his star witness. And besides, the kids were cute, and throughout the duration of the case, he found himself growing more and more attached to them.

Not unexpectedly, the trial, which began on May 10, 1984, was a sensation for the media. It lasted six weeks. The case looked like it could go either way, until Hugi brought in his star witness. Little Cheryl Ann could speak again, and she took the stand against her mother. Her testimony clinched it, and Diane was sentenced to life. In 1987, Diane made a break for it, but the law caught up with her.

Steve Downs relinquished custody of Cheryl Ann and Danny—who these days gets around in a wheelchair, thanks to his mother—and they were adopted by Fred Hugi and his wife, Joanne, in 1986.

Ruth Eisemann-Schier

KIDNAPPING, EXTORTION

Not much is known about Ruth Eisemann-Schier except that she was involved in several crimes, the most famous of which she committed with a partner, Gary Krist.

In 1968, Miami heiress Barbara Mackle was kidnapped from a motel in Decatur, Georgia. She was buried alive inside a "fiberglass reinforced plywood capsule," to quote the survival instructions left by the kidnappers, who demanded a $500,000 ransom. After her family paid up, the FBI received a call that led them to Mackle, who had spent 83 hours buried in the coffin. The kidnappers, Gary Krist and Ruth Eisemann-Schier, fled to Florida together, then went their separate ways. Krist was caught soon after, but finding Schier proved to be more of a challenge for the FBI, who put her on their Ten Most Wanted list.

Schier first went to Texas, but eventually settled in Norman, Oklahoma. Under the alias Donna Sue Willis, she found work as a waitress. What finally led to her capture was that she (none too wisely) applied for a state job and had to give her fingerprints, which were then sent to the Oklahoma State Bureau of Investigation. The fingerprints were processed, and as it turned out, they matched those of fugitive Ruth Eisenmann-Schier. In March of 1969, she was arrested by FBI agent Jack Burns at the restaurant where she worked.

Gary Krist was sentenced to life in prison. As his accomplice, Ruth Eisenmann-Schier received only seven years. She was the first woman to appear on the FBI's Ten Most Wanted list, as well as the first woman on the list to be caught. Her whereabouts are unknown at the time of this writing.

Ruth Ellis *(1926–1955)*

MURDER

Ruth Ellis is a prime example of Shakespeare's generalization that hell hath no fury like a woman scorned. Of course, being scorned wasn't the only factor that may as well have made her a character in one of the Bard's plays. While she wasn't a woman one could call solid and stable by any stretch of the imagination, that she could actually be capable of murdering the scorning party in cold blood was a complete and utter shock to anyone who knew her. Still, Ellis's grounds for defense, killing as a crime of passion, was all but pooh-poohed when her case went to trial, and Ellis, a 28-year-old mother of two small children, became the last woman to be hanged in England.

It was an average autumn day in Wales when Ruth Neilson was born. The third of six children, Ruth grew up slightly overweight, mousy, and severely nearsighted. Ruth's mother, Elisabertha, was a Belgian refugee who had fled her home country for Wales during the First World War. Her father, Arthur, was a musician. His real last name was "Hornby," but he and his family all went by his professional last name,

Neilson. Arthur wasn't exactly successful either. As time went on, he got fewer and fewer gigs and spiraled downward into alcoholism. By the beginning of the Second World War, Arthur was all but completely washed up. And his marriage to Elisabertha as good as over.

Ruth had spent many years essentially being raised by her older sister, Muriel. This relationship would prove to be stronger than the relationship she shared with either of her parents. Ruth had always believed she was going to be something special in life, and in 1941, when she was barely 15, she quit school to take a job as a waitress. She had to start somewhere, after all. She also moved out of her mother's house and left the nurturing environment created by Muriel to move in with her father, who had by then given up on his music career and found work in London as a chauffeur. While staying in Wales would have been better for her psychologically and emotionally, special things just didn't happen to small-town Welsh girls. She had to find her star, and where better to look than the big city of London?

When Ruth left Wales behind, she also left behind her mousy self. By the time she was 16, the five-foot-two-inch Ruth would forever be blonde and brassy. In the spirit of her new persona, Ruth took to the London nightlife like her father had taken to booze.

For years, she was a veritable maenad, jumping from bacchanal to bacchanal. But it caught up with her. By 1942, she had become rundown and was hospitalized for two months.

Upon her recovery, she jumped right back into her crazy life and by 1944, at the age of 17, she got entangled with a French-Canadian soldier and became pregnant. Entangled would be the perfect word to describe any of Ruth's relationships with men. She never "fell in love," she was never "swept off her feet." She just always managed to get tangled up in questionable situations with men who were completely wrong for her.

Here's what she didn't know: Her Canadian sweetheart was married. He had already made his exit from Ruth's life before their son Andy was born in September 1945. Andy was essentially "given" to Muriel to raise.

Back to work and back to her old life, Ruth was ready to become entangled in her next doomed affair. Morris Conley was 44 in 1944; Ruth was only 18. Conley hired Ruth to manage several social clubs he had in the area. Exactly what it meant to be a "manager" or "hostess" at one of these clubs was vague at best. For years they continued their "professional" arrangement, and then, in 1950, Ruth became pregnant again—and the father was not Conley, but one of Ruth's customers (hence the suspicion about what it meant to be a hostess). But this time, Ruth had an abortion, which sent her into the same sort of spiral her father had fallen into when he realized his career was over. Ruth became a full-blown alcoholic.

Around this time, Ruth met George Ellis. George was a dentist, and also an alcoholic. He had a reputation among patients and colleagues alike for being more than just a bit off. Closely following her devotion to older men, Ruth became entangled with Ellis, who was nearly 15 years older. He was smitten with her; she was lukewarm on him, but by November 8, 1950, George and Ruth were married.

Early the next year, Ruth and George moved out of the city to the Hampshire coast. George continued his drinking and also began to have extramarital affairs. For a year, Ruth moved back to her family, then back with George, then back with her family, then back to George again. In late 1951, Ruth gave birth to a daughter, whom she named Georgina. But the marriage was still in severe trouble. Right after the birth of his daughter, George filed for divorce. Ruth did not allow him to divorce her for quite a while, however. She depended on his money to support her two children. She was destitute. As a last resort, Ruth went back to Conley and her old career as a "hostess."

In 1953, Ruth met David Blakely, a younger man, and a terminally spoiled product of a broken marriage. He loved cars, drinking, and infidelity. He and Ruth developed a near earth-shattering attraction and lived together on and off, even though she was still legally married to George and David was engaged to another woman.

Not surprisingly, the relationship was a volatile one. And soon, in 1954, there was a new man in Ruth's life: Desmond Cussen. Five years Ruth's senior, he, like David, had a penchant for cars. But unlike David, most biographers agree, Desmond was actually in love with Ruth.

Desmond did whatever he could for Ruth, including taking her in. While David was not exactly happy about this living arrangement, he didn't do anything to prevent it. David and Ruth continued their relationship, however, which became more and more strained—until it finally reached the point of no return.

In early 1955, Ruth got pregnant again, and as she was sleeping with both Desmond and David at the time, there was no way for her to know who the father was. She had another abortion. This set her on her final downward spiral of alcoholism, pill popping, depression, and madness.

By Easter weekend, Ruth's hold on sanity had finally reached a nadir. She had left Desmond, and she and David were supposed to spend the weekend together. Except that he blew her off to spend it with his friends, Anthony (Ant) and Carole Findlaters. He had had enough of Ruth's dramatics, of her alcohol-soaked raves, of her altogether. Had he any idea how far gone she was, however, he probably would have been more careful about how he handled the situation.

On the night of Easter Sunday, 1955, David and his friend Clive Gunnell left the Findlaters' home on a beer run. Ruth was parked outside the house waiting for any sign of David. She was looped up on antidepressants and alcohol and was mad as hell at this final straw from David; this was the last time he was ever going to disrespect her. She wasn't driving her own car. There has always been speculation about whether Ruth took a cab to follow David, or if she was escorted by Desmond Cussen. Whatever the case, Ruth's car pulled out behind David's, and she followed the men into town.

It was about 9:15 P.M. when David and Clive emerged from the bar to see Ruth standing there, staggering, and pointing a gun at David. Before anyone could speak, Ruth began firing. Within minutes, David's corpse lay in a bloody heap at the curb.

The case went to trial within two months. While Ruth's attorneys begged her to tone down her hair and dress more conservatively, Ruth felt that this was the moment to shine that she had been waiting for. Her appearance garnered her no sympathy from the jury box. When she admitted that she had intended to kill David Blakely when she shot him, the jury had no choice but to convict her.

On July 13, 1955, at 9 A.M., Ruth Ellis was led from her cell to the gallows. In less than 10 seconds from the time she was hanged, Ruth Ellis was dead.

Freydis Ericksdottir

MURDER

The most famous Viking of the eleventh century A.D. is explorer and adventurer Leif Ericson. But one of the most infamous Vikings came from Ericson's own family, too: It was Leif's sister-in-law, Freydis, the wife of Leif's brother Thorwald. In the early colonization efforts of Greenland, Freydis cunningly and murderously thwarted the efforts of anyone but the brothers Ericson from claiming the new land.

Not much is known about Freydis's life and background, but it hardly matters. What is known is that she was a clever and scheming woman who put no price on human life when it got in the way of power and glory.

Greenland was first colonized by a band led by Ericson's brother Thorwald. (Leif himself had already returned to Europe at the time.) Eventually dissidence rose up through the ranks, and soon two other brothers, Helgi and Finnboggi, decided that it was time to split from Thorwald and try and build their own civilization. This did not sit well with Freydis, who conceived of a plan not only to thwart them, but which would inevitably lead to their deaths.

One night, Freydis snuck out of her husband's bed and made her way to Helgi and Finnboggi's camp, where she met with the brothers under the pretense of working out an amicable alliance between the two camps. When she returned to her husband's bed, she woke him, and when he wondered where she was, she lied to him and told him that she went to visit the dissenting brothers and their followers to try and arrange an alliance—and that they were not only unreceptive to her peacemaking efforts, but that they verbally and physically abused her as well.

Thorwald was not going to have any of that, and so he rounded up his troops and ambushed the brothers and their camp, capturing them and bringing them back to his own camp. There, all the men were axed on Freydis's orders, but when Thorwald decided against chopping up the five women in the group, the bloodthirsty Freydis commanded that she be given an ax and tore into them with an unspeakable fury.

Freydis and Thorwald soon returned to Europe and never admitted the horror that became of other half of the settlement expedition.

Amy Fisher *(1974–)*

ATTEMPTED MURDER

It was one of the most sensational trials of the 1990s—perhaps even of the twentieth century. The 16-year-old lover of a 36-year-old mechanic goes to his home with a loaded gun, confronts his wife about the affair, and when the wife does not give the girl the proper reaction, the girl clubs the wife over the head with the gun; on the third hit, the gun goes off, and wife Mary Jo Buttafucco crumbles to a heap on her front porch.

This is not the agenda of the typical Long Island teenage girl. But Amy Fisher was not your typical girl. And while Amy had a pretty good handle on her sexuality and how to use it to get what she wanted from older men, she was still an immature and mixed-up kid who was allegedly abused by her father growing up and was, therefore, horribly susceptible to the manipulations of an older man.

Whatever the impetus that led Amy Fisher to the Buttafucco doorstep on that fateful day in 1992, the act successfully robbed her of her childhood, whatever she had left of her innocence, and her self-respect and dignity in one foul swoop. And although today, Amy is out of jail and trying to make a life for herself, going to school and working—both full time—it is not likely that she will ever be able to escape the stigma of the "Long Island Lolita," even as Joey resides in Los Angeles and even plays small roles in film. At least his wife has finally left him.

Amy Elizabeth Fisher is the only child of Roseann and Elliot Fisher, a couple who ran a successful business and lived on the South Shore of Long Island, New York. Amy came into the world on August 21, 1974; by the time she was in eighth grade, the Fishers were doing so well that they moved into a pricey house in the upscale town of Merrick, Long Island. She did fine in school, had friends; everything was normal. Amy had everything she wanted from her parents, and as is the custom for many upper-middle-class Long Island kids, she was given a used car for her sixteenth birthday. It was this white Dodge Daytona that lead to her acquaintance with Joey Buttafucco. He was co-owner of Complete Autobody and Fender, the fix-it shop Elliot and Amy brought her car to after her first accident.

By July 1991, after lots of flirtatious behavior on both sides, when Amy brought her car in for various extras, like pinstriping and other frivolities, Amy and Joey's relationship was consummated as a sexual one, and lasted for nearly a year. During that period, Amy totaled her car, and Joey told her he would help her make the payments on a new one. But within a couple of months, he reneged, claiming that the business wasn't doing all that well. Amy was stuck; Joey had a plan to unstick her. He hooked her up with an escort service where she could make $150 for an hour's, um, work.

Amy worked for the service and continued to see Joey for six months, but she was getting impatient with her lover for not leaving his wife. So she broke off the relationship, and within a few weeks, she was involved with another older man, Paul Makey, who co-owned a gym. Makey also happened to be Joey's personal trainer. As was her style, Amy had a highly charged, highly sexual relationship with Makey, the antics of which, to her horror, would come back later to bite her in the butt in court.

True love apparently conquers all, and soon Amy and Joey were back together. She thought she could live with him staying married to Mary Jo. But apparently, she could not.

On May 19, 1992, Amy paid Mary Jo that infamous visit. She brought with her a T-shirt she claimed was Joey's, but Mary Jo would not believe her, as it was several sizes too small to fit over Joey's meaty build. The T-shirt—or at least Joey's admission of whom it belonged to—lead the police to Amy. Her "true love" betrayed her; she was arrested on May 22.

The New York media had a veritable field day with the Amy Fisher story. She made national and even international headlines. She was arraigned and bail was set at $2 million. Amy had to sell the rights to her story in order to post it.

Amy Fever spread like an epidemic. Everyone wanted a piece of the action. Everyone wanted to be part of the story. In January 1993, each of the major networks ran a made-for-TV movie about Fisher, attracting such visible starlets as Drew Barrymore, Alyssa Milano, and Noelle Parker to play the lead role. A day did not go by that Amy was not featured in the news, and even on news magazine programs. It was *Hard Copy*, in fact, which bought the exclusive on the sex tapes Paul Makey made with Amy, including one featuring the teen performing a wild striptease. And then there were the instant books, the comic books, and even an off-Broadway play.

Amy's trial was a circus. Pamela Smart (page 191) whined about the way the media depicted her. It could have been worse. She could have been Amy Fisher.

Amy went through two lawyers until she finally ended up with Bruce Barket. Her first lawyer, Eric Naiburg, pushed the limits of his professional responsibilities and made a few passes at Amy while he was defending her. While Naiburg claimed he treated her "like a daughter," he also admitted to writing her some inappropriate poetry. And he didn't win her case. Amy was sentenced to 5 to 15 years at Bedford Hills Correctional Facility.

As for any celebrity inmate, jail was a living hell for Amy, more so than for a typical inmate. She reported being constantly harassed by other prisoners and even to being raped by guards. She tried to bust one of the guards, presenting a pair of semen-stained panties as proof, but the accused guard resigned just a few days before she filed her complaint. Many people didn't believe Amy—they were already distrustful of the emotionally disturbed teenager who hardly showed any remorse for her crime during her trial. But it was the person who had the right to be the most distrustful of Amy who was responsible for finally getting her out of jail.

On April 22, 1999, Mary Jo Buttafucco appeared before the parole board to appeal for Amy's release. This was the same woman who appeared during Amy's sentencing in 1992, the right side of her face paralyzed from her wound, telling the court that Amy should serve the maximum possible sentence for ruining her life, putting her marriage in jeopardy, and making the lives of her children unbearable. Some gentle coaxing from Mrs. Fisher, appealing from one mother to another, as well as several attempts at begging forgiveness from Amy, and Mary Jo's Christian beliefs all came together to bring Mary Jo to forgive Amy.

On May 10, 1999, Amy was released from the Albion Correctional Facility (where she was moved to during her sentence), now a 24-year-old woman. Since that time, Amy has kept a low profile, doing interviews from time to time, but essentially just trying to finish school and get on with her life. She still lives in Long Island with her mother; her parents divorced when Amy was in jail.

Heidi Fleiss (1966–)
a.k.a. "The Hollywood Madam"

MADAM, TAX EVASION

When Heidi Fleiss was busted in June 1993, many people believed she got the short end of the stick, that it was more a case of Hollywood studio executives wielding their power than a legitimate reason to be behind bars. Heidi, like the great madams before her, ran a business. She provided a service that folks were willing to pay for. Someone who buys illegal drugs will be as likely to serve time as someone who sells them. Why, then, were Heidi's customers not also indicted?

Perhaps Heidi's biggest mistake was making the offhanded comment that she would sell her "little black book" if someone met her price; and perhaps there were several people in high places who feared having their name revealed in said little black book. Perhaps Heidi would have been better off if she had taken a cue from the last high-profile madam who got busted: Sidney Biddle Barrows (page 10). When she was caught, she immediately—and perhaps smartly—pled guilty to protect the discretion of her clientele. If Heidi had done the same, well, who knows.

As a child Heidi Fleiss had a privileged lifestyle. Her father, Paul, was a prominent pediatrician; her mother, Elissa, a former schoolteacher. Heidi was the third of six siblings. Her older and younger siblings all did well in school, pulled top grades, and attended top schools. Heidi had a different agenda. A high-school dropout, Heidi learned early that she didn't "need" school. It held no interest for her anyway. She much preferred partying, or hanging out at the racetrack, or shoplifting, or stealing car stereos. She also managed to make some money selling the pot she grew in her parents' garden. She was enterprising and resourceful. There was no doubt in her mind that she was going to be someone big some day; why waste her time sweating it out in school?

At age 18, Heidi had a pretty severe reality check. She was out partying with a few friends, including her younger sister, Shana. Heidi was drinking and doped up on pills. She should not have been driving, but she was. She rolled her Jeep, in which she was driving around five other passengers, including Shana. No one was killed, but Shana's arm was almost torn out of its socket. Still today, Heidi's younger sister doesn't have full use of the limb. Heidi somehow avoided punishment for the accident, and her parents even bought her a new Jeep; but she realized that perhaps it wouldn't be such a bad idea to start taking life a bit more seriously.

Heidi eventually got her GED, and then tried out community college. Two community colleges, actually, and she didn't last a semester at either one of them. She was trying, to be sure, but she still had other plans.

In 1984, Heidi was working as a waitress when a friend invited her to a house party. It turned out to be hosted by Bernie Cornfeld, a wealthy—and much-older-than-Heidi financier. The two hit it off and began an affair that would last four years. Heidi's time with Cornfeld gave her a taste of the good life: extravagant dinners and vacations, the best clothes and jewelry—anything she wanted. She knew she had to find a way to have this life for herself one day.

Heidi and Bernie ended their relationship on great terms, and continued to be friends up until his death. In fact, they were still such good friends that Bernie was going to help Heidi finance her trial. Unfortunately, he died before he could kick in one red cent.

Heidi's next relationship was not as fulfilling as the last. Ivan Nagy was a Hungarian-born director who was also much older than Heidi. Older men didn't bother Heidi. She's even been known to say that she prefers them because "the sex is better." But no matter how good the sex was between Nagy and Heidi, the relationship was torrential at best, and short-lived. However, it was through Nagy that Heidi would find the next stepping-stone on her infamous path to fame.

Heidi Fleiss didn't set out to become a madam. It just happened. In fact, before she fell in with Nagy, who would introduce her to Madam Alex, the top madam on the Hollywood scene at the time, she was pursuing a real estate license. But that was not to be. Nagy got Heidi working for Madam Alex to pay off a gambling debt. Alex was very impressed by her protégé: Heidi learned the business very quickly. So quickly, in fact, that by 1991, she was able to strike out on her own. It was almost too quick as far as some people were concerned. Did Heidi steal contacts from her mentor—and then put her out of business? Anything's possible.

Heidi's business was extremely successful. Her girls liked her because she was "their age"—well, nearly their age. Even if she was a little older, she still liked to go out and party with them. Heidi had about 100 college-aged girls working for her who were able to keep 60 percent of the take. Compared to other madams, who generally kept 60 percent for themselves, that was nothing to shake a stick at. The average price for one of Heidi's girls was $1,500 per night, which paid the tuition bill a lot faster than a job flipping burgers. And just *who* these girls got to go to bed with was the icing on the cake.

The business ran exceedingly well for a couple of years. Heidi made enough money to move into Michael Douglas's former home. But then it all came crashing down.

The Los Angeles cops were dead set on nailing Heidi, so to speak. She had never been known for her discretion, and her big mouth got cops hot on her trail. They

actually took the time and financial resources to plan a sting operation to bring her down like she was some sort of drug lord. Her arrest went down typical Hollywood style. As Heidi told Jessica Yellin in a 1995 article for *Los Angeles Magazine,* "The day the vice cops came to my house [was the weirdest day]. I had a premonition that something wasn't right. I was just hanging out, and then two helicopters fly over, and 30 officers start kicking down my doors, storming in with guns and dogs. Then the FBI comes in with the IRS. They were acting like I was some big, dangerous thing." Yeah. That was necessary.

That was June 1993; Heidi was finally arraigned on August 9. The charges brought against her included pandering as well as tax evasion and even drug trafficking. The drug charge didn't make it to trial.

Heidi's case went to court September 10, 1993. Several high-profile witnesses were called, including *Spin City* actor Charlie Sheen, who had spent about $54,000 in one year on Heidi's girls. Amazingly, he walked away unblemished and without even a slap on the wrist.

Heidi's trial went down just like her arrest. The media was all over her. It was as if she was on trial for drowning a busload of school children on their way to church—after she'd doped them up on drugs, sadistically sodomized them, and shot them full of holes with a machine gun, that is.

After her arrest, the ever-entrepreneurial Heidi started a new business, Heidi Wear, to finance her trial.

Heidi was convicted for pandering and tax evasion. On January 20, 1997, the former madam was sentenced to 37 months in federal prison. In typical Heidi fashion, she shocked the world by falling into a sexual relationship with another inmate on her very first day beyond bars.

Heidi ended up serving 20 months of her sentence. On November 19, 1998, she was transferred to a halfway house to complete it.

Since getting out of prison, Heidi has not vanished from the spotlight, although lately she's flying under the radar. In April 2000, she gave her journal to Michael Ovitz's Artist's Management Group for possible publication. In 2001, Heidi joined the cast of a new Showtime series, *Chromium Blue,* which, at the time of this writing, has not yet gone into production. When it does, however, Charlie Sheen is expected to make a cameo appearance. Bygones?

Heidi told friends long ago, "They're going to be writing books about me one day. I'm going to be a legend." Okay, Heidi. Here's a start.

Mary Frith *(1584–1659)*
a.k.a. Moll Cutpurse

PICKPOCKETING, FORGERY, ROBBERY

One of the most notorious pickpockets in history—albeit not the slightest of hand, or build, for that matter—was also one of the most famous cross-dressers ever. Moll Cutpurse, as she came to be known in her 75 years, was loyal to her fellow marauders, who kept her in their gang because of her steadfastness and cleverness. Through her own craftiness, she would eventually rise through the ranks of small-time crooks to establish a virtual empire of trafficking fenced goods.

Mary Firth was born an only child to a shoemaker and his wife in London, England, in 1584. Not much is known of Mary's father, but Mary's mother doted on her daughter, providing her with everything their modest living could afford the child, placing her in the best schools and trying desperately to teach her the necessary skills and attributes of womanhood. But Mary wasn't having any of it. While other girls were learning to quilt and sew, Mary was out roughhousing with the boys and earning a reputation as something of a bully.

She wanted to be where the boys were, but not because she was boy crazy; in fact, it has been said that, especially as she got older, she rather fancied the ladies. This was a fact that became increasingly disturbing to Mary's family, and various members tried to take action. One of these family members, Mary's uncle, a minister and her father's brother, tricked her into signing on to a "merchant ship" for work. Once the poor girl realized she was instead on a ship bound for a convent, she jumped overboard and swam back to shore. She never spoke to her uncle again.

It was this adventure that turned Mary Firth into Moll Cutpurse. She renounced her womanhood and began dressing entirely in men's clothing. She learned she could eke out a living deceiving folks as a fortune-teller, but it wasn't good enough for her. Eventually, she fell in with a group of cutpurses, and committed all kinds of crimes, from pickpocketing people on the street to full-fledged highway robbery. While Moll wasn't the most skilled in her band, she was certainly one of the most beloved, and even though Moll's skill (or lack thereof) paled in comparison to the other members', they kept her around.

Moll was a thinking woman, and eventually she learned she could make more money less dangerously in other pursuits. (Moll had almost been busted when she robbed General Fairfax on the road, shot him in the arm, and killed two of his horses. She was brought before the courts,

but she managed to buy her freedom for £2,000, which was quite a hefty sum in the seventeenth century.) After her close call, she moved from highway robbery to the more discreet occupation of fencing stolen goods.

Moll excelled in this pursuit, and it is how she came by most of her money. Her connections with her former robber brothers were very useful in her new profession. They would rob people; she would sell the victims' possessions back to them. She became so powerful, in fact, that the thieves came to rely entirely on her for their income. No one would dare even dream to perform a robbery without her involvement. She quickly went from dearly loved to sorely feared, although due to her essentially jovial nature, she still managed to keep many friends among the thieves. In fact, she harbored them if ever they needed a safe haven from the law.

In addition to loving her masculinity, Moll loved her ale and spirits and prided herself on being the first-ever woman to smoke. She was never one to say no to a night out with the boys, but all of her hard living had no affect on her longevity. Moll lived to be 75 years old, quite a feat for the 1600s.

In her lifetime, it is believed she amassed a fortune of about £5,000; but by the time of her death, that sum had been whittled down to just about £100, which she divided between two of her maids (who some say she may have been romantically involved with) and a few of her close friends.

Lynette "Squeaky" Fromme *(see Manson Women)*

Caril Ann Fugate *(1943–)*

MURDER

In *Homicide: 100 Years of Murder in America* author Gini Graham Scott says of the relationship between Caril Ann Fugate and Charles Starkweather: "Psychiatrists maintain there are some disturbed people who need a partner to validate their fantasies. In effect, the acts of the accomplice make the fantasy element real. Usually such people have 'borderline personalities,' but the label does not matter. Starkweather and Fugate never should have met …" Such a statement may be true for more than this couple. Surely Martha Beck (page 15), Charlene Gallego (page 86), Carol Bundy (page 46), and numerous others in this volume may have lived a fairly normal, violence-free life had they not been swept away by the wrong men. But the difference between these gals and Caril Ann Fugate was that they were all grown women when they acted; Caril Ann was barely 14 years old.

Caril Ann grew up in the same small town as Charles Starkweather: Lincoln, Nebraska. She lived a fairly uneventful schoolgirl's life with her mother, Velda Bartlett, her stepfather, Marion Bartlett, her older sister, Barbara Fugate, and her half-sister, the toddler, Betty Jean Bartlett. For all intents and purposes, they were a normal working-class family. They were poor, but the typical issues of alcoholism and divorce—catalysts that have been blamed for sparking many a lethal romance both before and since—were nonexistent in the Bartlett/Fugate household.

Charles Starkweather entered Caril Ann's life because he was buddies with Barbara Fugate's boyfriend, Bob Von Busch. Charles was immediately smitten by the dark-haired, freshly scrubbed, and borderline-tempestuous Caril Ann. And while Charles was already 19 years old and she only 13 when they met, the two were somehow permitted to date.

Chuck, as he was generally called, worshipped Caril Ann because she made him feel good about himself. There's nothing quite like a 13-year-old-girl-hero-worship crush, yes? While he was a pretty good-looking guy, and oft compared to James Dean (who he downright worshipped and fancied himself to be), let's just say that old Chuckie had more than a few troubles. For one, he was a less-than-stellar student. He also suffered from a slight speech impediment, which got him teased enough to cause him to drop out of school. On top of that, Charlie started out with some pretty severe emotional problems, and being the third of seven children born to Guy and Helen Starkweather, was always very conscious of getting enough—of getting his share. And as he was at this time working as a garbage collector, with no hope of riches in his future, he had been fantasizing a lot about becoming a bank robber some day.

Suffice to say, Charles may have been a crook without Caril Ann's love; whether he would have been a cold-blooded spree killer, however, will always be a mystery.

In any case, Charlie eventually made his first kill for Caril Ann—or at least to make himself look worthy in her eyes. One day, when he and his child-lover were getting gas for his car, he wanted to buy his sweetie a stuffed animal for sale at the gas station, but he didn't have enough money. He felt humiliated by the gas station attendant, Robert Colvert, even though it cannot be proven that Colvert treated Starkweather with anything but friendly, good-natured attendant-to-customer respect. Starkweather dropped Caril Ann off and went back to the gas station several times that day. The last time, he pulled a gun on the unsuspecting Colvert and robbed him. Then he took him for a ride, and ended up

shooting the 21-year-old new father in the head.

That initial killing would be the bond that brought Caril Ann and Charles together, till death they do part. Or at least as far as Charles was concerned. Now all fired up, Charles finally felt worthy of the love of his jailbait girlfriend. Of course, Caril Ann's family had a different sense of Charlie's value when it came to their daughter. And this without knowing about the killing. Caril had gained a few pounds, and they feared the worse: that she might be pregnant with the spawn of Satan. They felt it was time to step in and politely ask Charlie to get out of their daughter's life. It did not turn out as they planned—nor in their wildest small-town-Nebraska dreams could they ever conceive what the outcome was to be.

On January 21, 1958, the entire family—with the exception of Barbara, who had since married Bob Von Bosch and moved out of the house, and Caril Ann, who wasn't home at the time—would learn just how well Charlie would tolerate being told that he was not to see Caril Ann again.

While this conversation was going on, apparently, Velda began pounding Charlie with her fists, and so he retaliated: hitting her with his gun. When Marion came to his wife's defense, Charlie shot him in the head. Then he grabbed a knife out of Velda's hand and threw it at her, killing her. But the most cruel and brutal death would come to the baby. It wasn't good enough for Charlie to just shoot the baby. Oh, no. When baby Betty began to cry, he hit her with the butt of his gun. Then, he shoved the barrel down the baby's throat and pulled the trigger.

By some accounts, Caril sat back and watched as her wayward Romeo defended her honor and fought off any who would dare keep them apart. Other accounts say that she came in once the carnage was complete. In either case, she helped Charlie move the bodies to the outbuildings and clean up the living room. The couple stayed in the tainted house for over a week. When neighbors and friends came by to see the Bartletts, Caril would shoo them away, explaining that the family had the flu.

Caril and Charlie finally left the Bartlett house when visits from neighbors and friends became more frequent and insistent. The police were finally called in, and Chuck and Caril officially became fugitives. Which was fine by them. They were young. They were in love. And most important, they were together.

Now having the smell of blood in his nostrils, Chuck was ready to kill again. And Caril was ready to be by his side throughout, no matter what. Although later, in her confession, Caril explained, possibly in an attempt to save herself, that Chuck had

been holding her hostage, she also admitted to doing a fair share of her own killing.

The next victim was an elderly "friend" of Chuck's: August Meyer. In a true gesture of friendship, Meyer let the kids stay with him; to thank him, Chuck shot a bullet through his head. Next came a couple of high school kids, Carol King and Robert Jensen, who picked Caril and Chuck up hitchhiking. Their reward: death. King had the added bonus of being raped by Chuck; a jealous Caril mutilated the genitals of her corpse. Next, they struck an estate on Chuck's garbage collection route, killing C. Lauer Ward, his wife, Clara, and their maid, Lillian Fencl.

On January 29, just over a week after the madness began, Chuck and Caril were captured and brought to justice. Both were tried as adults, and had Caril not turned on Chuck, both would have faced execution— even though Caril was only 14 years old. Chuck was sentenced to death and went to the chair on June 25, 1959; Caril was also found guilty, but received merely a life sentence. Caril was paroled in 1976 and is reportedly trying to live a normal life. At the time of this writing she would be 57 years old.

The events of that January 1958 rampage have inspired several Hollywood fictionalizations, including the films *Badlands* (1974), *Wild at Heart* (1990),

True Romance (1993), *Kalifornia* (1993), and *Natural Born Killers* (1994).

Charlene Gallego *(1956–)*

MURDER, KIDNAPPING

Is Charlene Gallego an example of what happens to child geniuses when they don't get enough mental stimulation? Was it boredom that led this seemingly normal, upper-middle-class, sun-kissed California girl into drugs and promiscuity by the time she was 12 years old? And how does a remarkably talented classical violinist barely get through high school—and then drop out of college before she completes the first semester? How does a woman with such purported intelligence find herself involved in two marriages, destined to fail, before her early 20s, and then meet up with the man who will transform her from underachiever to full-fledged murderer?

Profilers of Charlene Gallego dispute how much involvement she had in her third husband's brutal murders and molestations of young girls and women. Some depict her as a spineless go-along; others like to paint her not only as a willing accomplice but as the instigator of the heinous atrocities that took place on the West Coast between 1978 and 1980.

Charlene Williams was born in October 1956, in Arden Park, an affluent section of Sacramento, California. Her mother, Mercedes, was a housewife; her father, Charles, was an executive in a national grocery chain. Charlene was an only child who never wanted for anything, from the undivided attention of her parents, to any material possession she desired. Perky and petite, Charlene was barely five feet tall, blond, and, with a 160 I.Q., full of potential. But Charlene couldn't get out of her own way.

By the time she was still just 20 years old, she had already been through two marriages. Her first husband was a heroin addict; her second was anti-drug, but also anti-Charlene. He hightailed it out of the marriage within a few weeks and took up with another woman. So when Charlene met up with Gerald Gallego in a bar in September of 1977, her self-esteem was pretty dented. Somehow, the average-looking Gallego managed to win over the sprightly young Williams. He sent her a dozen roses the day after he met her; within a couple of weeks, they shacked up together.

Almost right away, he treated her in the way she had become accustomed to being treated by her lovers: like crap. Not only did he not work, he also had other lovers, whom he waved in front of Charlene like trophies. Perhaps had she gotten to know him a little better, she would not have been so quick to leap into love with him. But she did. And married him the very next year—right after their first kill.

Gerald Gallego had a pretty extensive background for criminal behavior and, well, marriage. In fact, when he met Charlene in 1977, Gallego had already been married five times—and he was only 31. He had been arrested more than 23 times, had been involved in chronic altercations with the law since age 6, and essentially grew up in various boys' homes.

But the cherry on the sundae was Gerald's lineage, which makes a pretty good argument for nature rather than nurture. Gerald's father, Gerald Albert Gallego, was executed in the gas chamber in Mississippi the year before Charlene was born for killing two police officers. This after he had already been released from prison on parole, which is where he was when his son and namesake came into the world in 1946. But Gerald's father wasn't the only criminal in his bloodline. Gerald's mother's side included murderers and child molesters, and she herself had served time for prostitution.

At some time during their romance, the passion began to fade. Gerald began to have problems getting erections, and he blamed Charlene for not being sexy enough to arouse him. There are two points of view that explain what happened next. The side that wants to depict Charlene in a cold and callous light claims that it was Charlene

who suggested that the couple go after young sex slaves to satisfy Gerald's fantasies. The other side contends that it was Gerald who demanded that Charlene help him find young girls to fulfill his fantasies, and made her feel horrible enough about her own sexual desirability that she finally broke down.

The first of the 10 victims they would claim were Kippi Vaught and Rhonda Scheffler, two 16-year-old Sacramento girls. Vaught and Scheffler were lured to the Gallego van by an innocuous-looking Charlene, who enticed them with the promise of smoking pot. Once there, Gerald pointed a gun at them, forced them into the van, and brutally raped them in the back of the vehicle, while Charlene drove around the neighborhood. Again, a conflicting account states that Charlene might have taken part in the molestation of the girls, but it has not been substantiated. When Gerry had had his way with the girls, Charlene stopped the van in a deserted area. Gerry led each away from the van separately and shot them dead.

Charlene and Gerald celebrated the slayings by heading to Reno and getting married. They decided to stay in Reno, and this time each got a job: Gerald was a driver for a meat distributor; Charlene worked for a competing distributor. It would be several months before Mr. and Mrs. Death struck again.

In June 1979, they did, this time hitting the junior-high set in Reno. Fourteen-year-old Brenda Judd and 13-year-old Sandra Colley were minding their own business when a pretty, friendly blonde invited them to help her hand out leaflets. They were greeted at the van by a gun-toting Gerald, who raped and sodomized them, then led each away separately to bludgeon them to death with a hammer. They were buried in a shallow grave. It would not be until 1982 that the girls' bodies were found.

Sometime between the last murder and this one, the couple felt it was safe to return to Sacramento—but under a different name. In an effort to protect their daughter, but also to protect their family name, the Williamses helped Gerald change his name to Stephen Feil. It was also around this time that Charlene learned she was pregnant—for the second time. (She had terminated an earlier pregnancy already at Gerald's insistence.)

The next murders didn't happen until almost a year later. On April 24, 1980, the Gallegos hit the Sunrise Mall, located about 20 miles outside Sacramento. The next two victims, Stacy Ann Redican and Karen Twiggs, both 17 years old, were enticed to the van by Charlene and never heard from again, meeting the same fate as the unfortunate victims before them.

Only about six weeks passed before the Gallegos struck again, in Oregon. This crime didn't fit the typical Gallego killing profile. This time, the victim was a 21-year-old pregnant woman named Linda Aguilar. (The Gallegos had always attacked pairs before, and Aguilar was much older than their other victims.) Not only was Aguilar beaten and sexually abused, but her corpse, when it was found about two weeks later, showed signs that the woman was probably buried alive.

Five weeks after they slaughtered Aguilar, the Gallegos were back in Sacramento, getting drunk at the Sail Inn, where 34-year-old Virginia Mochel worked as a bartender. This time, they took their victim, the bartender, back to their apartment, where they tortured and murdered her.

By this time, the police were beginning to become suspicious of the Gallegos, but it wasn't until the couple's final murder that they would be able to pin the killings on them.

Only three days after the murder of Mochel, Gerald and Charlene kidnapped a college-aged couple: Craig Miller and Beth Sowers. Having no use for the man, Gerald killed him almost immediately. Beth's body was not found until November 22, 1980. It was this murder, however, that would trip them up.

Sensing danger, Craig's fraternity brothers copied down the license plate of the car that took their friend away. The car was traced to Charlene's parents. Gerald and Charlene fled Sacramento, and might have been able to get away again if Charlene hadn't wired her parents for money. Knowing they had to bring their daughter to justice for her own safety, the Williamses tipped the FBI off about where the Gallegos were, and they were finally brought to justice.

In the tradition of all great madmen, Gerald Gallego decided to defend himself. Charlene, on the other hand, struck a plea bargain that would only mean about 17 years in the slammer. These two factors ensured Gerald would face the ultimate penalty, and he was sentenced to death on June 22, 1983.

Charlene served out her sentence and was released from prison in August 1997.

Rita Gluzman (1949–)

MURDER

There's a remarkable irony that surrounds the murder case of Russian-born Rita Gluzman. She was convicted under the Violence Against Women Act (VAWA), 18 U.S.C., which was enacted to prosecute wife beaters to the fullest extent of the law if they crossed state lines to terrorize their wives. Naturally, the law stands ready to protect men who are subjected to injury, harassment, and intimidation on the part of their wives, and Gluzman was the first woman prosecuted under VAWA since it was put into effect in 1994. The law had no sympathy for a woman who crossed state lines to murder her husband and hack his body into tiny pieces.

Backtrack for a moment: What could provoke a woman to commit such a horrible crime, after more than 25 years of marriage peppered by a strong and dutiful sense of commitment—or so it seemed—on both sides? Just 20 years earlier, Rita Gluzman had attained some romantic celebrity when she fought for her husband's—famed scientist Yakov Gluzman—release from the former Soviet Union by staging an 18 day hunger strike. The couple also owned a successful electronics company together: ECI Technology, Inc.

But that was all to sour. Over the years, the marriage became strained. Yakov Gluzman's parents were known to feel that Rita slowly sucked the life out of their son over the course of the marriage. Yakov himself felt that Rita was a financial strain on him, even blaming her for the faltering success of their company. A year before his death, he moved out of their $530,000 Saddle River home and filed for divorce.

Rita never accepted any responsibility in the breakup of the marriage: She blamed his leaving on an affair he was having with an Israeli woman.

The divorce proceedings terrified Rita. She was afraid that she would lose everything—including an $11,000 per month living allowance—as well as be kicked out of the business.

On Easter Sunday, April 6, 1996, 48-year-old Rita Gluzman and her cousin, Vladimir Zelenin, ambushed and murdered Yakov Gluzman at his apartment. Then, with a dullish knife, they cut his body into 65 different pieces—ears, toes, lips, his nose, and countless more gruesome parts. They also removed his fingertips so his body could not be identified.

Rita disappeared; Vladimir took the many body bags to the Passaic River, where he began to dump their contents into the murky water. While he did this, he was approached by police. When they saw what he was wearing—blood-spattered pants, bloody latex gloves—and then realized what he was doing—dumping, um, bio waste into the river—they detained him and searched the area. They found two cars close by, which contained eight more bags of body parts between them. Vladimir was taken into custody, and whatever loyalty or allegiance he felt to his cousin melted away when he realized how much trouble he was

in. He sang like a canary, and soon enough, the police were hot on Rita's trail.

Rita was finally found nearly 10 days later hiding out in the visitor's cabin at the Cold Spring Harbor laboratory in Cold Spring Harbor, Long Island, New York, the lab where she and her husband had worked 10 years earlier. She was found with travel brochures about Australia and Switzerland, as well as with more detailed travel information about the latter. Rita was arrested for burglary and given an opportunity to confess what she had done before they threw Zelenin's testimony at her.

The trial commenced a year later in Westchester County, New York. Zelenin gave a repeat performance of his testimony to the court, and the federal jury had no choice but to find Rita guilty for the brutal dispatching of her husband. Zelenin was convicted of conspiracy and murder charges, but at a reduced sentence because of his cooperation. Rita was sentenced to life imprisonment based on VAWA. Her attorney pleaded for a reduced sentence, based on Rita's standing in the community. She was not a criminal, just a person who in the heat of a murderous passion perpetrated a criminal act, he said. But he was denied.

The case went to appeal in August of 1997 as Rita's attorney deemed it unfair that she was tried by a federal jury, but that appeal, and another made in December of 1999, were both rejected. At the time of this writing, it is unknown if another appeal is in the works.

Sandra Good *(see Manson Women)*

Barbara "Bonnie" Graham
(1923–1955)

MURDER, PROSTITUTION

If there's a case to be made for unhappy childhoods leading one down the path to a life of crime, Barbara "Bloody Babs" Graham is certainly it. Between her mother's utter lack of love for her, and her time spent in foster care, juvey homes, and the streets, it's not hard to understand why Barbara fostered relationships with many of the wrong men and developed the heroin addiction that, in its own twisted way, ultimately landed her in the gas chamber.

Barbara Elaine Wood was born into poverty in Oakland, California, to her teenaged mother, Hortense Wood. There was a trend toward general misconduct in her mother's family. Even after giving birth to her daughter, Hortense was to serve time in a juvenile facility. Young "Bonnie," as Barbara was called, was bounced around from family member to family member, foster home to foster home. When her mother was finally freed, she took Barbara back,

and soon found herself pregnant again—twice in fairly quick succession. If her mother had little interest in Barbara before—and a whole lot of disinterest at that—she had even less after the other two children were born. Barbara continued to bounce from living situation to living situation, barely completing elementary school.

When Barbara was 12, she had an opportunity to start a new life with a welfare worker who was quite fond of the little girl and wanted to adopt her. Hortense would have none of it, however, which meant that Barbara would have to find her own way, or be forever in the clutches of her loveless mother.

Hortense, perhaps in an act of spite, turned Barbara over to a juvenile home just a year after the adoption debacle. Already pretty intolerant of authority, Barbara was not an ideal ward of the Ventura State School for girls. She was hotheaded and defensive, and she learned quickly how to fit in with her fellow "students." Barbara ran away several times, and soon Ventura realized they wanted to hold on to Barbara about as much as she wanted to be beholden to the school. So they struck a deal with her: If she could successfully complete just one year of high school, she was free to go.

Barbara was not educated, but she wasn't dumb either. She bided her time and tried to keep her nose clean. When her time was up, she resolved not to end up like her mother. She was determined to make something of herself. So she headed back to Oakland, but not back to her mother and younger sister and brother. Instead, she did whatever she could to support herself. The year 1939 was hard enough for a single woman making her way in the world. For Barbara, uneducated and unskilled, it meant relying on the only thing she had: her body. Barbara fell in with some of the girls from her Oakland neighborhood who picked up sailors at the navy yard in the San Francisco Bay area. They were coined "seagulls" because they hovered around the area, scavenging what they could. While hanging out with lonely servicemen didn't always mean having sex with them, Barbara still learned to exchange herself for money.

Barbara grew tired of the life she was leading, and as soon as she was able to squirrel away some extra money, she enrolled in a business school, where, as fate would have it, she met her first husband, who was taking night classes to further his career. They were married when Barbara became pregnant, and she gave birth to a son. Within a short time, the couple had another son. Married life went by peacefully—until her husband learned of Barbara's past. He couldn't hack it. They were divorced and her husband won custody of their two sons.

Alone again, Barbara hit the streets to make some quick cash. She headed down to Long Beach where she resumed her career as a seagull. It was fully wartime by now, and any innocence of the previous decade was all but lost. Barbara became a full-fledged prostitute and began to rack up an impressive arrest record. In 1942, one of her johns fell in love with her, and they married. But alas, this was also not to last, and within a few months, Barbara was on her way back to San Francisco.

Barbara became a pretty well-established hooker in San Fran, and did fairly well for herself. Until she made the mistake of lying on the witness stand for a couple of "friends" in 1944. She got caught in the lie, which resulted in her doing a year's time for perjury and being put on probation an additional five years.

Once she was sprung from the joint, Barbara decided to leave California altogether, and took a job as a nurse's aid in Tonopah, Nevada. Here she married her third husband—but this time, fearing the worst from past experiences, it was her turn to leave. In less than a year, she quit her job, divorced her husband, and hightailed it back over the state line, this time to Los Angeles.

Barbara was heavily back into prostitution when she met her fourth husband, Henry Graham. From this marriage, she would not only have another son, she would also be introduced to heroin—and then to the man who would lead her from prostitution into robbery and murder.

Henry Graham was heavily into heroin; Barbara had retained it as a casual habit, but by the time she was 28 years old, she was a full-blown junkie. When she found out that her husband was stealing from her stash, she packed her bags and shacked up with Henry's friend, a fellow ex-con named Emmet Perkins, who was also a drug addict. Not even a year later, Barbara would sail into a life of crime beyond her wildest imagination.

Emmet Perkins had a few buddies who knew of an elderly woman living in Burbank who supposedly had a large stash of cash hidden in her home by her son, a notorious gambler. On the night of March 10, 1953, Barbara, along with Emmet Perkins, and three of his bad-boy-buds, Jack Santo, Baxter Shorter, and John True, busted into Mabel Monohan's home in search of the money. As the story goes, Barbara posed as a woman with car trouble and pleaded with the old widow to let her use the phone. When she gained entrance to the home, she beat the woman to death with the butt of her gun. The money wasn't what they had hoped it would be, but they wrapped the dead woman's head in a pil-

lowcase, dragged her halfway into a nearby closet, and headed back to Los Angeles.

The next day, the woman's body was found, and the police, who were already trailing Baxter Shorter on another lead, decided that he was a prime suspect. They questioned him, and he sang, but only named the first names of his partners: Jack, John, Emmet, and Mary. When he was released, he was abducted from his home by his fellow gang members and never seen or heard from again.

As soon as the police figured out who they were looking for, they tracked them down and brought them in. (Mary was a name that Barbara generally used as a prostitute. As soon as they figured out that Emmet was Emmet Perkins, it was pretty much a dead giveaway who Mary was.) They decided their best plan of action was to take one in the group and turn him or her against the others. Baxter would have been their first choice, but he was MIA. So they went after Jack Fine, as he had no prior arrest record. With his testimony, they were able to nab the others.

In custody, and held without bail, Barbara developed a love affair with one of her fellow inmates. Donna Prow was a 20-year-old divorcée who was serving a short sentence for vehicular manslaughter under the influence. A corrections officer posing as an inmate got Donna's ear and promised her a reduced sentence if she could break Barbara down and make her confess to Monohan's murder. The two women concocted a scheme whereby a "friend" of Donna's would offer to lie on the stand for Barbara and provide an alibi for the night in question. Barbara didn't realize her scheme with Donna was a set-up until the "friend," Sam Sirianni, appeared in court as a witness for the prosecution. Sirianni was an undercover cop who had worn a wire in his meetings with Barbara to arrange her "alibi." Now he testified against her that she had been trying to stage an alibi with him.

Barbara had been betrayed by the only person she felt had ever truly loved her. That breach, along with John True's testimony, meant doom for all the perps, except True, who was granted full immunity for his betrayal of the group. Barbara, Jack Santos, and Emmet Perkins were all sentenced to death.

After 18 months of failed attempts for appeal, the three were set to be executed on June 3, 1955. Barbara was scheduled to visit the gas chamber alone and first. When she was escorted from her cell at 10 A.M., she had made peace with her maker and was fully prepared to die. Then, phone calls starting coming in from the governor's office. First, the execution was called off. And then it was on again. And then it was off again. And then finally, at 11:18, the final decree was made. After more than an hour of torture inflicted on Barbara by the governor's indecisiveness, it was time for Barbara Graham to die. At 11:34, she was strapped into the chair in the gas chamber. When a guard told her to count to 10 after she heard the cyanide tablets drop, because it would make the end easier for her, she uttered her final words: "How the hell would you know?"

Gwendolyn Graham (see Lethal Nurses)

Belle Gunness
(1858–1908?) a.k.a. Lady Bluebeard

MURDER

As the popular legend goes, "Bluebeard" was the moniker of a wealthy French nobleman. He was charming and handsome, and never had trouble attracting a young and beautiful wife—which he needed to do quite often: For some reason, his many wives eventually disappeared. A new bride would always inevitably take pity on the poor man, but in a matter of months, she too would be gone. One day, a young maiden became the new bride of Bluebeard. He had to go out of town a lot, so before he left his latest bride for the first time, he told her she could visit any room she wanted in their enormous mansion, but she was not to enter the room at the end of the corridor—even though he gave her the key. Her curiosity got the better of her, however, and she unlocked the door. What greeted her therein was a horror beyond words: The many former wives of Bluebeard were strung about the walls, strangled.

So why did Belle Gunness earn the title "Lady Bluebeard"? Well, like the popular character, she was charming and irresistible. And while she didn't marry all her suitors, she was able to lure many into her home and into her life—whereupon they always seemed to vanish. The townspeople felt sorry for the poor woman and her increasingly bad luck with men. But after her "death," that would change. The grounds around her burned-down home were excavated, and the mystery of what had happened to all those men was finally solved.

Belle Gunness was born Brynhild Paulsdatter Storset in a Norwegian fishing village on November 11, 1859. While the family didn't live in poverty, all of Brynhild's siblings had moved—many of them to the United States—to make better lives for themselves. Brynhild's sister, Anna, was living with her husband in the American Midwest, and she invited Brynhild to come and live with her. In the early 1880s, at age 24, the young woman set off to begin her life.

By 1885, Brynhild had Americanized her name to Belle, and married Mads Sorenson, a fellow Norwegian immigrant. Mads and Belle tried for a long time to conceive children, but were not successful. The couple adopted several children, but not all lived to adulthood. In 1896, their oldest daughter, Caroline, died. Within two years, eldest son Axel also succumbed. The reason for both deaths was cited as "acute colitis." Then, in 1900, Mads died. As Mads had had heart trouble, the cause of death was attributed to a heart attack—although all three deaths suggested poisoning.

Belle collected the insurance monies and relocated the remaining members of her family to La Porte, Indiana. The cash she made on the deaths of nearly half her family meant she was able to afford a mansion. In fact, Belle had made more money than perhaps she would have otherwise been entitled to. Her husband had had two insurance policies, which overlapped, conveniently, on the day of demise. Belle was entitled to a double payout!

Belle and her family—daughters Myrtle and Lucy, and foster-child Jennie Olson—were all quite well liked in their new town. And by 1902, Belle found true love and married again. Peter Gunness was also from Norway and a farmer. Belle at last became pregnant, but the joy was short-lived. Before the end of the year, Peter was dead; a sausage grinder, with what seemed a mind and malice of its own, had fallen off a shelf and struck him on the head. Belle collected his insurance money, but had grown comfortable in the house in La Porte, so she decided not to uproot her family.

After Peter's death, Belle ran ad after ad in several Norwegian-language publications, looking for farmhands who might also become lovers. Over the next few years, many of these strapping young bucks came along. And then suddenly went. When Belle's foster child Jennie wondered why the men always seemed to leave in the middle of the night, Jennie also went. Belle told folks that she had been accepted to a San Francisco college and was off getting her degree.

In springtime 1907, Belle "hired" a fellow by the name of Ray Lamphere. He seemed to last longer than most of the hired hands, and he and the town's beloved Belle became something of an item. They were a delightful sight: He was tall and thin as a rail; she was about five-seven and weighed almost 300 pounds. Eventually, the romance soured and Lamphere resigned his post on the farm. But he didn't get over Belle. In fact, he was often seen loitering at the edges of the estate or quarreling with Belle's new lovers.

One of these suitors, Andrew Helgelin, had answered Belle's ad for a man to marry.

Even though he seemed quite smitten by her, and even though he had signed over all his money to her, Helgelin eventually "took off" on Belle, too.

In the ensuing months, Belle began to spread rumors about Lamphere—how he was menacing and scaring her and her children, and how she feared he would soon burn her house down because he was such a hateful man. On April 27, 1908, Belle re-wrote her will, leaving everything to her children, or, in case she out-survived them, to a local orphanage. The next morning, the Gunness house burnt to the ground, taking the entire family with it. Prescience? Or premeditated murder and arson?

Once the smoke cleared, within the rubble were found the bodies of Belle's three children, and a headless female corpse that was guessed to be Belle. The problem was that the headless body was that of a woman of about five feet four inches tall, and of considerably less girth than Mrs. Gunness (even factoring in how much weight the fire would have been able to, um, burn off). Suspicion was roused, but the prime suspect, Lamphere (just as Belle had orchestrated it?), was taken into custody.

Eventually, a dental bridge containing several gold teeth was recovered from the rubble, and identified by Belle's dentist as hers. There were those who were skeptical that the dental work would have held up in a massive fire. An experiment was conducted and it was proven that it wouldn't have held up the way it did—that it must have been planted. However, the authorities decided to let it rest at that. Until Asa Helgelin came looking for his brother Andrew, that is.

Asa surmised that there was no way that Andrew would have run off on Belle after he had cleaned out the brothers' savings account for the woman. He, and others, began to notice all sorts of men's paraphernalia scattered among the ruins—wallets, cufflinks, watch fobs—and suspected foul play. He begged the authorities to dig around the grounds for anything suspicious. What they found was not to be believed. Under a dusting of lime, Andrew's body, chopped in various pieces, each put in a different burlap sack, was the first of the missing to be discovered. Also in the pit, Jennie Olson, and many others.

What never turned up, however, was Belle Gunness's head.

Despite the evidence pointing to Gunness still being alive—and suspect— Ray Lamphere was put on trial for murder and arson. (Many suspected that if Belle had committed these horrible crimes, Lamphere had helped. While in jail, he confided to his cell mate that he had had a hand in some of the murders after all.) On November 26, 1908, he was convicted only of the arson

charge, and sentenced to 2 to 20 years. He didn't live out his sentence, however, as he died from tuberculosis within the first two years.

No one ever found out what happened to Belle Gunness. For years after the fire, Lady Bluebeard sightings sprang up like modern-day Elvis sightings in white-trash America. If she survived, she lived out her life in anonymity.

Camille Hall (see Symbionese Liberation Army Women)

Emily Harris (see Symbionese Liberation Army Women)

Jean Harris (1923-)

MURDER

The case shocked a nation: The headmistress of an elite private school murdered her long-time lover in an act of passion and was facing life in prison. She claimed she was innocent. She admitted going to Herman Tarnower's Scarsdale home on the night of March 10, 1980, with a gun, but it was not for killing him; it was to take her own life.

Things had not been going well for Jean Harris the couple of years before the murder. She was having a lot of difficulty with work, her self-esteem was shot to hell, and her typically philandering boyfriend seemed to be getting more and more serious with one of his other lovers. She didn't think there was any reason to live; but what prosecutors had to prove was that she didn't think there was any reason for Herman to live.

How did this grandmotherly, seemingly together, pillar-of-the-community, who was even known as "integrity Jean," become such a notorious murderess? Behind every criminal, there is a story. And Jean Harris's story starts simply enough in a suburb of Cleveland, Ohio. In 1923, Jean Struven was born the second of four children to Albert and Mildred Struven. He was a successful civil engineer whom his children both feared and revered for his stern nature; she was a housewife and a Christian Scientist. While the family always attended Episcopalian services, Mildred's Christian Scientist beliefs were adhered to within the family.

Jean took after her father, with a hot temper and stubborn nature, but she also managed to be the picture of good behavior—that is, if you didn't cross her. She did well in school, had many friends, and worked her way into Smith College, from which she graduated in 1945 with honors. Shortly after graduation, she met and married Jim Harris. Even though she majored in economics, Jean spent her married life tending house and raising the

couple's two children, David (b. 1950) and Jimmie (b. 1952). After the children had begun to grow up and start having their own lives, it became painfully obvious to both Jean and Jim that their marriage was based on little more than a fan-tasy of domesticity; they divorced in 1965. Jean parlayed the home kindergarten she ran for extra money while raising her own two children into credentials for becoming a schoolteacher, and she was set.

And it wasn't that long after her divorce that she was back on the dating scene again. She was introduced to Herman Tarnower, a doctor with a successful practice, within months of her divorce. When the two met, they clicked right away. Unfortunately for Jean, Herman, or "Hy" as he was called, was a shameless womanizer. She accepted his indiscretions, however, as long as none of them became serious, and he became so smitten by her tolerance, that he proposed marriage to her in 1967. She at first accepted, but soon decided that they should put off the wedding until her sons finished the school year. This sadly proved to be a mistake, as by the time she was ready to talk about marriage again, Hy had changed his mind—forever.

No matter for Jean. She had been married before, after all. And she loved Hy. She could put up with his other affairs and one-night-stands. Or so she thought.

Jean and Harris continued their affair for years, and in the time they spent together, their professional lives began to soar. Already a top physician with a wealthy clientele, Hy's success and popularity increased. Jean left teaching behind to pursue the more administrative avenues of education. In the early 1970s, she became headmistress of Thomas School in Rowayton, Connecticut, but she was also becoming increasingly depressed. Hy prescribed Desoxyn for her, a drug with a makeup fairly close to speed, which would really catch up with her later. For a while, though, the drug seemed to smooth out life's roughest edges; but not enough. In 1974, Jean was relieved of her duties at the school.

Jean's professional life wasn't the only thing going to hell in the mid-1970s. Herman had hired a new secretary, Lynne Tryforos, with whom he almost immediately began a serious affair. Jean was used to Hy's infidelities, as long as many anonymous, nondescript women were the target of his affections; one significant woman was one too many as far as Jean was concerned. Furthermore, according to Jean, Lynne would call her incessantly in the middle of the night and taunt the older woman. Jean accused her of stealing her jewelry and of destroying the possessions that Jean kept at Hy's home. Lynne never testified in the Harris trial, so no one but Jean and Lynne know whether or not Lynne did the things Jean accused her of.

Jean floated around for several years in the miasma of jealousy and the idleness of unemployment, devoting herself to helping Hy compile information for and write his *Complete Scarsdale Medical Diet* book. At last, in 1977, she was appointed headmistress of the Madeira School in Washington, D.C. But the administration wasn't pleased with her performance, and by 1979, it looked like she was going to be on her way out.

Jean Harris had had enough of life. Her career was a failure. Her love life was a failure. As far as she was concerned, she herself was a failure. It was time to take matters into her own hands, she figured, so she purchased a gun with the intent of killing herself. Apparently, as a suicide, she was also a failure.

The proverbial last straw came in 1980, when Hy informed Jean that she would not be sitting at his side at a dinner in his honor. Lynne would also be attending the banquet, Hy told her, but not to worry, she would also be sitting in the audience. Jean was so demoralized by this that she wrote a letter to Hy, telling him how horrible she felt about his association with Lynne, and all the terrible things the other woman did to torture her. The letter fell on deaf ears.

On March 10, 1980, Harris drove up to Hy's home to say good-bye, and then to shoot herself in his garden. It didn't unfold as she had intended, however. She arrived at the house in the middle of the night. Hy was annoyed and didn't want to let her in, but he did anyway.

Once inside, Jean noticed a number of Lynne's things taking up residence in Hy's home, and she flipped her lid, smashing mirrors and knocking tables over and such. After nearly 14 years, Hy had had enough of Jean's fiery emotional outbursts and was essentially unsympathetic to her. According to Jean, the rest of the events happened as follows: (1) Jean decided it was time to take the gun out, so she did, and pointed it at her own temple; (2) Hy attempted to wrestle the gun away from her, but it went off, shooting a bullet right through his hand; (3) Jean begged for the gun back, but he wouldn't give it to her, which resulted in a tug-of-war; (4) Jean's memory goes blank from this point, but the next thing she knew, Hy was lying motionless in a pool of his own blood.

The prosecution had a different tale to tell. According to them, Jean forcibly broke into his house and shot Hy four times in his bed before he had a chance to defend himself. In fact, the only measure he could take to protect himself was to shield his face with his hand, which explains that wound.

Jean was found guilty of second-degree murder. In prison, she authored and published three books. After serving 12 years, then-governor Mario Cuomo commuted her sentence. On December 29, 1992, Jean Harris was a free woman. At the time of this writing, Harris lives in Westchester County, New York, where she devotes her time and energies to improving the condition of women's prisons.

Dr. Linda Burfield Hazzard
a.k.a. "Doctor Death"

EMBEZZLEMENT, MANSLAUGHTER

If her methods, ends, and means had been different, Dr. Linda Burfield Hazzard may have been remembered as a woman who established herself in the alternative medicine field in an era when such a thing was nearly unheard of. But her criminal behavior and passive-aggressive cruelty toward her patients ended up bringing her an entirely different sort of notoriety.

During the early part of the twentieth century, Dr. Hazzard was a staunch proponent of fasting as a way to achieve health and well-being, and she ran a sanatorium in Olalla, Washington, that specialized in her controversial treatment.

In 1911, two British heiress sisters, Claire and Dora Williamson, visited Dr. Hazzard for a cleansing, invigorating experience. The sisters had heard of Dr. Hazzard's internationally known treatments, and as they had just inherited a large sum of money from their Scottish-born grandfather who had recently passed away in Australia, they felt the time was right to make a trip to the States to clear up the abdominal discomfort and general "female troubles" they had been experiencing.

They were immediately taken by Dr. Hazzard's personality and zest for life, and signed up for their treatments. The sisters stayed in a small apartment in close proximity to the doctor, and five days a week, they underwent their health regime of broth consumption and up to three-hour-long enemas. They began to feel weaker, but chalked it up to the euphoria their bodies were experiencing at being purged of all their toxins.

The girls became so frail after a few weeks that Dr. Hazzard decided it was time for them to reside full time in the sanatorium she had just finished constructing. A steely, manipulative woman, Dr. Hazzard had more in mind than healing the hapless sisters. Her plan, the prosecution later revealed, was to gain control of the sisters' estate in order to turn her sanatorium into a state-of-the-art facility.

Hazzard instructed Dora and Claire to give her their jewelry and sign over their papers and possessions to her. The girls were naïve, to be sure, but after three weeks of living on tomato and asparagus broth, with whatever nutrients they provided being purged from their bodies through frequent enemas, they were also too weak to argue; most definitely, their minds had become as frail as their bodies. Both girls had willingly checked in; Claire would never check out.

Claire, possibly with near-death clarity, had begun to get wise to Dr. Hazzard. She sent a cryptic telegram to Margaret Conway, the Williamson family nurse, in Australia, pleading that she come to the sanatorium quickly, but gave no details why for fear that Hazzard might intercept the note and that she and Dora would surely die. Conway got word to their uncle, but by the time John Herbert arrived to pick up his nieces, Claire was dead. Dr. Hazzard produced paperwork to prove that both girls consented to the treatments and signed away any responsibility that would befall Dr. Hazzard if the treatments didn't take or if either girl was harmed. Herbert claimed Claire's body, helplessly leaving Dora behind.

Claire weighed less than 50 pounds at the time of her death, but Dr. Hazzard vehemently denied that her patient's weight had anything to do with it. An autopsy revealed Claire's death to be caused by cirrhosis of the liver, but later investigation found Claire's jewelry and clothing in Dr. Hazzard's possession and the last entry in Claire's diary to have been forged by Hazzard. The cause of death officially became foul play.

Having lost her sister and realizing the treatments would likely have the same effect on her, Dora was utterly relieved when Margaret Conway finally arrived. The nurse forced her charge to eat more and little by little she regained her strength.

After stealthily nosing around in Hazzard's papers, Conway discovered that Claire was not the first person to be killed in her care, and that Hazzard had also tricked several other patients out of their money. She contacted John Herbert, who contacted British Vice Counsel C. E. Lucien Agassiz. His investigation into the sanatorium revealed that more than forty patients had died under Dr. Hazzard's care. Death certificates issued by Dr. Hazzard stated a variety of different causes of death. Certificates issued by other doctors, however, nearly all stated the same cause: starvation.

It was discovered that Hazzard was (1) not a legally practicing M.D., but an osteopath; (2) trained to practice medicine only as a nurse; and (3) not legally married to her husband, Sam Hazzard, who was still technically married to another woman. In fact, the two had fled Minneapolis when Linda lost yet another patient to her starvation cure.

The ensuing trial garnered so much attention that today it would be considered a media circus. Accusations were made of the defense attempting to bribe witnesses. Claire's personal documents were ransacked. Even the vice counsel's home was broken into. There was also talk of an international conflict as the American had taken advantage of British citizens. Hazzard's sanatorium was dubbed "Starvation Heights," and Hazzard's behavior in court was nothing short of confrontational.

Ultimately, on February 4, 1912, Dr. Hazzard was convicted of manslaughter and sentenced to 2 to 20 years at Walla Walla State Prison. She was released eight years later in 1920. She returned to Olalla and picked up her business as if nothing had ever happened.

Bonnie Heady
(c. 1912–1953)

KIDNAPPING, MURDER

Not much is known about Bonnie Heady's early life, except that she was born Bonnie Emily Brown and was probably raised in the American Midwest. It has been said that she grew up in a wealthy family. Her name change, and the fact that the FBI files documenting the heinous kidnapping and murder of six-year-old Bobby Greenlease consistently refer to her as "Mrs. Heady," suggests she was married, though whether she was married when she met up with Carl Hall in the early 1950s is not known. What is known is that getting mixed up with good ole Carl was quite possibly the worst thing this woman of questionable self-esteem could have done for herself.

Bonnie Heady, though by no means ugly, was not a beautiful woman, and when she fell in with Carl Hall she was already middle-aged, semi-plump, and lonely. Before meeting Carl, her worst offense against the law was occasionally prostituting herself to make some extra money. Bonnie was also known to have a taste for "the sauce," a passion she shared with Hall. Somehow she managed to own her own house, in St. Joseph, Missouri—perhaps through a divorce settlement? Heady, though possibly a bit rougher around the edges than your average 1950s woman, was for most intents and purposes average.

Although also painfully average, Hall differed from Heady in that he did more than just *dabble* in criminal activity. When he met Bonnie, he had just been released from Missouri State Prison, where he was incarcerated after robbing a few cab drivers. His $38 haul had cost him several years. Ironically enough, Hall had also grown up in a wealthy family, and when his father died, he inherited a pile of dough that should have kept him comfortable for the rest of his days. But Hall was greedy and not a very good businessman. He invested and lost every penny of his inheritance, and turned to crime in an attempt to get it back.

Hall and Heady decided together that it was time to get back to the good life, and they concluded that the only way they were going to get there was through one good kidnapping. They had no qualms about it. In fact, Heady has been quoted as saying that kidnapping "is better then sex." Because of his early privileged life, Hall knew more than a few wealthy guys from school who could be targeted. Robert Greenlease and his family would never be the same.

Hall and Heady followed the Greenleases around for the entire summer of 1953. They learned the family's routines, where their children were during the day, who picked them up and took them home. The plan at first was to abduct the Greenleases' 11-year-old daughter, but after their surveillance period, it seemed the 6-year-old son, Bobby, would be a much easier target.

The grim events of the last day of that child's life actually began the night before, when Carl Hall dug a shallow grave in

Heady's backyard in which to bury the tiny body. Yes, they already knew that no matter what happened, they were not going to return the child. The following morning, on September 28, 1953, Bonnie nonchalantly walked into Bobby's school, told the principal that she was his aunt, and had come to pick Bobby up because his mother had just had a heart attack. She walked off, hand-in-hand with the small trusting boy.

They took a taxi to a local drugstore, where Hall was waiting for them. The three drove across the state border into Kansas and into an empty field. Bonnie took a walk while Carl ended the little boy's life with a bullet through the head. Bonnie returned and they took the minute corpse to its predetermined final resting place and planted flowers on the site.

Once Bobby was dead, Hall contacted the Greenlease family, telling them he had kidnapped their son. If they ever wanted to see him alive again, they would have to pay him a ransom of $600,000. (This sounds like an odd figure, and it is, but there's a reason Hall decided on it. He wanted the money in $10s and $20s. This amount in $10s and $20s would probably weigh about 80 pounds—or just as much as he felt he could comfortably carry. A million dollars—well that would probably be a burden at, what, 150 pounds?)

The family rounded up the funds and delivered them to the agreed-upon drop-off spot. Hall and Heady immediately left town and rented a small apartment in St. Louis. It was there that Hall got Bonnie so drunk that she passed out. After slipping a couple grand in her bag, he absconded with the rest of the haul.

Hall got very sloppy after he abandoned Heady, and blabbed his exploits to the wrong people. He got himself arrested, and then told authorities where to find Bonnie. Hall couldn't keep his mouth shut once he opened it in custody, so by October 7, 1953, barely two weeks after the boy was murdered, his remains were dug up out of Bonnie's flower garden. The only thing that wasn't determined was what happened to the other half of the money Hall and Heady extorted out of the Greenleases (the first half of the money was found by the police when they arrested Hall). Though Hall pointed the finger at a couple of the cops involved in the investigation, nothing was ever proven. The whereabouts of the money is to this day a mystery.

Hall and Heady confessed, and it is documented that Bonnie actually smiled when she received her sentence of execution. Perhaps the smile was triggered by a sense of remorse, which is what most believe. That both parties didn't seek an appeal suggests that perhaps both were sorry—though most people don't give Carl Hall that much credit of character.

On December 18, 1953, Bonnie Heady became the first woman executed in the gas chamber. The executions were to be simultaneous, so an additional chair was installed in the chamber for Bonnie, who, according to most reports, was bright and chatty until a morose Carl Hall told her to shut up. She did.

Patricia Hearst (see Symbionese Liberation Army Women)

"Heavenly Creatures"
Pauline Parker (1938–)
a.k.a. Hilary Nathan
Juliet Hulme (1938–)
a.k.a. Anne Perry

MURDER

On June 22, 1954, police were summoned to Victoria Park, in Christchurch, New Zealand, at the request of two young women: "Please help us. Mummy has been hurt—covered with blood." The mother of one of the girls had slipped and fallen down the ridge and they were afraid she was terribly hurt, perhaps even dead. When the police found the body of 45-year-old Honora Mary Parker, there was no question that she was dead. But there was also no question

that she did not sustain her injuries from falling. A brick wrapped in a stocking found a few yards away from the murder scene seemed a more likely killer. But who had swung the brick at the woman? The horror of the answer to that question would reveal itself in just a matter of days.

Pauline Parker was 16 years old when her mother was killed. She was living with her mother, her sisters, and her mother's common-law husband, Herbert Repier, in Christchurch. Pauline was a dumpy, sickly girl. Due to suffering osteomyelitus when she was five, Pauline walked with a limp. Pauline's younger sister was mentally challenged; her younger brother died at birth.

As a result of her sickly condition, Pauline had few friends. She couldn't partake in any of the physically demanding activities kids her own age were engaging in, so she had little opportunity to develop a social life. One girl, however, regularly rode her pony over to visit with Pauline. This girl, Juliet, came from a fairly wealthy family, and soon Juliet had secretly arranged for Pauline to have a pony as well.

Juliet Hulme was the opposite of Pauline: she was five foot seven inches tall, to Pauline's five foot three inches, and she was healthy, robust, and beautiful. Originally from London, Juliet and her family moved to New Zealand in 1948. Actually, Juliet, who was a neurotic child from suffering bomb shock in the war, moved to New Zealand before her family—to a sanatorium. Juliet was extremely shy and reserved and had few friends. When she first took up with Pauline, her parents were pleased. Pauline had a way of bringing the other girl out of her shell. But as time passed, neither Juliet's nor Pauline's parents thought their relationship was altogether healthy.

Pauline and Juliet spent all of their time together. They had sleepovers as often as possible, where they would sleep in the same bed. The girls' main pastime whilst together was to write novels and poetry. It came out in their trial that the literature was highly charged, and demonstrated without a doubt that the girls considered themselves above other humans; they were "heavenly creatures." In fact, in a poem by Parker called "The Ones I Worship," which was about her and Juliet, she writes:

> I worship the power of these lovely two,
> With that adoring love known to so few
> 'Tans indeed a miracle, one must feel
> That two such heavenly creatures are real
> Both sets of eyes though different far,
> Hold many mysteries strange
> Impassively, they watch the race of man decay
>   and change
> Hatred burning bright in the brown eyes for
>   fuel
> Ivy scorn glitters in the gray eyes, contemptu-
>   ous and cruel

> Why are men such fools they will not realize
> The wisdom that is hidden behind those
>   strange eyes
> And these wonderful people are you and I.

The girls dreamed of saving enough money to move to the United States, where they thought they could publish their work. But their parents started getting in the way.

Hornora was the first to see that perhaps the relationship between Pauline and Juliet was becoming a bit too intense, and she started to interfere with them, making them spend less time together. For this, Pauline would write entries in her diary to the effect that other people's parents die all the time, why couldn't hers. As time went on, the murderous wishes started to become murderous plots.

Resistance to the girls' friendship was also growing at the Hulme home, which was going through its share of problems in the early part of 1954. Juliet had found her mother in bed with another man, and she told her father. The couple decided to divorce, and Dr. Hulme was going to move to South Africa. Seeing this as a great opportunity to split Juliet and Pauline up, her parents decided that Juliet would move to Africa with her father. Juliet insisted that Pauline should move with her, but both sets of parents refused to allow this.

Pauline believed that her own mother was the biggest naysayer of her moving with

Juliet, and she decided she had to do something to remove the obstacle. Pauline and Juliet planned to take the woman to a secluded place to "rationally discuss" why Honora would not permit Pauline to go with Juliet. They were going to bring a brick in a stocking to shake her up; they claim they had not really intended to hit Honora with it until it was happening.

On June 22, 1954, Pauline, Honora, and Juliet took a walk in Victoria Park on Cashmere Hills. Pauline pulled the brick out and started to swing. She hit her mother across the head with the makeshift weapon. "As soon as I had started to strike my mother I regretted it, but I could not stop," she later admitted in court. But then Juliet grabbed the weapon and started to do some swinging of her own. The girls tossed Honora's body down a hill and ran for help.

Their story didn't hold much water; later that same evening, Pauline was arrested for her mother's murder. Juliet was arrested the very next day.

The case went to trial on August 23, 1953, and lasted for six days. Teams of doctors tried to prove that Juliet and Pauline were insane, but the court wasn't buying it. As the prosecutor declared, Honora's murder was "a callously planned and premeditated murder, committed by two highly intelligent and perfectly sane but precocious and dirty-minded girls."

Because they were both under age 18, they would not face death. Rather, they would be imprisoned "at the Queen's pleasure," or in other words, until the Crown saw fit to release them.

Their prison terms began immediately. Pauline was incarcerated at Arohata Borstal and Juliet at Mount Eden. Each girl was released in 1959. After their release, both girls claim not to have had any contact with the other.

No one knew what happened to the girls after their release until 1994, when crime novelist Anne Perry admitted she was Juliet Hulme. She said that after she served her time, she moved to London and pursued her writing career. Parker wasn't outed until 1997, when she was discovered posing as Hilary Nathan, a very religious former teacher living in Hoo, just outside Rochester in Kent. Although both women are living in England, neither has any desire to contact the other.

In 1995, the release of *Heavenly Creatures*, a movie based on the girls' crime, starring Melanie Lynsky as Pauline and Kate Winslet as Juliet, reminded the world about the creepy case.

Virginia Hill *(1916–1966)*

MOB MOLL

Tough broads aren't born; they're made. And if ever there was a tough broad, it was the voluptuous and glamorous, icy and aloof, scheming and plotting, trash-talking, slutty, and sexily vulgar Virginia Hill. Although the beautiful starlet may have aspired to be in pictures in the 1940s, her biggest and most famous role would be the one she played off-screen as a mafia queen consort to infamous gangster Benjamin "Bugsy" Siegel. Virginia was a woman who pulled herself out of a white-trash existence and catapulted herself to fame and fortune. And it all started with a frying pan bubbling over with hot sausage grease.

Virginia had a tough childhood. She was born Odie Virginia Hill, the seventh of 10 children, on August 26, 1916. Her family lived in Lipscomb, one of the poorest cities in Alabama. Her father, W. M. "Mack" Hill, was probably the main reason that Virginia became what she did. He was a horse and mule trader who could have run a very successful business—if he hadn't been drunk all the time, that is. He had great business sense, but his insatiable craving for the sauce made him a good-for-nothing wife- and child-beater.

Virginia claimed that her father took most of his abuse out on her, and one day she finally decided she wasn't going to take it anymore. He came home particularly drunk and came at Virginia in the kitchen. She grabbed a frying pan from the stove, which was still full of hot grease from the sausages that had been cooking in it, and hurled it, full force, at her father's chest. He never went near her again.

Virginia would always remember this moment as the reason her life would be lived without fear—and without developing too many close attachments to people, either.

Virginia's mother, Margaret, was a woman ahead of her time. By the mid 1920s, she decided she had had enough of Mack's crap, and packed up her children and moved the family to Marietta, Georgia, her hometown. There, she ran a boarding-house, which her kids, especially Virginia, helped her to maintain.

Virginia was a reckless child, who had fully sexually matured by the time she was 12 years old. She freely slept around, sometimes taking money for sex, until she realized that she was never going to get anywhere in her life unless she moved out of Marietta and into a big city. She chose Chicago as her destination, and when she was 17 years old, Virginia left home to realize her dreams of wealth and fame.

Virginia got a job waiting tables in an Italian restaurant that attracted members of the mafia. She and another waitress used to crash parties, especially gangsters' parties, and it was at one of these parties that an admirer from the restaurant approached her. Joe Epstein worked as an "accountant" for Al Capone and his gang. Soon he had Virginia working as a money courier. She blazed up the ranks of the mob within a few years. Virginia never bothered to socialize with the mob wives; she was smart. She knew who to ingratiate herself with in order to get ahead. And they all hated her—the wives that is. Quite possibly as much for her disinterest in them as for the sexual favors she frequently granted to their husbands.

Joe Epstein would play a huge role in her life. In addition to getting her involved with the mob, he also saw to it that she lost her white-trash edge and developed a fashion flair, helping to transform her into the glamour-puss she will forever be remembered as being.

Soon Virginia was acting as liaison between Al Capone's group in Chicago and Lucky Luciano's crime family in New York. It was during one of her assignments in New York that she allegedly first made the acquaintance of Benjamin "Bugsy" Siegel. She almost compromised her position with Capone when she slept with Bugsy.

By 1938, Virginia needed a break from the organized crime life, so she moved back home to Marietta for a spell to chill out. But she didn't stay for long. That same year she recruited her brother, Chick, and the two headed to Hollywood. Organized crime had made its way to Tinseltown, and Virginia was ready to get back into the action.

Virginia became a starlet in Hollywood and even clinched minor roles in several films. One of them was a film called *Manpower*, which starred George Raft. Coincidentally, or by fate, George was a good friend of Siegel's, who had come to Hollywood the year before. While Siegel was visiting the set one day, he and Virginia became reacquainted and started up a relationship that would last five years and then some.

Bugsy and Virginia were the Hollywood-Mafia "it" couple. The paparazzi followed them around as if they were movie stars. Reputedly, Bugsy was smitten; Virginia was on the job, getting information for her employers. Whatever the case, both admitted it was the best sex of their lives.

By 1947, Virginia had had her fill of Bugsy. He was obsessed with his Las Vegas dream and with building his hotels. She would still see him from time to time, but never in Vegas. Somewhere along the line, some of Bugsy's investors' money went missing. Virginia was suspect, but the investors only cared about Bugsy. Most people who did business with Bugsy hated him, so this was a great opportunity to wipe him out.

On June 20, 1947, Bugsy was shot to death in Virginia's Beverly Hills mansion. She was out of town at the time. Although Bugsy's death had little to do with it, it was also about this time that Virginia Hill's life was starting to unravel.

In February 1950, Virginia met Hans Hauser, an Austrian ski instructor working in a ski resort in Sun Valley, Idaho. Their relationship would not be without its troubles, but it marked the only time that Hill would marry (within months of their meeting) and reproduce (her son, Peter).

By the 1950s, the government was starting to crack down on the mob big time. In 1951, the Kefauver Hearings brought members of various crime groups in to testify. The authorities had still not gotten to the bottom of Benjamin Siegel's murder, so many people were called in for questioning about it. As one might expect, Virginia Hill Hauser was called to testify. At first she declined the request, but the government got INS on hubby Hans, and she soon had no choice. Her testimony provided her inquisitors with useful information about organized crime, but she also managed to put her foot in her mouth when she talked

about her income. The IRS suspected she had been cheating them; now they knew for sure.

Virginia tried to work out several deals with the government, including handing over the diary she kept throughout her years in the business. They took the diary, but they didn't let her off the hook. All of her property and possessions were auctioned off. And, by this time, she and her husband had separated.

In 1951, Hill renounced her American citizenship, moved to Austria, where she became a citizen, and was reunited with her husband and son. The marriage wasn't really working out, and Virginia spent most of her time drinking. In 1956, she wanted to come back to the United States, but there were conditions. Most of them she could live with; testifying against Joe Epstein was not one of them.

Eventually, Virginia was able to work something out, and then, penniless, she began extorting money out of Epstein and other mob members. One of them, Joe Adonis, became especially fed up with the aging mob moll, and it's likely that he ordered her hit in 1966.

Virginia Hill's body was found by hikers in Austria on March 24, 1966. The cause of death was deemed a suicide by poisoning—and there was even a suicide note purportedly in Virginia's handwriting saying it was just that. Of course, anyone who knew Virginia Hill would never believe that she took her own life. Most people believe that she bit the hand that fed her, and that it had finally struck back.

Audrey Marie Hilley
(1933–1987)

MURDER

It's hard to pin down exactly what went wrong with Audrey Marie Hilley—why she murdered her husband, possibly her own mother, and why she was hell-bent on poisoning her own daughter for years. Most crime historians slate her in the "enigma" category, as she had been without motive or typical malice. It might be that she was simply insane, or that she was just plain evil.

Audrey had a typical Depression-era childhood. Money was short, and in order to give their only child everything they could, both her parents, Huey and Lucille Frazier, worked very long hours at the Linen Thread Company Mill.

Aside from seeing little of her parents, Audrey had a normal childhood. Sure, she was spoiled, but she managed to get good grades, and she was very popular. Audrey's parents were dead set on her getting a good-paying secretarial job when she graduated from high school, so when Audrey's future

husband, Frank Hilley, entered her life when she was only 12 years old, they were understandably ambivalent, particularly because Frank was already a junior in high school at the time. But he was in love and would wait for Audrey to grow up. Luckily, after he completed high school, Frank enlisted in the Navy, buying a little time for Audrey to grow up some. But by May 1951, they were married.

The Hilleys had the same problems as most married couples but added to those was Audrey's compulsive spending. Her parents had trained her early on to expect to receive everything she ever wanted; Audrey expected the same from her husband. Except that there wasn't that much money. They were both just starting out, and neither of them was on the fast track to a windfall of cash anytime soon. He held a nondescript job in shipping; she worked as a secretary, much to her parents' delight.

In 1952, Audrey became pregnant with her first child, Michael. After his birth in November of that year, Audrey stopped working for a while, but she never stopped spending. Her spending became so out of control, in fact, that she even registered a PO box, where she had bills re-routed so her husband couldn't see what she was up to. In 1960, the overspent couple welcomed their second and last child, their daughter Carol. Audrey eventually returned to work, but her office life, while bringing more money into the household, also brought other stuff into the household. Like the day that Frank Hilley came home early from work because he wasn't feeling well and found his wife in their bed with her boss. This infidelity would not be an isolated incident.

Year by year, the marriage began to unravel. Audrey seemed to be taking a downward spiral into a certain pitfall. By 1974, the problems could no longer be swept under the rug. Frank Hilley finally came clean to his now-grown son, Michael, about what had been going on with Audrey. When Frank died after a long, unidentified illness, Michael accepted his mother's invitation for him and his wife, Teri, to live with her and Audrey's ailing mother, Lucille, for a while. Lucille soon died; Teri had to go to the hospital several times for stomach trouble. Michael, becoming suspicious, decided that it was time to move out again.

Wherever Audrey Marie Hilley went, catastrophe seemed to follow. On top of her husband's unexplained death, her mother's death, and her daughter-in-law's chronic illness, her house had also burned down for what seemed like no reason at all. And then Carol started getting inexplicably and violently ill.

Audrey never denied that she favored her son over her daughter. She and Carol were always at odds, and as Carol grew older, and Audrey suspected her daughter was a lesbian, the problems did not get better. Far from it. Audrey had taken out life insurance policies on both her children: $25,000 for Mike; $39,000, with no explanation as to why it was so much higher than Mike's, for Carol. Essentially, Audrey spent a couple of years trying to poison her daughter, just as she had done with her own husband.

After each of Carol's bouts with illness, her mother would administer to her special "injections," which were not prescribed by the doctor. And upon learning this, a concerned doctor let Mike in on what his mother might be up to. Although he didn't flat out believe that his mother was trying to kill his sister, he knew something wasn't quiet right, and he asked his mother not to visit Carol for a while. Sure enough, Carol recovered.

In October 1979, when it could no longer be denied, Mike submitted a formal request to have his father's body exhumed and tested for arsenic. The tests proved that Frank Hilley had been poisoned. Audrey's mother's body was also exhumed, and while the cause of death was cancer, the body had extremely high levels of arsenic. Audrey was indicted on January 11, 1980, for the murder of her husband. And then she disappeared.

Audrey Marie Hilley fled, but she resurfaced in Fort Lauderdale, Florida, as Lindsay Robbi Hannon. There, she met a man, fell in "love," married, and then moved with her new husband to New Hampshire. She got a job as a secretary and kept her co-workers somewhere between entertained and horrified with her tragic tales, especially the one about how she herself was dying from a rare blood disease. She told them all kinds of fictitious stories about her life, including that she had a twin sister named Teri. Then—true story—"Teri" showed up and "Robbi," as she was known, just disappeared. Teri told her co-workers that her sister had left her husband to move back to Florida, where she died. The hubby, who was obviously out to lunch, bought the story, and soon Teri shacked up with him to "grieve." But her co-workers were perhaps a bit savvier than the hubby. They saw right through the act, reported her to the police, and in January 1983, she was picked up as Audrey Marie Hilley, fugitive from justice, and dragged back to Alabama.

Audrey was sentenced to life in prison for the murder of her husband, plus an additional 20 years for the attempted murder of her daughter. Inmate Hilley was incarcerated at Tutwiler State Prison on June 9, 1983. In 1985, she was given minimum-security clearance, thereby entitling her to take passes. She was such an exemplary prisoner, in fact, that in 1987 she was granted a three-day pass. A mistake: She never returned to the prison. A few days later, she was found delirious, sitting on a neighborhood porch. She died of hypothermia in the ambulance on the way to the hospital on February 28, 1987.

Myra Hindley *(1943–)*

MURDER

Myra Hindley had all the early childhood indicators that she would grow up to lead a life of crime. She grew up in a poor family. Her father was a drunk. She was "given up" to live with her grandparents when her sister was born because raising two children was just too much to bear for her parents. She never had a good relationship with her father. She wasn't a model student; in fact, she hated school so much, she would often make excuses to stay home, which her coddling grandmother allowed. And, when she met Ian Brady, she was barely getting by at work as a typist. She had no defined sense of self and no goals. So Ian Brady, in the great tradition of the psychopathic boyfriend, went in for the kill.

But we'll come back to that later.

Myra Hindley was born on July 23, 1942 in Manchester, England, to Bob Hindley, a one-time paratrooper, and his wife, Nellie, also known as Hettie. Bob's post-war career left a lot to be desired, and his drinking, combined with the meager living he was able to eke out between binges, meant that raising even one child was a burden for the Hindleys. When Myra's sister, Maureen, was born in 1946, four-year-old Myra was sent to live with her mother's mother, Ellen Maybury, who lived fairly close by, so Myra was still able to see her parents. But she didn't see that much of her daddy. In fact, many experts have pinned Myra's devotion to Ian Brady on her underdeveloped relationship with her father.

Myra was not a dim girl. She somehow got As and Bs in school, and probably would have done even better if she hadn't skipped school so often. But her grandmother coddled her, possibly feeling sorry for the little girl whose parents didn't want her. When a dear friend died when Myra was 15, the girl lost interest in school altogether and eventually dropped out. She got a job as a typist for a chemical supply company in Manchester.

Myra had no big dreams. Not even any desire to leave the town she grew up in. So it was easy for Ian Brady to sweep her off her feet with his big ideas about the world: no matter how deranged they were, they were better than anything she could have imagined for herself.

Myra was 19 when she first met Ian Brady. She loved him first. They were both outsiders, and she could sense this. He had a bad-boy quality she was completely drawn to. He had a past that made him rugged and cool, having grown up as Ian Stewart in the toughest part of Glasgow, Scotland. As a child, he got his kicks torturing and maiming all things smaller than him, children and animals alike. The illegitimate son of a waitress, Ian grew up in foster care until he was 16. At that point, his mother married, so he moved in with her and her new husband and took his stepfather's last name.

Ian was a few years older than Myra, and she had an enormous crush on him. She prayed for the day he would finally notice her and ask her out. One day, he did. Their first date? A movie: *The Nurmemberg Trials*. From that day forward, this ex-con, alcoholic, Nazi-worshipping, sadistically perverse young man was Myra Hindley's very own boyfriend. Although she had briefly been engaged before she met Ian, she was allegedly a virgin at this point. With no other sexual experience to draw from and decipher what was normal from what was not, she did whatever she could to ensure she'd keep her catch, including shearing off her hair and dying it bright blonde to look as Aryan as possible, dressing in leather, and wearing Nazi-style boots. But the changes she made were more than just physical. Myra started reading Ian's Nazi propaganda, and in no time, she passionately embraced his beliefs. She even swooned when he called her by her pet name, Myra Hess, after Hitler's henchman Rudolph Hess. That's what can happen when you have no belief system of your own.

Ian was tired of his job as an invoicing clerk and was always on the lookout for a way to make quick money—legally or illegally. He tried to break into pornography, taking obscene photos of his willing girlfriend, but no one wanted to buy them. He also tried to get them involved in armed robbery, fantasizing some English version of Bonnie and Clyde, but the Hindley-Brady brain trust was not able to pull it together. Like Bonnie Heady (page 102) and the Barker-Karpis gang (page 9), they also considered kidnapping as a way to make some quick cash, but they were never really successful with this either. The main reason: They were much happier having sex with their victims and killing them than collecting a ransom. This is how the horrific Moors Murders began.

Within two years of their first date, Brady and Hindley stalked their first victim, a 16-year-old girl. The next two victims were young boys. And then a 10-year-old girl disappeared. Unlike most partner-sex-and-murder teams, Hindley and Brady didn't just go after girls. Brady also liked to molest and rape young boys.

The Moors Murderers, the moniker they were given because they buried their victims' corpses on the moors, killed for nearly two years before they were caught. They were already in trouble for the murder of 17-year-old Edward Evans (Myra's brother-in-law reported them to the police for that one), when the body of another of their victims was discovered. Police eventually searched the house that Myra and Ian shared, and they found several pornographic photographs involving the sicko couple and their child sex pets, as well as tapes featuring audio recordings of the killer couple documenting their crimes.

Once they were nailed, Brady and Hindley still swore, despite all the evidence, that they were not guilty of the crimes. The trial, which shook up the United Kingdom, began on April 27, 1966; they were found guilty of first-degree murder, and neither of them showed any remorse. Lucky for them, the death penalty had just been abolished, so they were given life sentences.

By 1970, the "love" had worn off for Myra as she realized where her relationship with Ian Brady had taken her. She desperately tried to get paroled in the mid-1970s; he issued a statement saying he would not try to get parole, as both he and Myra were guilty as sin and he was prepared to spend the rest of his life repaying his debt to society. Myra continued to fight back, saying that she was a victim of Ian Brady's mental machinations and manipulations, but even at the time of this writing, she still has not been able to free herself from prison and the bad decisions she made as a young girl, full of (and, admittedly, a fool for) love.

Karla Homolka *(1970–)*
a.k.a. Karla Teale

MURDER

It could have been an episode of a show called *Canada's Sickest, Most Depraved Home Videos,* as footage of the Teales's—otherwise known as Karla Homolka and her husband Paul Bernardo—raunchy and repulsive sexual exploits were played, audio only, in a Canadian courtroom in the early 1990s. The contents of those tapes were hard to believe. How could such a clean-cut, Barbie-doll cute, young, upper-middle-class couple be responsible for the acts they were accused of performing? Without the taped evidence, perhaps only Paul would have been convicted for the crimes. But after hearing the evil role that Karla played in all the acts, including voluntarily taking part in the rape of her own sister—even performing sexual acts on the 16-year-old girl herself—there was no choice but to convict both. Should Karla Homolka's flimsy defense of being a subservient wife who had lost herself in the will of her husband have

stood up in court? That all depends on how you interpret the story of Karla Homolka.

Born to an upper-middle-class family in 1970, Karla was the oldest of three Homolka daughters. The Homolka household was a permissive one. This was the place where all the neighborhood teens came to hang out. They could drink if they wanted to, and there was little parental supervision, so they could do whatever else they wanted, too. All the sisters, Karla, Tammy, and Laurie, grew up in seemingly loving competition with each other, each trying to forge her own identity apart from the others. Karla, in particular, was obsessed with having her own identity; some psychiatrists have even argued that she was a narcissist, or someone who saw a fantasy reflection of herself in someone else. According to Patricia Pearson, in a 1995 *Saturday Night* article titled "Behind Every Successful Psychopath," "If Hell ran a dating service, narcissists and psychopaths would top the list of perfect pairs. Theirs is a union of grandiose, immature egos, with the narcissist projecting her fantasies of success, power, and romance onto the flat, reflective surface of the psychopathic soul." Enter Paul Bernardo, psychopath.

Bernardo came into the relationship with more than a few problems of his own. He was the illegitimate product of the brief union his mother, Marilyn Bernardo, had with a man who was not her husband when her husband, Kenneth Bernardo, became unmanageably abusive toward her. She eventually returned to Kenneth, who helped raise Paul as his own son. It's not known whether Kenneth abused Paul Bernardo, but he did sexually abuse his only daughter. Simply put, the Bernardo home wasn't a happy home. One day, in an effort to hurt Paul, with whom she was having a fight, Marilyn told him that Kenneth wasn't his biological father. Paul never forgot this, and even cried about it at trial, citing it as at least one of the reasons he later led a life of crime.

Paul was a very good-looking guy, a successful accountant (and stolen-goods trafficker), who ran through women like water; or, it might be said that they ran from him like gazelles from a ravenous cougar, because he was a bit of a psycho and had very sadistic carnal urges. When he met Karla, who was willing to get into anything he wanted, provided he would love her and be her perfect boyfriend, the deal was struck. The couple consummated their relationship—in full view of the friends who would be the witnesses at their wedding—within hours of their first meeting. And their lives would go downhill from that point.

Actually, Paul's life, along with his morality, had already begun its long downward slide. Although it wasn't common knowledge when Paul met Karla in 1987, Paul was already making a reputation for himself as a prolific rapist, having already earned for himself, albeit anonymously, the moniker of the "Scarborough Rapist." When Karla learned of his activities, she didn't leave.

The two were inseparable. They spent lots of time in the Homolka home, where they would have sex in Karla's bedroom, which was right behind the recreation room where the family watched TV. Karla was Paul's goddess; Paul was Karla's very breath. She would do anything for him, which she was about to prove in the summer of 1990, and, in a more brutal fashion, at the end of that fateful year.

Paul had developed something of a crush on Karla's younger sister, Tammy. Karla was jealous, but seemed to understand Paul's disappointment that, because Karla wasn't a virgin and was so old (um, almost 21), it was increasingly difficult for him to get excited by her. So when Paul took a ride with Tammy that July and later admitted to Karla that he made out with her, Karla was hurt but understanding.

For Christmas, she thought she'd give him a very special present: her 16-year-old sister's virginity. Karla worked in an animal hospital, so she had access to plenty of tranquilizers. Before the holiday, she grabbed a solution called Halcion. The family went about their Christmas Eve festivities, the kids having as much to drink as their parents, and then the youngsters retreated to the rec room, where Karla slipped her sister a mickey. While Karla held a rag soaked in halothane over her baby sister's already-passed-out nose and mouth, her loving boyfriend brutally raped the child, camera pointed at Tammy in hand. When he was done, he insisted that Karla also have sex with Tammy. While Karla was going about her business, Tammy awoke, vomited, then choked to death on her own vomit. No one else in the family ever found the tape. They just thought they lost their daughter/sister to an unfortunate choking accident.

Months later, Karla and Paul would tape themselves lying in bed, nude, about to have sex, and talking about the incident. This, a tape on which Karla is heard cooing about how sexy it was when Paul raped her now-deceased sister, is one of the tapes that would be played in court.

Life went on, however, but now that Paul's favorite sex toy was dead, Karla took it upon herself to bring him more young girls for delightful evenings of good food, fine wine, and sodomy. They also managed to get married, throwing themselves a lavish wedding for 150 guests, with no expense spared. They changed their name to "Teale," a less ethnic-sounding name than Bernardo. A Hawaiian honeymoon followed, during which, Karla would later claim, Paul brutally beat her. (In the honeymoon videotapes, however, Karla had nary a bruise on her improbably tan, string-bikinied body.)

The tapes revealed that the Teales raped and killed at least three people, but there may have been several others who never made the videos. In the meantime, police were starting to catch up with the Scarborough Rapist, a.k.a. Paul Teale. They had a fairly detailed police sketch and were lucky enough to come by some great DNA samples. It was just a matter of time before Paul would be found out. Except that Karla helped speed the process considerably.

One day in 1992, after a rather vicious beating, Karla phoned the cops and reported Paul's domestic violence, but when the police arrived, she also confessed the couple's crimes. Their movie-making days were over.

As soon as the case went to trial, the Teales immediately turned against each other. Both blamed the other: Paul said that Karla was an insatiable lesbian and that he was never around for any of the killings; Karla said that Paul had complete control of her mind and that she acted out of fear of him. The tapes, of course, told a different story.

Karla's trial began in 1993. And although certain details of the trial were not released, to ensure Paul a fair trial (his case, for various reasons, did not go to trial until 1995), there was an inevitable escape of information. The Canadian press was given a gag order and couldn't release any of the details, but the American press was chomping at the bit, and right on the Canadian border after all. Paul's attorneys would later argue that the information leaked by the American press from Karla's trial could prevent Paul from having a fair trial. But his defense proved to be as soggy as day-old cereal in a bowl of milk: Paul Bernardo was sentenced to life in prison on September 1, 1995.

Karla acted like a stoic matron at her trial. According to some accounts, she read somewhere that a jury responds favorably to an emotionless defendant, so she played the role of brainwashed wife flawlessly—or so she thought. The jury, though, was horrified by the tapes, including one that featured Karla striking a coquettish pose while her husband asked her what she liked and she answered: "Showing off. Licking little girls. Making my man happy." She got life in prison.

Karla was eligible for early release in 2001, but as she was still seen as someone who would undoubtedly kill again, early release was denied. She will be up for another hearing in 2005. Authorities are doubtful that she'll be let loose, which, in some ways, is fine with her. Karla receives plenty of hate mail, many containing death threats, and there's also a website on the Internet that features a Karla Homolka deathwatch. She thinks that if she gets out, she will probably move to another country, but as *Maclean's* pointed out in January 2001, "Immigration lawyers say with her record and notoriety, there are few countries that would let her in, even as a visitor."

Lady Frances Howard
(c. 1590–c. 1629)

MURDER

Many people have been involved in a love triangle; but not many can boast of being involved in two ... at the same time. But Lady Frances Howard, whose sanity was questionable, not only simultaneously found herself part of two triangles, but used murder to dissolve at least one of them.

There are two ways the legend of Lady Howard typically unfolds. In the first, she is depicted as a manipulative bitch, a woman who would stop at nothing to keep her business private. In this tale, the Lady has Sir Thomas Overbury thrown into the Bloody Tower so he will keep quiet about her affair with Viscount Rochester. Over the course of three months, Lady Frances arranged to have Overbury slowly poisoned, thus assuring he would never speak of her infidelities. Two years later, one of the Lady's maids was so overcome by guilt, she had no choice but to confess the crime. Lady Howard was arrested and held prisoner in the Bloody Tower for a short time and then released; all of her accomplices were executed.

The second tale, however, has decidedly more intrigue and perhaps even seems more feasible. In this version of the story, Lady Frances Howard, at the time a child of 15, falls in love with Robert Carr, a handsome bisexual who was a regular consort of King James I. She was already married at the time to the Earl of Sussex, but as the Earl had been abroad since the wedding, the marriage had not yet been consummated. Once she fell in love with Carr, it never would be. When her husband returned, she withheld sex from him, and the Earl had no choice but to have his marriage annulled.

Which meant that now she could easily marry her beloved, except that in addition to his sexual liaisons with the king, Carr, a popular young lad, was also sexually involved with the writer Sir Thomas Overbury. Overbury was completely enamored of his Robert, and while he could deal with sharing the boy with the king, he wasn't about to share his young lover with a woman.

Frances and Robert both knew it was time to remove Overbury from the equation, but how? The king, not liking the mood Overbury was putting his Robert in, decided to offer Overbury a post abroad. Frances, knowing that if Overbury refused the position he'd be imprisoned, told Robert to strongly advise Overbury to decline the king's offer. Overbury turned down the king's offer, and off to the Bloody Tower he went.

Carr got his hands on some poison; Lady Frances Howard found a willing servant to administer it; and on September 15, 1613, Sir Thomas Overbury died. Lady Frances Howard and Robert Carr were married shortly thereafter, and Frances, predicting that they might need his protection someday, allowed the king to share her husband's favors with her.

It was a good prediction. In 1615, one of the accomplices of the crime confessed his part—implicating Frances and Robert as well—and the young couple was arrested. They were both to be hanged, that is, until they threatened to "out" the king. Instead of serving a death sentence, they were imprisoned in the Bloody Tower for six years, after which they were free to live their lives. Lady Frances Howard died at age 39 of ovarian cancer; Robert Carr lived for many years after his bride perished.

Juliet Hulme *(see "Heavenly Creatures")*

Helene Jegado *(1803–1851)*

MURDER, THEFT

"Wherever I go, people die." These are the famous words of the French-born cook Helene Jegado, who made her way across France in the early to mid-nineteenth century, working for various families as a cook, and leaving a trail of poisoned corpses in her wake.

Born in Brittany, France, in 1803, Helene was an orphan by the time she was seven. She played out her childhood in various orphanages, and by the time she was a teenager, she was making her living as a servant. By the end of the 1820s, Helene found her true calling: murder.

Once she got started, there was no stopping her. Her first victims were an entire household of seven, which she wiped out over a three-month period. As she moved on, she got more ravenous in her quest for death, and less and less time would go by between when she was hired, usually as a cook, and when she started taking out members of the families for whom she worked.

By the beginning of the 1930s, Madam Jegado was feeling a tad out of control, so she decided to hole up in a convent for a while to protect herself from poisoning folks and, more importantly, getting caught. As it turned out, Sister Helene found herself jumping from convent to convent; she kept getting kicked out for stealing this and that. Lucky for her, no one connected her to the mysterious deaths of her fellow sisters.

By the end of the decade, Helene had either run out of convents to hole up in or had grown tired of the nun's life, because she resumed her career of serial-killer cook. But she began to lose her killer touch. Although several victims of her poisonings obediently succumbed to death, others only became violently ill and eventually recovered.

By the beginning of the 1850s, Helene was beginning to get sloppy. In 1851, she took her final position as a cook in the household of Professor Theodore Biddard. There she was only able to poison one servant before the gig was up. The authorities had grown wise to Helene, and this time an autopsy was conducted to determine the servant's cause of death. She was, indeed, poisoned. The authorities swooped down on the Biddard household to discuss the poisoning with the professor. Helene, who thought she was busted, put her own foot in her mouth by exclaiming, without prompting: "I am innocent." The officers, who had not accused her of anything, realized that they had found their killer. Helene Jegado's protests of innocence bought her own one-way ticket to the guillotine.

At the trial, the long list of victims Jegado was accused of murdering astonished everyone. The worst of it was that there was no motive; Helene poisoned people simply because she enjoyed poisoning them. Case closed. And she didn't limit her poisonings to employers and other distant associates: one of her victims was her own sister, Anna.

Because of the statute of limitations, Helene could only be tried for the crimes she committed after 1833. No matter: They were still able to pin at least 23 deaths, 6 illnesses, and countless thefts on her. She was executed the same year she was convicted for her crimes.

Christine Keeler *(1942–)*
a.k.a. C. M. Sloane

PERJURY, PROSTITUTION, ALLEGED ESPIONAGE

In 1989, a movie premiered in London that revisited the details of one of the most shocking sex scandals of the 1960s in Great Britain. The aptly named *Scandal,* based on former call-girl Christine Keeler's own tell-all memoir of the same title, is the story of the 1963 Profumo Scandal. The scandal involved then–War Secretary John Profumo, who denied allegations of having an affair with a prostitute, Keeler; when it was discovered that he actually did have an affair

with Keeler, he was forced to step down. Many believe this guffaw cost Prime Minister Macmillan to lose the election, thus putting England's conservative party out of office. But just who was this babe whose open legs sunk a thousand political ships?

Christine Keeler was born into a poor, poor family in Berkshire, England, in 1942. Her childhood was far from idyllic; by age 16, she had already been raped twice and had had an abortion. When she was 17, she left home and supported herself working in London as a topless dancer. One of the regulars started coming to the club just to see Christine. Dr. Stephen Ward, an osteopath who was nearly 20 years older than Christine, befriended the coquettish brunette, and soon enough, Christine quit her job and moved in with the older doctor. This was not a sexual relationship in any way, however. Not between Christine and Ward. However, he would use her to gain the favor of the influential people he so loved to rub elbows with.

One of these influential people was John Profumo, the War Secretary. Ward tried to fix Christine and John up at a party at the Cliveden home of Ward's good friends, the Astors. While Mr. Astor and Profumo, both very married, each took a noticeable liking to Christine, so much so that Profumo tried to make a pass at her at every chance he could get, nothing would occur between Christine and Profumo that weekend.

A few days later, Ward introduced Christine to Russian diplomat Captain Eugene Ivanov, who had stopped by Ward's flat on business. (It had been suspected that Ward was working as a Russian spy, and that Ivanov was actually either bringing or taking government papers at this meeting. The details are not available; in fact, the details of the espionage element are contained in sealed records that won't be opened until 2045.) Ivanov became entranced by the lovely Christine, and as everyone had been dipping into the sherry, as it were, Ivanov ended up in bed with Christine.

Within a matter of days, Christine once again met up with Profumo, and they consummated their affair. They only got together about five times, but this, combined with her liaison with Ivanov, was enough for many to suspect that Profumo was mixing military secrets with bodily fluids, and that Christine was reporting what she learned back to Ivanov to help the Soviets. Profumo vehemently denied to Parliament being sexually involved with Christine, but the truth could not be covered up. The randy politician shamed the entire conservative administration and was forced to resign from the House of Commons.

But while some may have fun seeing Christine as one part Mata Hari, one part Monica Lewinsky, she denied having anything to do with passing secrets to the Soviets. She stated that she and Profumo hardly talked, and when they did, it was not about government secrets. "If I had asked, he would have had me arrested," she would later say of Profumo.

The scandal was not only going to affect the conservative party. As soon as it erupted, the authorities went after Ward for pimping Christine and another woman who was living at his London home, Mandy Rice-Davies. On July 31, Ward overdosed on Nembutal and died within days of his conviction. Someone needed to take the fall, and it was going to be Christine. She was arrested in December of that year for committing perjury by lying about being attacked a while back; she was given nine months in the slammer to reflect on her actions.

Sadly, Christine never really pulled it together after the scandal, until the book and the film more than 25 years later, that is. Her own mother even disowned her. With nowhere really to go, she fooled around a lot, got married a couple of times, and managed to bear two sons. One of her sons, James, is completely estranged from her; the other, Seymour, is not.

Kathryn Thorne Kelly
(1904–??)

KIDNAPPING, BANK ROBBERY

One can't help but wonder what Kathryn Thorne Kelly might have become if she hadn't been seduced by a life of crime. She played the role of glamorous gangster's wife with more sophistication, more suave, more skill than most politicians' wives play politicians' wives. A master of public relations and marketing, Kathryn built her husband up from small-time crook to FBI-most-wanted-caliber bad guy, all in just a couple of years. Indeed, Kathryn was the brains—and the guts, really—behind legendary gangster "Machine Gun" Kelly. She was as shrewd as Eleanor Roosevelt, as stunning as Jackie Kennedy. But she was as notorious as Lady Macbeth herself.

Kathryn's obsession with the glamorous life was apparent from an early age. "Kathryn" was not, in fact, even her given name. She was born Cleo Brooks, in Saltillo, Mississippi, in 1904, and was married to a blue-collar worker named Lonnie Frye by the time she was 15. It was a short marriage, but it produced one child: a daughter, Pauline. After the marriage ended, Kathryn decided that "Cleo" was not a glamorous enough name, so she started calling herself "Kathryn." She then married and divorced another husband, Allie Brewer—all this by the time she was barely 20 years old.

Cleo Brooks did not come from money or position. In fact, she didn't even come from the right side of the law. Her entire family was forever mixed up in some criminal activity or other, from robbery to prostitution. Even her mother, Ora Brooks, was not immune. About the time that Kathryn divorced her first husband, Ora divorced Kathryn's father, James Emory Brooks, and took up with and married Robert K. G. Shannon, a known Texas bootlegger. Both Ora and Kathyrn got involved in the business, and soon daughter found a Texas bootlegger of her own to marry: Charles Thorne.

Charles was the first husband Kathryn did not have to divorce when she grew tired of him. One day, he was simply found dead in his home. Foul play was alleged, and Kathryn was almost a murder suspect. One reason police suspected her was that, while coming home from visiting relatives just before her husband's death, she told a gas station attendant that she was "bound for Coleman, Texas, to kill that God-damned Charlie Thorne" because she heard a rumor that he was cheating on her. The death was deemed a suicide when a scrawled note from Charles was found that read: "I cannot live with or without her." Whether this was Charles's actual note or a quick attempt at covering up by Kathryn remains a mystery.

When she met George Kelly in 1930, Kathryn finally saw a project she could sink her teeth into. George Kelly, born George Kelly Barnes in 1895, was a small-time crook with more brag than balls. George had been involved in small-time hold-ups of liquor stores and the like. He had served time in Leavenworth for smuggling, and when he got sprung, he joined a gang and began dabbling in bank robbery and bootlegging. But he was a handsome and charismatic fellow, and Kathryn saw enormous potential in him.

In the years between Thorne's death and this fateful meeting, Kathryn had accumulated quite a rap sheet for herself, from shoplifting and prostitution to robbery and bootlegging. The year was 1930, and Kathryn was playing mistress to bootlegger "Little Stevie" Anderson. George was working for Anderson when he met Kathryn, but nothing would ever be the same after that meeting. George and Kathryn fell instantly in love, ran off to Minneapolis together, and by September of 1930 were married.

It was Kathryn who pushed George out of the realm of petty crime into the big time. First, she worked on his image. She bought him his first machine gun and attached to him the "machine gun" moniker. Then, she played up his "legend" to anyone whose ear she could catch, even handing out used-up machine-gun cartridges as souvenirs.

Kathryn was also known to have masterminded many of Machine Gun Kelly's bigger crimes—most notably the 1933 kidnapping of oil magnate Charles Urschel in Oklahoma City, which would bring the couple's crime spree—and love affair—to an abrupt end.

In a carefully configured plan, Kathryn and George lined up several accomplices, including Kathryn's mother, stepfather, and 20-year-old stepbrother, Armon Shannon, to assist in the kidnapping that eventually brought them a $200,000 ransom.

On July 22, 1933, George Kelly and his partner Albert Bates kidnapped Charles Urschel from his home at 11 at night. Urschel was held—sometimes blindfolded, bound, and gagged—for nine days, while Kelly's gang awaited delivery of the ransom money. Urschel tried to take in as much as he could with his senses impaired, and was able to give authorities enough information after his release to point them in Machine Gun Kelly's direction. Kathryn's family and the other accomplices were all taken into custody by the middle of August. George and Kathryn fled, and were not captured until September 26, 1933.

Both George and Kathyrn were obsessed with looking good and enjoying the finer things in life. A wildly fashionable pair, the two looked more like film stars than crooks at trial. And why not? They were all glamour and all show, and the public ate them up. It was, after all, not only the Golden Age of Hollywood, but the Golden Age of the Midwestern gangster. Kathryn played herself in the trial like a Silver Screen goddess playing Kathryn Kelly, always fashionable and never missing a photo op. Her adoring husband doted at her side.

But so much for love. During the trial, Kathryn essentially denied that she had anything to do with George's crimes—even though members of her own family were being dragged down in the mess and were facing life sentences for the roles they had played. She tried to convince the jury that it was all George's doing, and that he had coerced the family into acting with him.

But the law saw through her. A threatening note sent to the Urschels in Kathryn's handwriting was turned in as evidence, and into the slammer she went, along with the others. Only Armon Shannon got off lightly, with a 10-year suspended sentence because of his age. On October 13, 1933, the Kellys were sentenced to life in prison. Kelly was headed back to Leavenworth, Kathryn to a federal prison in Cincinnati. Despite her turning on him, George promised the press that he would break out by Christmas and then break out his wife, and that they would spend Christmas together.

The big breakout was never to be, however. George's infamous big mouth got him transferred to the maximum security Alcatraz. He was returned to Leavenworth after a few years, where he suffered a massive heart attack and died in 1954. Kathryn hired a new lawyer and managed to get herself and her mother released from prison in 1958 on the basis that during the trial, she was never able to bring in a handwriting expert of her own to dispute whether the threatening note submitted as evidence was actually hers. The last anyone heard of her was that she was working as a bookkeeper somewhere in Oklahoma.

Constance Kent
(1844–1944)

MURDER

Kids sometimes have a strange way of showing that they do not approve of a parent's choice for a new spouse. Before Lizzie Borden (page 35) chopped up her father and stepmother in their New England home at the end of the nineteenth century, 16-year-old Constance Kent murdered the product of the union of her father and his much-disapproved former housemaid. It wasn't confirmed for many years after, and once the girl confessed, many believed that she had inherited her mother's insanity.

Constance Kent came from a well-to-do Victorian family that hailed from Rode, a quaint English village situated eight miles from Bath and about four miles from Frome. She was born in February 1844, the eighth of eleven children of Sayville Kent and his first wife, Mary Anne Kent nee Windus. Six of the children would not live to adulthood, however. By the time Constance Emile came into the world, her mother was already quite ill with tuberculosis and had started to lose some of her mental capacities, many say due to the loss of all those children. A year after Constance was born, Mary Anne gave birth to her last child, William. Because they were so close in age and so far apart in age from their older siblings, William and Constance were as close as two siblings could be, without the trappings of incest. They were not that close to their older sisters, who were more than 15 years older, but they both looked up to their brother, Edward, who was only nine years older than Constance.

The Kent children were not exactly popular. In fact, because their mother's insanity was well known in the small village, William and Constance were essentially ostracized, causing them to spend ever more time together.

As Mary Anne became increasingly ill and insane, Mr. Kent hired a woman to look after the house for his ailing wife. Mary Anne died of a bowel obstruction in 1853; that September, Kent announced his engagement to the housekeeper. The two children both hated their new stepmother so much that the duo ran away together once. Constance cut off all her hair to look like a boy. Eventually they were found and brought back "home."

The family had more than its share of problems. Shortly before William and Constance's escape attempt, they received news that their beloved brother Edward was lost at sea. Then, to make matters worse, their parents decided that William was going to be sent away to school, making an already morose, melancholic, and unpleasant Constance all the more so. The only high point of this time in young Constance's life was that her dear brother Edward had at last been found.

But Constance's new stepmother was increasingly getting on her nerves, churning out new, healthy babies almost once a year. The middle child of these new babies, who, as it seemed to Constance and to William, were favored above everyone else in the family, was Francis Sayville, who was reputed to be the favorite of even the favored. Constance had had enough. It was time to strike back.

During the night on June 29, 1860, favorite little Francis disappeared from his crib. The nurse had looked in on him in the night and noticed he wasn't there, but she hadn't worried about it, because Mrs. Kent was known to take Francis to her own bed in the night. But the next morning, Francis was still missing from his crib. The toddler was found in the privy, with his neck slashed so deeply that his tiny head was barely attached to his little neck.

Accusations abounded. The prime suspects became the nurse, for being suspiciously inattentive, and Constance, because of her attitude and behavioral problems. The police believed the crime to be an inside job, and it was no secret, inside or outside the household, how much Constance hated her stepmother. But the most incriminating bit of evidence was produced by the parlor maid. She had taken Constance's nightgown to be washed the day after the murder, and it was inexplicably damp.

Constance was arrested, and the case went to trial, but the evidence was too flimsy to hold up in court. The nurse was arrested again, but a case could not be built against her, either. The murder remained unsolved. The family went about their lives, miserable. Constance was sent to live in a convent in France where she registered as "Emile" Kent.

During her time at the convent, Constance became almost fanatically religious and, possibly overcome with guilt and remorse, confessed her crime on April 25, 1864.

At the trial the following July, Constance pled guilty to the charges, and was sentenced to death. However, because she was only 16 years old at the time she committed the murder, her sentence was commuted to life in prison. She ended up serving only 20 years of that term.

Many people have speculated about what happened to Constance after she was released from prison. The wildest of all accounts suggests that Jack the Ripper was really Jill the Ripper, and that Jill was actually Constance, who, having inherited her mother's insanity, went off the deep end when she murdered her half-brother and never lost her taste for blood. Other accounts say that she went to the United States. Still others say she took off for Australia after her release, changed her name to Ruth Emilie Kaye, became a nurse, and even received a one-hundreth birthday telegram from the King, the first convicted murderer ever to receive such a salutation. Per this account, she died two months later on April 10, 1944.

Sante Kimes (1935–)

MURDER, SWINDLING

Imagine leading such an insidious life, that when you go on trial for murder, you are convicted—even though a body had never been recovered. That was the fate of Sante Kimes and her youngest son, Kenneth, in 1998, when they were each given a life sentence for the murder of their New York City millionaire landlord, Irene Silverman.

Irene had been complaining about her $6,000-a-month tenant, Kenneth Kimes, to various friends before she disappeared: "I have this tenant who's driving us all crazy!" she'd say. "We can't get into the room to clean, and I suspect he's hiding something in there. He's not nice, and he's rude, and I suspect that something very bad is going on." Her suspicions were warranted: Kenneth and his mother, Sante Kimes, were planning to bilk the woman out of all of her money and then do away with her. It's too bad no one understood what the Kimeses were up to in time to save Irene.

Sante Kimes was the mastermind behind all the duo's schemes. She was, after all, the mother. Kenneth Kimes, like most men who had ever encountered Sante, was simply caught under her spell. And oh what a spell that was. Circe herself had nothing on Sante. Her power was not limited to men, but it was on the "frailer" male sex that her magic worked best, especially in the case of Kenneth, who had been involved in a life of crime with his mother since he was old enough to spring a slingshot. It was part of the raising process, after all.

Just ask Sante's older son, Kent Walker, who, in 2001, published a memoir about his childhood with mommy dearest. In *Son of a Grifter,* Walker remembers: "It was exciting to be with mom when she was good, but it was more fun when she was bad."

One time, Kent remembers going with Mom to "buy" a car. She convinced the dealer to let her take it for a spin with her little son, and she never brought the car back. Another time, when Sante was already married to Ken Kimes and little Kenny was already in the picture, Kent remembers running down the street with his family, evading a hotel manager after they had skipped the bill. "I've never been a cookie-baking type of mother," Sante has been known to say, "but I did the best I could."

This could be the truth. Sante, after all, had a pretty scary reputation for defending her boys. Once, when a bully attacked Kent, she confronted the offending boy's father, and he tried to laugh it off. Never laugh at Sante Kimes. She picked up a garden hose and proceeded to beat him with it until proper apologies were made.

And then there was the time that the house that Kent lived in with his mother burned to the ground. He didn't know that it was going to go up in flames; he'd like to think that his mother didn't know either, because she asked him to go back in the house to get something for her while they were leaving one day, and just as he had made his way out the front door, the house exploded.

No one really knows where Sante came from. The story that seems to hold the most weight is that she was born in Oklahoma to Rattan and Mary Singhrs. Rattan left the family when Sante was just two, and by the time Sante was 10, she was put up for adoption.

Records indicate that Sante Kimes began her life of crime in 1961, when she shoplifted a bag. For the next 35 years, Sante would pick up more than 20 aliases and swindle her way across the country. She would also find time to get married twice, and bear a son in each of those unions.

Her first husband was Floyd Walker, a builder. They would bring Kent Walker into the world. By the mid-1970s, Sante was restless. She wanted things that Floyd couldn't give her: riches, jewels, servants. So she dumped him and married a millionaire.

Kenneth Kimes Sr. was considerably older than Sante, but it mattered not. He was the owner of a successful construction company, and he had money. The Kimeses had three separate residences across the United States, and each of these residences was kept up by servants, who Sante, reputedly, did not treat well. In fact, it was proven in a court of law that the girls did not in fact even *want* to be there—that they were kidnapped from Mexico and forced to work for the Kimeses. Sante would serve three years for enslavement of her servants.

All the money in the world didn't keep Sante out of trouble. In 1985, just before her indictment for kidnapping her servants, Sante was caught lifting a $6,500 fur coat from the bar of the Mayflower Hotel in Washington, D.C.

Kenneth Jr., who was born in 1976, never had a chance. He was always extraordinarily close to his mother—he was even home schooled. He was completely under her spell and had no point of reference in the outside world to gauge that maybe Mama was not altogether normal. Before his father's death in 1994, like his half-brother Kent before him, Kenneth had engaged in some of Mom's shady dealings, but on a very minor level. After his father died, however, Kenneth became his mother's full-time cohort, consort, and, as many have speculated, especially considering the depths of despair that Kenneth fell into when he learned he would not be jailed anywhere near his mother, her lover.

In 1998, the Kimeses went in for the big kill. They targeted a New York millionaire, Irene Silverman, intending to steal all her assets as well as her $7.5 million town-house. Kenny rented an apartment in the space. Mother and son began their scheming. Irene Silverman officially disappeared in July; the Kimeses were apprehended just days later.

Police were lead to the Kimeses as suspects shortly after Silverman's disappearance. The FBI had been tracking the pair as they made their way across the USA, a trail of murder and fraud unfolding in their wake. Sante and Kenneth were already suspects in the vanishing of Syed Bilal Ahmed, a Bahamas millionaire, and California businessman David Kadzin. The Irene Silverman case looked pretty similar to the other two cases. What finally tipped them off, however, was the car that the Kimeses had purchased with a bad check just a few months before. The car, a green 1997 Lincoln Town Car, was seized shortly after Silverman vanished. Inside the police found rent receipts with Silverman's signature, blank power-of-attorney forms with Syed Bilal Ahmed's name filled in, and other incriminating papers. The police had enough proof to bring mother and son in.

On July 5, 1998, Sante and Kenneth were apprehended on the street in front of the Manhattan Hilton Hotel. The 22-year-old Kenny, the purported murderer in all the pair's con games, actually soiled himself. They were detained in different jails, which nearly put the already fragile Kenny in a tail-spin.

The case went to trial almost two years later. On May 18, 2000, mother and son were both convicted of murder, and yet, Silverman's body had not yet surfaced. They were also tried and convicted for 118 other offenses, including second-degree murder, conspiracy, robbery, and possession of stolen property. Because there was no body, there was no first-degree murder conviction, so they were able to escape the death penalty in New York, but they would both be looking at about 100 years behind bars apiece. However, in California, where they are suspected of Kasdin's murder, there is a body. If extradited and convicted, they would both face death.

This was too much for the young Kenny Kimes to bear. The separation from his mother had driven him evermore mad by November 2000, when he held Court TV producer Maria Zone hostage with a pen. He was offered a deal whereby he and Mom wouldn't have to go to California if he cooperated. The anxiety of pending death caused Kenny to confess that he, alone, had killed Silverman, and that his mother's only involvement was to help him dump the garbage-bagged corpse in New Jersey. It didn't matter. The two were still shipped to California to face the music for Kasdin's death in January 2001.

Sharon Kinne (1939–)

MURDER

Sharon Kinne was like a cat. She got herself stuck in any number of precarious situations, and then with grace and finesse, slinked away, virtually unscathed. To this day, it is not known whether Sharon perished after her successful escape from a Mexican prison, or if she is still among us, knocking off various husbands and lovers as they overstay their welcome with her.

The trouble in Sharon's life essentially began when she got knocked up at 16. In the mid-1950s, abortion wasn't a standard option for an unwanted pregnancy; marriage was. So Sharon married James Kinne in October of 1956, vowing till death do they part. As luck would have it, she miscarried the baby that forced her into the marriage she never wanted, but by that time, she was well entrenched in her married life. By 1960, she found herself living out the American dream with her house in suburban Independence, Missouri, and two darling children. And, oh yeah, that husband.

Sharon was barely 21 when the 1960s broke. She was full of fire and life, unlike her increasingly boring husband who was five years her senior. So she started having an affair with a friend from high school, John Boldizs. But it wasn't enough. Sharon

wanted to enjoy all the delights life had to offer. James found out about Sharon's extra-marital activities and told her he was going to divorce her. This would not help matters at all. If she was divorced, she'd be even less free, bringing up her two little children on her own. At least if her husband died, she could have his insurance money on which to get by. There was only one solution: murder.

On March 19, 1960, Sharon Kinne shot her husband in the head, and when the police came to investigate, she played off her shock and despair so very well that everyone accepted her story that her two-and-a-half-year-old daughter Danna done it. According to Sharon, while James was taking a nap, Danna went up to him, gun in hand, and asked "How does this work, Daddy?" Sharon said she was in the bathroom at the time, that she didn't know her daughter was playing with one of her husband's many guns. And then she heard it go off.

Before James's body was cold, Sharon cashed in his life insurance policy and bought a brand new Thunderbird. The salesman, Walter Jones, was intrigued by the frisky young widow, and the two began an affair—hardly a month after her own husband had been put in the ground. Walter was known to seduce his customers regularly, but he was also known to have a wife, named Patricia. Neither of these mattered much to Sharon. By May, she told Walter that she was pregnant and that he was to divorce his wife and marry her. He wasn't having any of it.

A couple of days later, Patricia Jones mysteriously disappeared. Oddly enough, Sharon found Patricia Jones's body, with four holes shot in it, and reported it to the police. The police were pretty confused by how Sharon ended up in the secluded area where the body was found, but she explained that her "friend" Walter was suspicious that his wife was cheating on him, and that she was trying to help Walter nab Patricia in the act.

It didn't take long for the police to learn that Walter was, in fact, more than a friend to Sharon. She became a suspect. And while they were at it, they had never been altogether comfortable about her daughter accidentally slaying James Kinne. Sharon was arrested for both murders.

But charges just seemed to roll off Sharon. They couldn't get her on Patricia Jones's death because ballistics tests could not prove that the bullets that killed Mrs. Jones came from Sharon's gun. (Sharon had several guns, it should be noted. Her deceased husband was something of a gun nut. So who knows if Sharon wasn't just able to dispose of the murder weapon in time.)

Then, when her husband's now-murder case went to trial, the jury could not come to a decision. Sharon skipped town before the next trial, which was set for October 1964. By this time, she already had herself a new beau; she and Frank Puglise took off for Mexico.

Life South of the Border was no honeymoon, however. Frank and Sharon fought constantly. One night, when she had to get away from him, she went to a local bar for a couple of drinks. There she met Francisco Ordonez, a Mexican radio announcer who invited her back to his hotel room. She accepted. And bang: murder number three took place. Sharon shot him twice through the heart, and when the manager broke into the room after hearing the shots, she said she killed in self-defense.

Sharon wasn't slinking out of anything this time. She was already a fugitive in her own country, so she couldn't expect any help from there. Sharon was locked up in a Mexican jail. The Mexican press called her *La Pistolera*. She was sentenced to 10 years.

Sharon tried to appeal, but her efforts only bought her three more years of hard time. No matter for the cat. On December 7, 1969, Sharon disappeared from the prison, and has never been heard from again.

Patricia Krenwinkel *(see Manson Women)*

Helen Kroger
a.k.a. Lona Cohen

ESPIONAGE

Little is known about Helen Kroger. Her real name was Lona Cohen, and she was married to Morris Cohen, who went by the name Peter Kroger. Russian-born, the Krogers moved from their native country to America in 1951 to act as spies.

At one time, the Krogers had been involved with Julius and Ethel Rosenberg (page 177), but had moved away from the Rosenberg spy ring in time to escape indictment. In fact, before they had even moved to the States, Helen Kroger is credited with having been the person who received the "Kleenex Box" from Ted Hall (one of the spies involved in the spy ring), which contained blueprints for the atomic bomb. The Krogers took off for London in the mid-1950s, and used their antiquarian bookstore as a front for sending secret documents to the USSR.

In 1961, their luck ran out. The Krogers were discovered, indicted, and sentenced to 20 years in jail. However, in 1969, they were traded for a British citizen and lecturer, Gerald Brooke, who had been arrested in the Soviet Union for distributing anti-Soviet literature in Moscow for an extreme Russian émigré organization. He was being held in the USSR and the Russians offered his return for the Krogers. Britain's Prime Minister, Harold Wilson, was not initially satisfied with the exchange, citing that Brooke was not, in fact, a spy. However, the Russians did not plan to give up without a fight and threatened to retry Brooke, God only knowing what they would find him guilty of. Wilson relented and Brooke was finally returned to Britain. The Krogers were sent to Russia three months later.

Not much is known about the Krogers after their return to Russia, except that Helen died in a Moscow hospital shortly afterward.

Playwright Hugh Whitemore produced a play in 1997 called *Pack of Lies,* which was based on the seemingly simple suburban lives of the Krogers and how they were regarded by their neighbors until they were exposed in 1961.

Polly Adler signs copies of her just-published memoir, A House Is Not a Home, *at a promotional party at New York's 21 Club, June 1953.*

(Photo courtesy Bettmann/CORBIS)

Martha Beck, following her arraignment for the murders of Delphine Downing and her daughter, Rainelle, in Detroit, Michigan, March 3, 1949.

(Photo courtesy Bettmann/CORBIS)

Ma Barker with friend Arthur Dunlop just months before she and her son Fred were shot dead by the Feds in their Florida hideout.

Iva Toguri D'Aquino (a.k.a. "Tokyo Rose") in custody in Japan, July 9, 1945.

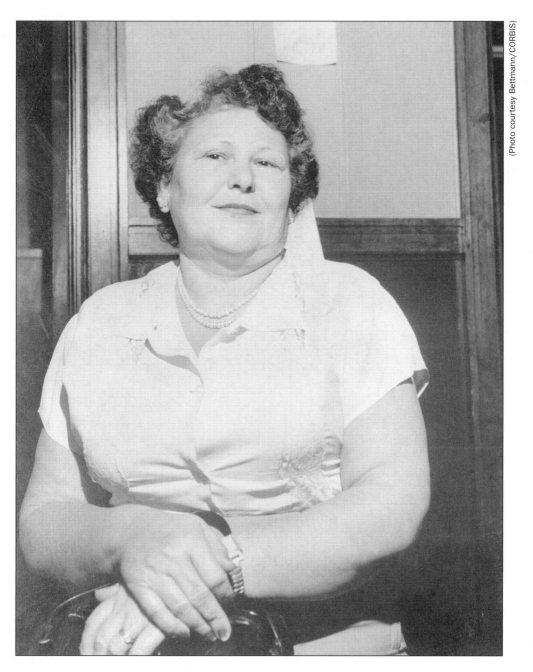

Nannie Doss, the "giggling grandma," after her arrest in November 1954.

Ruth Ellis on a night out on the town with lover and future victim, David Blakely.

Virginia Hill glamour shot, 1947.

"Machine Gun" Kelly and his wife, Kathryn Thorne Kelly, at trial in Oklahoma City, October 9, 1933.

Mata Hari at the peak of her popularity before the First World War.

Melita Norwood reads her statement outside her Bexleyheath storybook cottage on September 11, 1999.

Bonnie Parker hams it up for the camera on the road with Clyde Barrow (taking the photo).

Public enemy number two, Ethel Rosenberg, keeps house after her husband's arrest in July 1950.

Lethal Nurses

MURDER

Gwendolyn Graham (1963–)

Catherine Wood (1964–)

Throughout the history of murder, caretakers have always emerged as killers. Sometimes these homicidal custodians are mothers, which can in a twisted sense be explained or understood through an emotional connection that exists between killer and killed. But in the case of nurses who murder their patients—what's the motive? Martha Beck (page 15), Judi Buenoano (page 43), Amy Archer-Gilligan (page 2), Jane Toppan (page 203), and Carol Bundy (page 46) were nurses by profession. Two of these women—namely Jane Toppan and Amy Archer-Gilligan—made a career of using their positions to kill those entrusted to their care.

Perhaps the oddest lethal nurses were two who worked in a Midwest hospital as a sex-and-murder team in the late 1980s. Gwendolyn Graham and Catherine Mae Wood were lovers who, together, murdered six elderly female patients during their stint at the Alpine Manor Nursing Home in Walker, Michigan.

The relationship between these two women was not unlike the lethal combination of Beck and Fernandez (page 16) or Bundy and Clark (page 46) or Fugate and Starkweather (page 83); one of the pair was desperate for approval from the other, who was an undeniable psychopath with murderous sexual fantasies. As in all these cases, it's hard to tell if Graham would have killed if she had not been involved with Wood. Like Beck, Bundy, or Fugate, however, Wood would most likely never have been involved in such a situation had she not been involved with Graham.

Gwendolyn Graham was born in California in 1963. She grew up in Tyler, Texas, where she experienced a melancholy childhood. It is alleged that her father sexually abused her, but he denied it, and the abuse has never been conclusively proven. Gwen left her unhappy past behind her when she moved to Michigan in 1986 at age 23 to take a job as a nurse's aid at Alpine Manor.

Catherine Mae Wood was already installed in the hospital, as the supervisor to the nurse's aids. A native of the Midwest, Wood had lived most of her life in Grand Rapids, Michigan. When she was barely seventeen, she married, but it proved to be far less than "happily ever after" for her and her husband. Catherine coped with her marital problems in the form of the food she began to overconsume. By the time Gwen came into her life, Catherine weighed nearly 450 pounds, and her marriage had all but ended.

At first, Gwen was a boost to Catherine's faltering self-esteem, but she later proved to be a nightmare who preyed on Catherine's fragile sense of self. Their sexcapades generally involved Gwen tying Catherine up and practically asphyxiating her—in fact, Catherine nearly blacked out during one of the rougher bouts. But Catherine never complained. She was losing weight, feeling great about herself, and knew she owed everything to her darling Gwen. It's fairly certain she had no idea just how far the sex games would go, however.

It was Gwen's idea to bring their (read: her) snuff fantasies out of the bedroom and into the sick room. If the thought of murder was getting them hotter than ever before, why not commit a few to see how the carnage could improve their already ecstasy-enriched sex life? As they dwelt daily among the elderly and the infirm, they had an orchard of easy victims. Not only would the old broads be unable to put up much of a fight, suspicion of foul play would be minimal as old people typically stop breathing on their own—no need for a murder investigation.

Their first idea was to knock off six patients whose initials, put together, would spell "M-U-R-D-E-R." Would the police get the, um, joke? But this plan didn't quite work out. The "M" patient proved to be more resilient than they imagined, so they were forced to scrap the M-U-R-D-E-R game and simply prey on the frailest patients.

The murders weren't complicated. The victim would simply be smothered by a pillow in her sleep. No blood. No poison. No mess. Gwen was the actual killer; Catherine was the lookout. Once the murder was committed, the two women would get so turned on that they'd run to the nearest supply closet to celebrate with intense sex. It is rumored that one time the women got so hot washing the corpse of one of their victims that they had to have each other right then and there.

Eventually, love faded. Gwen moved to a new hospital, where she fell in love with another woman. She and Catherine still kept in touch by phone, however. It was because of these conversations that the women were finally busted for their crimes. Once, Gwen boasted to Catherine that she was getting really anxious to "smash a baby" (her new job was taking care of infants). The thought of that was so deplorable to Catherine that she decided it was time to come clean and confess to her husband. Interestingly, he didn't do anything about it until more than a year later, when he called the police.

The lethal lesbians were arrested in December 1988. The case went to trial in the latter part of 1989. Catherine plea-bargained to testify against Gwen, which meant a conviction of second-degree murder and 20 to 40 years in the slammer. On November 2, 1989, Gwen was handed six consecutive life terms, without possibility of parole.

Diana Lumbrea *(1957–)*

MURDER

Either Diana Lumbrea was suffering from a serious affliction of Munchausen by Proxy Syndrome, or she was just an evil woman who gaveth life so she could taketh it away. At 17, she married Lionel Garza, and within 3 years she had produced 3 offspring. By February 1978, within months of the birth of her third child, Jose Lionel Lumbrea, all three children were dead.

None of Diana's children ever made it to school age, but for some reason, this didn't tip off the staff at the Texas emergency room where the terrified, overly emotional mother would always bring them.

Perhaps it was because they were always fighting, or perhaps it was because Lionel saw that his wife was not exactly "mother material," but Diana and Lionel divorced in 1979. She never remarried, but Diana continued to reproduce.

In the 1980s, she bore three more children, all with different fathers, and none of the kids lived to blow out the candles on their fifth birthday cake. The one who lasted the longest was Jose Antonio, who was born in 1986. Somehow this child managed to survive until just after his fourth birthday. Even children who weren't the fruit of Diana's loins were not safe. In 1980, Diana was watching the six-week-old daughter of a friend. Soon enough, Diana showed up in the emergency room with the lifeless child, telling her usual story, that the child had died of "lethal convulsions."

Finally, in 1990, hospital workers decided there was something decidedly wrong with Diana, so they called the police. An investigation revealed that Diana had taken out insurance policies on all her children right after their births—and she even took out additional policies before some of their deaths.

Diana was tried and convicted in both Texas and Kansas. The verdict in each: Guilty of murder in the first degree. Neither state, however, handed down the death sentence. She is presently serving a life sentence, with a chance of parole in 15 years.

Margaretha Geertruida Zelle MacLeod

(1876–1917) a.k.a. "Mata Hari"

ESPIONAGE

Was the most famous stripper of all time actually a double agent, working for France and for Germany during the First World War? Or was she simply a woman who found a way to live well, providing special "favors" to hundreds of powerful men in exchange for money, furs, and jewels? It's only in recent years that information has surfaced that perhaps Mata Hari was merely a scapegoat, and not the loathsome traitor she had for so long been believed to be.

Whatever she was or turned out to be, the woman who would become the notorious Mata Hari did not grow up with fantasies of spydom and international intrigue. And she did not grow up in an Indian temple where she learned the secrets of exotic dance, as her self-created PR machine professed. Her life started simply, and until she was about 29 years old, it was pretty much as ordinary a life as a woman living in turn-of-the-century Europe could have lived.

Mata Hari was born on August 7, 1876, as Margaretha Geertruida Zelle in the Netherlands. Her father was a prosperous milliner. It was a comfortable life, but like most young women, Margaretha wanted to see the world, even if that meant finding herself a husband.

When Margaretha was 19 years old, she answered a personal ad placed by Captain Rudolf MacLeod, a 38-year-old Dutch colonial army officer who was looking for a wife. Margaretha and Rudolf were married within a couple of months in 1895, and they moved to MacLeod's post in Java, an island of Indonesia, south of Borneo. It was here that Margaretha learned some of the seductive dances that made her an international sensation in later years.

The marriage lasted several years—and probably several more years than it should have. MacLeod proved to be a less-than-ideal husband. He was a drinker, an abuser, a neglecter, a philanderer. Margaretha had two children with MacLeod: a son, Norman, who was born soon after the marriage took place, and a daughter, Non.

In a tragedy that ultimately ripped apart the already fragile family unit, in 1902, Norman was poisoned by the MacLeods' servants. It was allegedly an act of retaliation against MacLeod for raping one of the servant's daughters. The MacLeods headed back to Amsterdam where Rudolf resigned his commission. But the wound was too deep for the marriage to withstand. Margaretha and Rudolf divorced shortly after their return.

Margaretha left her daughter, who was still just an infant, in the care of relatives, and took off for Paris. There, she supported herself in various ways, from being an artist's model to giving horseback riding instruction. But the sporadic income she made from these ventures was not enough to provide her with the lifestyle she had grown up in and married into.

Margaretha was 29 years old. Gravity had already begun to tug at her body. Her breasts sagged. She was thickish around the middle from bearing two children. But she radiated an undeniably raw sexuality, and men were quick to notice it. Margaretha supplemented her meager earnings with donations from various benefactors—in other words, she gave sex for money. It wasn't really prostitution. There were no official deals made. But she allowed men to shower her with money and gifts for the privilege of enjoying her body all the same.

It was with one of the "sugar daddies," the Baron de Marguerie, that Margaretha got the idea to start exotic dancing to make a living. Together they invented an exotic persona, Mata Hari, meaning "light of day." Margaretha had dark hair and a dark complexion, so there would be no problem passing herself off as an Indian princess who had learned the secret dance of the veils from her ancestors.

Mata Hari's first gig was at Emile Guimet's Museum of Oriental Art. On March 13, 1905, she writhed before the six-armed statue of Siva, removing articles of clothing with each maneuver of her body. By the time the last veil dropped to the floor, Mata Hari was an international sensation.

Mata Hari continued her infamous striptease throughout her 30s. But as famous as she got, she still relied upon the generosity of her many, um, benefactors, to keep herself comfortable. In fact, as the novelty wore off, as her body aged, and as other, younger, more lithe women began to imitate her act, Mata Hari relied on their kindness more and more. But these relationships, which once kept her afloat, were in part what led to her downfall.

Although of Dutch descent, Mata Hari had by this time adopted France as her home and pledged her allegiance to the country. So when World War I broke out, the French were understandably wary of Mata Hari's relationships with German officials and the like. That she was receiving money and gifts from such officials was enough for the French to suspect treason. By 1915, Mata Hari was put under 24-hour surveillance by the French government; by 1917, she was arrested for being a German spy.

She denied the charges vehemently, and even offered to spy for the Allies. But she made a huge mistake during her initial interrogations: She let slip a German code number that only a German spy would know. Now, whether this was grounds for execution hinges on the question of whether Mata Hari was actually a spy or just a scapegoat for a larger operation. Mata Hari had many lovers, and men didn't share her bed just for something to do. Men worshipped her. She was a sex goddess. It's feasible that one of her many lovers could have leaked that information to her between the sheets. But the French government was not convinced.

On October 15, 1917, Mata Hari was marched before a firing squad of 12. As folklore presents it, she went to the firing line wearing a fur coat with nothing underneath it. When her executioners raised and pointed their guns, the woman was said to have opened her coat, flashed her killers, and blew them a kiss. Another legend states that only 11 of the 12 bullets fired hit the woman. The soldier who missed approached the corpse and blew a hole through her gorgeous head.

While no one will ever really know what transpired that day, or whether Mata Hari was in fact innocent, one thing's for certain: The name Mata Hari remains synonymous with mystery and intrigue and sexuality to this day.

Manson Women

MURDER

The Manson Family is not really so much a family as it is a cult. Its leader, Charles Manson, has been serving time since the early 1970s, but still, the family continues.

To understand the family, and the motives behind their crimes, it is necessary to understand their leader. Born "no name Maddox," the son of teenage prostitute Kathleen Maddox, in Cincinnati, Ohio, in 1934, Charlie didn't get the ideal start in life. He got the name "Manson" by taking the surname of one of his mother's boyfriends, one who he liked.

By the time he was four years old, his mother was in the clink for armed robbery for knocking over a gas station with her brother. Charlie was sent to live with another uncle, who was always finding new and creative ways to humiliate the boy, including sending him to school in girl's clothes. By 1947, Charlie, who had been in and out of trouble throughout his childhood, paid his first visit to a juvenile detention facility. The boy was nothing if not charismatic, and during one of his stints behind bars, he even befriended Alan Karpis, the only surviving member of the Barker-Karpis gang (page 9). It was Karpis who introduced Charlie to one of his main passions: playing the guitar.

By 1967, Charlie was out of jail, thoroughly enmeshed in the San Francisco drug culture, and aspiring to become a famous singer-songwriter. This is not a joke. Charlie even had a foot in the door of the music business—he was good friends with Dennis Wilson of the Beach Boys for a while; that is, until Dennis sensed there might be more than a little something wrong with Charlie and blew him off. Charlie's big "in" to the music biz was trashed. He also had a contact with Doris Day's son, Terry Melcher, another recording "in," but that, too, soon fell through. Charlie needed something else to do.

He was already 33 when he descended on San Fran, but somehow, he was able to fit in well with the 18-to-24 set. Eventually, he amassed a group of followers, whom he convinced that "the black man" was going to rise up and violently take control of society from "the white man." It was Charlie and his followers' responsibility to stop this from happening. He called the movement "Helter Skelter," believing that the inspiration for it had come from The Beatles song of the same name.

Throughout the late 1960s, Manson recruited family members, men and women alike. They all lived together in a commune, Spahn Ranch, which was taken from its original owner in exchange for sexual favors provided by the girls. Manson slept with all the women, and many of them, over the years, gave birth to Charlie's illegitimate children.

In the summer of 1969, Manson felt it was time to show society what would happen when the black man tried to take over, so he orchestrated a series of grisly killings that his family carried out. Charlie never soiled his hands with anyone's blood.

Two slaughters from that August stand out. First, the murders of Sharon Tate, who was eight months pregnant at the time, and her houseguests, Folgers coffee heiress Abigail Folger, Abigail's boyfriend, Voytek Frykowski, and Jay Sebring, a hairstylist with a thing for Sharon. (Sharon's husband, Roman Polanski, was away at the time, shooting, ironically, *Rosemary's Baby*.) The second slaughter involved a middle-aged couple, Leno and Rosemary LaBianca. Later, it was discovered why the Polanski-Tate residence was hit: It was the former home of Terry Melcher, who had let Charlie down with his recording career. No one really knows why the LaBiancas were targeted.

The Manson family might have gotten away with their killings had Susan "sexy Sadie" Atkins not blabbed all about them when she was doing time for another murder. But she did, and several of the members went on trial for the killings. Susan Atkins, Patricia Krenwinkel, and Leslie van Houten played the perfect little psychopaths, shaving their heads and carving swastikas into their foreheads for effect.

Manson, along with the three girls, and another male accomplice, Charles "Tex" Watson, were originally sentenced to death, but when the death penalty was abolished in California in 1972, all death sentences were commuted to life. None of them is allowed to be in contact with Manson, and even though they are in the same prison, just cells apart, Krenwinkel, Atkins, and van Houten do not communicate with each other.

It would be impossible to look at all the women who have been associated with Manson as his followers throughout the years. Therefore, here presented are brief profiles of some of the most significant and outstanding, as well as of his own criminally inclined mother.

Kathleen Maddox

The third child born to Nancy and Charles Maddox in 1918, there were no signs that Kathleen would go so terribly astray. Her parents seemed to have it together. Her father worked long, hard hours for the B&O Railroad. Her mother stayed at home with the children.

Perhaps young Kathleen began to march to the beat of her own drummer as a way of rebelling against her family's fanatical religion. Her grandmother, who lived with the family and who was also the family disciplinarian, was particularly obsessed with religion. Grandma was also extremely critical of Kathleen, which ultimately lead the girl to run away from home at age 15.

By the time she was 16, Kathleen was making her living as a prostitute, drinking heavily, and leading a devil-may-care lifestyle. That same year, she also gave birth to what many people believe is the spawn of Satan: Charles Maddox Manson.

Susan Atkins

Susan "sexy Sadie" Atkins fell in with Charles Manson in November 1967, when she was just 19 years old. Hailing from San Jose, California, Susan had no direction in her life when she found the Manson Family. She was supporting herself by selling drugs and stripping. So the idea of being a part of Manson's group looked pretty darn good to her at the time.

Susan is responsible for the murders at the Polanski-Tate residence and for the LaBianca murders. It was Susan who did Sharon Tate in, even as the pregnant starlet begged for her life and for Susan to spare her child. But Susan was not having any of it.

And thanks to Susan Atkins and her big mouth, the family was brought down in 1969. Susan was already in prison for killing Gary Hinman, and she simply could not keep her mouth shut. She told inmates Ronnie Howard and Virginia Graham everything, and they, in turn, told the police. She gave the women all the gruesome details of the killings, and proudly professed that when she was killing Sharon, the woman cried out "Please don't kill me. Please don't kill me. I don't want to die. I want to have my baby"; to which Susan replied "Look, bitch, I don't care about you. I don't care if you're going to have a baby. You had better be ready. You're going to die and I don't feel anything about it." When the horrified inmates asked her how she could live with herself for killing a pregnant woman, Susan was puzzled. "I thought you understood," she told them. "I loved her, and in order for me to kill her I was killing part of myself when I killed her."

Susan found God in prison, which is apt to happen, and she also married two times, most recently in 2000 to a Harvard-educated lawyer. She has been denied parole every time she comes up for it.

Lynette "Squeaky" Fromme

One of the first members of the family to fall in with Manson, Lynette met Charlie in Venice, California, in 1967 after she was thrown out by her parents. She had a normal childhood. She was a cheerleader in high school and even took ballet lessons. But Lynette's "flower power" values were more than her parents could bear, causing the rift. Charlie was taken in by Lynette, a tiny waif of a girl whom the family called "Squeaky."

Squeaky wasn't involved in the killings in the summer of 1969. But, when Manson and the others went to jail after their convictions, Squeaky became the official head of the family. She wrote to Charlie regularly, and he advised her how to carry his message out.

Squeaky's biggest claim to fame was that she tried to assassinate President Gerald Ford on September 4, 1975. She approached him wearing a white turban and her "red ceremonial gown," the one she typically wore when "cleaning the earth," which is what she thought she was doing by trying to kill Ford, whose environmental conscience was not strong enough to suit the Manson Family.

When she approached the president, everyone had his guard down. She was just this odd little thing in a crazy outfit. As Ford himself reported a couple of months after the incident, "I stopped because I had the impression she wanted to speak to me or shake my hand and as I moved to either shake hands or speak to her, I then noticed the gun ... in her hand, which was approximately two feet from me." The gun was not loaded, as the Secret Service was soon to discover, and as Squeaky tries to point out every time she's up for parole: How could it be attempted murder if the gun was not loaded?

On December 19, 1975, Squeaky was sentenced to life in prison, where she remains at the time of this writing.

Sandra Good

Older than the typical recruit, Sandra Good, the daughter of a successful stockbroker, was 24 when she met up with Charlie in 1968. She had no part in the murders of 1969, but she still did her part for the family.

After Squeaky got busted, Sandra released a list of 70 politicians and businessmen the Manson Family were targeting for the damage they were inflicting on the environment. Good was convicted for extortion in March 1976 and was sentenced to 15 years in jail; she served 10. She was paroled on the condition that she never have contact with any member of the Manson Family again.

Patricia Krenwinkel

A Sunday school teacher, Patricia Krenwinkel bonded with Charlie over the Bible when he met her while visiting a mutual friend in Manhattan Beach, California.

Patricia was involved in both the Tate and LaBianca murders. After LaBianca was killed, she jabbed forks into his stomach and then carved the word "WAR," into his gut. At the Tate crime scene, she was the one responsible for writing "Healther Skelter" [*sic*] and other deranged messages on the wall in the victims' blood.

Krenwinkel skipped her parole hearing in 1997; she will be up again in 2002. Since being in prison, Krenwinkel has publicly denounced Manson and all the madness of the summer of 1969.

Leslie van Houten

Leslie van Houten joined the gang in 1968. As legend has it, she one day quite casually wandered into the Spahn Ranch camp and decided not to leave.

Leslie van Houten was among the disciples who murdered the LaBiancas; she had no part in the Tate killings. In fact, part of Leslie's defense throughout the trial and her subsequent parole reviews was that she never actually did any of the killings, that she just mauled the corpses. Because of this, prosecutors were going to strike up a plea bargain with her to turn her cohorts in. They decided to bargain with Linda Kasabian, who had also been at the LaBianca killings, instead. Leslie has been denied parole 13 times already. Each time, she tries to appeal to the board on the same grounds: "No one at [the age she happens to be that year] is the same as they were at nineteen. I will live with that forever and I have learned to live with it the best way I know how." And every time, the board decides that she has not taken enough responsibility for the murders and denies her parole.

At her hearings, family members of the LaBiancas request that she stay in prison for life. Even her own father suggested that she not be paroled.

Leslie has not given up. Since she's been incarcerated, she's earned two college degrees. In 2001, she published a book about her learning experience in jail called *The Long Prison Journey.* In her last parole hearing in 2000, and of her education, book, and website she is compiling, Leslie said: "I don't know the world out there, but it felt like a good thing for a woman in her fifties to do. If that day ever comes, I want to become anonymous and live as quietly as I can. I believe what I did was inexcusable. You can never make it right and I sincerely apologize for all the pain the family went through."

Mata Hari *(see Margaretha Geertruida Zelle MacLeod)*

Louisa Merrifield
(1907–1953)

MURDER

They say good help is to hard to find, and for anyone who ever had the misfortune of having Louisa Merrifield on the household payroll, well, let's just say they'd know why.

Not the most ambitious worker, Louisa somehow managed to piss through 20 different jobs in fewer than 3 years before she signed on to work for Sarah Ann Rickettes, a wealthy old woman whom Louisa hoped to worm into her favor so she'd change her will to include Louisa and her 71-year-old third husband, Alfred, who was only half sane at the time but somehow would also work for Mrs. Rickettes.

Now Sarah Rickettes was not the picture of genteel old age; in fact, she was a bit of a crone, and was not well loved in her town of Blackpool, England. Sarah had simple needs and wasn't that hard to care for. She subsisted on a diet of glycerin and jam. And she drank like a fish. But she was a mean, cantankerous bird all the same.

Eventually, however, Louisa was able to convince the old dame to sign over the house to her and Alfred in her will. And Louisa did what she could to make it as official and seemingly on the up and up as she could. On April 9, 1953, Louisa called in a doctor to verify that Sarah was indeed of sound mind before she changed the will, and he confirmed that, in fact, she was. Once the ink was dry, it was time to act.

Louisa purchased rat poison and began mixing it into the old lady's jam, little by little. By April 14, Mrs. Rickettes' body had its fill of the poison, and she keeled over. Louisa believed that because of the woman's advanced age and her, um, popularity in the town, that there would be no autopsy. She thought wrong.

The autopsy revealed that Sarah Rickettes' death was caused by phosphorous poisoning, and the source of the phosphorous was traced back to the rat poison—and to Louisa. The authorities arrested both Louisa and Alfred, but during the trial, Alfred's mental derangement began to show, and it became obvious that Louisa had acted alone. What really tripped her up? Her big mouth. One day, while bragging about what she stood to inherit, a friend asked her when the old woman had died. Louisa replied: "She's not dead yet, but she soon will be." Needless to say, the person who heard this loose statement became a shoe-in witness for the prosecution.

The trial took place in July 1953. Alfred was let go and lived, believe it or not, in the deceased Sarah Rickettes' home, which he legally owned, until his death in 1962.

Louisa was sentenced to death, and on September 18, 1953, she was hanged at Manchester's Strangeways Prison.

Judith Ann Neelly *(1964–)*

MURDER

In many partner killing sprees, there's a stronger-minded partner who brainwashes the weaker-minded counterpart into doing his bidding. Martha Beck (page 15) smiled all the way to the electric chair, confident that she had done all she could to please the man she loved. Carol Bundy (page 46) thought it was perfectly acceptable to present 11-year-old girls to her lovers for their sexual pleasure. Karla Homolka (page 116) basked in the knowledge that she had sacrificed her own drugged-out sister for her lover's pleasure. Typically, it's the woman who falls out of her mind in love—or lust—with the man, succumbing to his will, no matter how despicable. In the case of the Neelys, Judith Ann and her much-older husband, Alvin, many have surmised that the shoe was on the other foot—that Judith Ann was the mastermind, and Alvin her too-willing servant. Was this simply a story concocted by Alvin's defense team, or the truth?

Judith might have been looking for a father figure when she took up with Alvin Neelly. After all, her own father died in a motorcycle accident when she was nine years old, leaving her mother alone to take care of Judith and her four siblings. But in looking for this "father figure," it didn't mean she was looking for a master. She had a mind of her own. Taking up with 26-year-old Neelly at age 15 meant Judith no longer had to share what little there was with her four siblings—and for the poverty-stricken in the 1970s deep, deep south, there wasn't much. Originally from Georgia, Alvin Neelly was 11 years older than Judith and had already abandoned one wife and three children by the time he met his Murfreesboro-bred babe. Within a matter of months, they eloped. Neither Alvin nor Judith was an angel when they met. Alvin was a drifter, and Judith had her own problems. So in the first months of their marriage, neither was corrupted by the way they made their living passing bad checks and holding up small stores, your typical petty fare. They enjoyed their own antics immensely, and even took to calling themselves "Boney and Claude." Later, when they communicated using CBs, they'd use the handles "The Nightrider" (his) and "Lady Sundance" (hers), referring to Butch Cassidy and the Sundance Kid.

In 1980, Judith was arrested for holding a woman up at gunpoint, and she, the good wife that she was, lead authorities to her husband so that he, too, could share in the fall. Both were incarcerated; but when Judith gave birth to twins just a couple of months later, she was transferred to a juvenile facility. A year later, Boney and Claude were once again let loose on the world, and that's when the real fun began.

Like all great murderous couples before them—and since—Alvin and Judith were addicted to having sex with each other. But it wasn't enough. The couple needed more spice in their sex life. And Judith especially, who craved having sex with other women, needed what her husband simply could not give her.

Judith met Lisa Millican at the arcade in the Riverbend Mall, the same mall where she had performed the holdup that led to her arrest. Lisa was on furlough from the Harpst Home, a home for emotionally troubled and disturbed girls. It wasn't the best possible life, and it has been concluded that Lisa probably decided to go with Judith because she didn't want to go back to the home that night. Whatever was in store, it certainly had to be better than what was awaiting her at "home," she thought. But, as she would soon learn, it was much, much worse.

Lisa found herself in a living nightmare that lasted for three days. When she left the arcade with Lisa, the two drove around aimlessly for hours, with Judith's young twins sitting in the backseat. Lisa spent her nights handcuffed to the bed in various motel rooms, where she was sexually molested by both Judith and Alvin, and in full view of their children. It was Judith who finally decided to kill Lisa, and it was Judith who carried through with the murder in the most bizarre manner imaginable.

Judith had once heard that injecting someone with liquid Drano would kill that person quickly, and that the cause of death would not be detectable. So she decided to try this out on Lisa. She drove the girl to a spot that overlooked a canyon. She explained to Lisa that all she wanted to do was give her an injection to put her to sleep so that Judith could have enough time to get away. It didn't seem to be working, so Judith injected Lisa again and again and again, giving Lisa's skin what the coroner would later describe as the "consistency of anchovy paste." When Lisa was finally dead, Judith tossed her body and all the crime paraphernalia over the edge of the cliff.

Shortly after Lisa was killed, Judith and Alvin struck again. This time, they went after a couple: Janice Chatman and John Hancock were walking down the road when a young mother of two pulled them over and asked them if they needed a ride. They accepted. As Hancock would later tell the police, Judith chatted back and forth on the CB with someone called "The Nightrider," with whom they would be meeting shortly. When they reached their destination, Judith pulled out a gun and shot Hancock in the back. They took Janice with them, leaving Hancock for dead. Judith and Alvin had their way with Janice, then Judith murdered her and left her corpse to rot.

Who knows how long Judith might have continued her lusty, murderous rampage, if she hadn't, for some reason, tipped off the police. Perhaps in an act of unconscious attrition, she called the police to tip them off on the whereabouts of Lisa Millican's body. As luck would have it, John Hancock, up and about after his own run-in with Judith, overheard the police playing the tape, and identified Judith's voice as that of the woman who shot him. He was shown police photos and picked Judith Neelly out.

On October 14, 1980, Judith and Alvin were picked up for check fraud, and the police figured out that they had found their murderers. Alvin admitted to one rape, but told police that his wife was not only the mastermind behind all the crimes, but that she alone had killed the victims. Alvin disclosed that there were probably about eight victims in all.

For the trial, Judith's lawyers decided to "clean her up," buying her new clothes, fixing her teeth, and otherwise making her more presentable than the "white trash" jurors would be chomping at the bit to send down the river. Her defense tried to depict Alvin Neely as a Svengali, but the jury wasn't having any of it. She was sentenced to death on April 18, 1983, and, at age 18, she was the youngest woman to ever be put on death row. Judith's attorneys tried to appeal several times, but all appeals were denied. However, the justice system works slowly: At the time of this writing, nearly 20 years after her first conviction, Judith Anne Neely still sits on death row, awaiting her turn in the chair.

Melita Norwood *(1912–   )*

ESPIONAGE

In the charming village of Bexleyheath, a suburb of London, England, there lives a kindly elderly lady who putters about her garden and sips tea from a Che Guevera mug. In late 1999, Mother England was knocked on her, um, arse, when the book *The Sword and the Shield* was put out by Cambridge University historian Christopher Andrew and former KGB archivist Vasili Mitrokhin. The book revealed the sweet granny—among other British citizens—to be one of Russia's top spies, who throughout her career fed Britain's atomic secrets to Russia in support of her own Communist ideals. Even more shocking was that the British government knew about her involvement as early as 1965 (although her total

involvement couldn't be fully confirmed until 1992). Even then, however, the government kept their knowledge under wraps so as not to interfere with other espionage investigations they were conducting.

Melita Norwood was born Melita Sirnis to a Latvian-born father and British mother in England. She had a normal childhood, growing up with her sister and half-brother. Melita had an especially strong bond with her father, whose left-wing ideals she wholeheartedly embraced. By the time she was hired by the British Non-Ferrous Metals Research Association at age 20, she was a full-fledged member of the Communist Party—but it would be a few more years before she became a spy.

In 1935, the NKVD, the name of the agency that would become the KGB after World War II, contacted the 23-year-old secretary to enlist her support for the strengthening of the Communist Party. Andrew Rothstein, one of the founders of the tiny British Communist Party, was the one who made the match. Melita was honored, and by 1937, she had officially begun smuggling secrets to Russia.

In 1936, Melita Sirnis married Hilary Norwood, a math teacher who was a fellow Brit and a fellow Communist, though not a fellow spy. Melita and Hilary were happy, for the most part, during their marriage that ended after 50 years when Hilary passed away in 1986. Their main point of contention: while he supported, and himself, followed, her politics, he didn't approve of her spying. He never tried to stop her, however, as he knew how important it was to her.

So from 1937 to her retirement in 1972, Melita, or as she was known by her comrades, Hola, photographed documents and plans and transmitted them to the KGB through indiscreet meetings that happened right in London. Among the information that she copied were the Tube Alloy files, files that contained the blueprints for creating nuclear weapons.

Unassuming Melita was the top female operative that Russia had. In fact, after her aid in securing and passing on the information that helped Russia catch up with the United States and Great Britain in the arms race in the early 1950s, the KGB and the GRU (Society Military police) fought fiercely for control of her. She stuck with the KGB. So highly regarded were Melita's efforts that in 1979 she was awarded the Order of the Red Banner. It entitled her to a lifetime pension of £20 per month, which she declined. Much like Julius and Ethel Rosenberg (page 177), Melita was never in it for the money, as evidenced by her modest bank account and the fact that she's lived in the same simple cottage for the past 50 or so years. In the mid-1960s, Melita

acted as a recruiter for a while, her passion for and faith in the Communist Party never dwindling.

Hilary and Melita had only one child, a daughter, Anita, who they never told about Melita's "second job." Anita, a grandmother herself when her mother's past was revealed to the general public in 1999, was blown away. "It seems so out of character, really," she told reporters. "As she says herself, she doesn't really approve of spying but her views were strong and she was able to do it."

Essentially, Melita did what she felt she had to do to keep something she believed in with her whole heart and soul alive. "I did what I did, not to make money," she confessed, "but to help prevent the defeat of a new system which had at great cost given ordinary people food and fares which they could afford, good education and a health service."

And that's the issue that left lawmakers and enforcers at a loss—whether they should prosecute the then-87-year-old media-dubbed "Red Granny." That, and, of course, how do you run a little old lady through the system without looking like a bunch of sadistic barbarians? Not quite civilized, is it?

Whether one could say "lucky for them" or not, British law offered the loophole by which Melita could not be prosecuted. Melita's unapologetic admission had gone to the wrong ears. Because she did not confess to police, but to the press, her confession was inadmissible under the 1984 Police and Criminal Investigation Act. The Act states, in effect, that a confession is inadmissible unless it happens under the proper circumstances, ideally meaning that it's made to the police. The act was put into practice to protect citizens' rights from corrupt cops.

At the time of this writing, the nearly-90-year-old Red Granny still lives in Bexleyheath, and is still unrepentant of her actions. "Older people, the ones who lived through it, might understand," she hopes. "I'm not sure about the young generation. I hope they accept it."

Papin Sisters
Christine Papin *(1906–1937)*
Lea Papin *(1912–1982)*

MURDER

Christine and Lea Papin grew up in France at the beginning of the twentieth century. Several members of the Papin family suffered psychological problems, but in those days, people didn't use terms like "schizophrenic," "depressive," "bi-polar," or even "alcoholic." All of these problems featured prominently in the patchwork quilt known

as the Papin family. The illnesses stemmed mainly from their father's side of the family. Their father's father had a violent temper and suffered from epilepsy. Many other relatives were living in asylums or had committed suicide. Christine and Lea's father, Gustave, drank profusely.

One day, drunk and delirious, Gustave stumbled home and, in a mad fit, raped Christine and Lea's older sister, Emilia, who was nine years old at the time. The Papin marriage soon fell apart, and Christine and Emilia were sent to live in an orphanage, while tiny Lea went to live with an uncle. He died, and Lea eventually joined her sisters. All the girls, especially Christine, were estranged from their mother at this point, even though the woman visited them frequently. When they were old enough to leave the orphanage, Emilia joined the convent. Christine got a job as a maid in a house in Le Mans, and when Lea came of age, Christine persuaded her employers to take Lea on as well. It was 1926. The two girls worked at the Lancelin household until 1933, when they murdered their mistresses.

No one in the Lancelin home knew the girls very well. They kept to themselves, went about their chores, and, as they were devout Catholics, they typically only left the house to attend church on Sundays. They shared a small attic room and even slept in the same bed. While they may have been considered odd, no one could have guessed what they were truly capable of.

The Papin sisters generally got along with the Lancelins, but liked Monsieur Lancelin the best. He didn't really bother with the details of the house, and therefore, had pretty minimal contact with the girls. The women of the house were another story. In typical aristocratic fashion, they were very particular about the way the chores were done and were quick to point out any and all imperfections. Finally, one complaint caused Christine to utterly snap. The result was gruesome.

On the night of February 2, 1933, Monsieur Lancelin was out at the club with his brother-in-law. He arrived home about 6:45 P.M. to find the house dark and completely locked up. He summoned police, who successfully broke into the house. What they found was the stuff of nightmares for many sleepless nights to come.

The bodies of Madam Lancelin and her daughter were strewn about the second-floor landing, mutilated, sliced, and with their faces completely torn to shreds and their eyes gouged out, as if they were clawed out with fingernails—or talons even. A light on in the attic led police to the small room that the Papin sisters shared. There they lay, huddled naked in bed together, and ready to face the music for the murders they had just committed. (Their state of dress and intimacy upon their capture led many to believe that in addition to a very strong emotional connection, the girls also shared a sexual connection. Whether this is true or not has not been conclusively proven; of course, it hasn't been conclusively disproven either.)

The Papin case was an absolute enigma. No one could fathom how these quiet and meek, church-going maids had so much venom, so much violence in them, to kill the Lancelin women so brutally. When the sisters were brought in for questioning, they explained that they had initially attacked the women with their bare hands, but had eventually picked up anything they could grab, including a kitchen knife and a hammer, to finish the job. According to the girls, the dispute had begun between Christine and the older Lancelin woman. When her daughter came to the rescue, Lea jumped in to help.

For a while, to protect her sister, Christine swore that she alone was responsible for the killings and that Lea was nothing more than an innocent bystander, but Lea would not let her older sister incriminate only herself.

The case went to trial and both sisters were sent to jail; Christine was sentenced to execution, while Lea was only to serve a limited number of years, as her crimes were not as brutal as Christine's, and it was obvious that without Christine's involvement, there would have been no murders to begin with.

In jail, Christine was prone to fits. She told her jailers about visions she was having, and how those visions propelled her into attacking the Lancelin women, but, as stated earlier, there was no such accepted term as "paranoid schizophrenic," and Christine's confessions fell on deaf ears. But that wasn't the worst of it. Christine and Lea were incarcerated separately, and this nearly killed Christine (whose sentence was commuted from execution to life imprisonment). The older sister would scream out and moan, as well as gyrate her body in erotic positions, begging to be with her sister. She started hallucinating regularly, and even tried to gouge out her own eyes. She persisted in proclaiming Lea's innocence, but Lea stood her ground that she was as guilty as her sister in the deaths.

Christine did not last long in prison. She stopped eating altogether, and by 1937, had died, literally, from wasting away to nothing. Lea served eight years of her sentence, and when she was released, she changed her name to Marie and reunited with her mother. She found work as a chambermaid, and lived in Nantes, France, until her death in 1982.

Bonnie Parker *(1910–1934)*

BANK ROBBERY, MURDER

In the world of women criminals, Bonnie Parker is perhaps the biggest name anyone can think of. But what few people realize is that her big name contrasted ironically with her tiny stature. At 4 feet, 10 inches, and barely 90 pounds, this perilous pip-squeak, along with her pint-sized paramour (Clyde Barrow was only five-seven and 130 pounds), terrorized numerous states and created a depression-era Robin Hood legend that still resonates in the beginning of the twenty-first century. Another thing most people don't know is that she was a smart and creative cookie, a humorist, and even a poet. If she hadn't fallen in love with the wrong man, she might have turned out like Dorothy Parker instead.

The blue-eyed, blonde-haired Bonnie was a looker. It's sometimes hard to tell in the photos she and Clyde took of each other during their crime spree, but her girl-next-door charms did not go unnoticed by her various suitors.

Born October 1, 1910, in Rowena, Texas, Bonnie was the middle child of three. She was exceptionally close to her mother, Emma. Bonnie's father died when she was quite young, forcing the family to move to Cement City, Texas, to live with Emma's folks.

Despite the bleakness and poverty of her personal life, Bonnie was an upbeat, bright, and energetic child. She attended her Baptist parish for services with her mother and grandmother every Sunday. She was also a great student with a flair for dramatics, spelling, and creative writing. She loved glamour and fashion. When she was a girl, Bonnie dreamed of becoming an actress, or a singer, or a poet. Unfortunately for Bonnie, however, she had a penchant for bad boys. This tendency, mixed with her loving and considerate, loyal and steadfast nature, would prove to be dangerous to Bonnie—and ultimately, lethal.

When Bonnie was 16, she married Roy Thorton, a lowlife her mother didn't approve of. But Bonnie always had a mind of her own, and even if she knew it was going to happen, there was no way Emma could stop her daughter from eloping. Bonnie quit school to devote all her time and energy to being Mrs. Roy Thorton. Which ultimately proved futile, as within a few months her husband was thrown in jail. Needing a means of support, Bonnie took a job as a waitress. She didn't leave her personality at home, however, and she made many friends in her customers—most notably Ted Hinton, a cop, who would be reluctantly responsible for ending the crime spree of Bonnie and Clyde.

Bonnie was not happy. Under her drab waitress uniform was the soul of a movie star, desperate to dress in glamorous clothes—as much red as possible. She dreamed of a better life, but was stuck in a working-class, depression-era limbo, with no hope of getting out. That is, until she met *him*.

In the moment that Bonnie Parker met Clyde Chestnut Barrow in December 1929 at a mutual friend's house, the earth stood still. Suddenly, everything was clear. In each other, they could see beyond who they were and into who they could be. It was, indeed, love at first sight. And while various chroniclers argue that it was Bonnie who was in love and Clyde who just kind of went along with it, the facts prove that the devotion was not one-sided.

Which is not to say they were immediately inseparable. After all, even though her husband was in the clink, Bonnie was still married. Nevertheless, they managed to spend a lot of time together in the first couple of months. Then, in February of 1930, Clyde was arrested for past petty crimes he had committed, small robberies of local stores. It was in this instance that Bonnie proved her love to her man. Remember, she was already married. And her husband was in jail. And he was staying there. But Clyde in jail? Not if she could help it. On a visit to

Clyde one day, Bonnie smuggled in a revolver. That night, Clyde escaped.

Bonnie thought that Clyde would probably leave the state, but she couldn't imagine he would leave without her. Yet he did. He and a fellow inmate, Frank Turner, who also blew the joint, took off for Illinois. Their freedom didn't last long. Because it had not occurred to Turner to change the license plate of the car they fled in, Frank and Clyde were soon back in the Waco, Texas, lock-up.

The law is never lenient on escapees, and Clyde was sentenced to fourteen years hard labor at the Eastman Prison working farm. It has been said that Clyde had sexual problems, and historians believe it was here where he developed them. Clyde was a pretty boy and the object of desire for many of the Eastham inmates. It is believed that one of them—Big Ed Crowder—took a particular liking to him. While Clyde never talked about it, he was apparently Big Ed's "bitch," and would be repeatedly raped and beaten by the man. Clyde, only 20 years old, reportedly one day lured Big Ed into the bathroom and beat him to death with a lead pipe. And that was the end of anyone else at the prison thinking of Clyde Barrow as a pretty piece of ass.

Clyde quickly grew tired of his time in prison and concocted a plan to get himself sprung: He convinced a fellow prisoner to chop off two of Clyde's toes, hoping he would be released for medical reasons. Unbeknownst to Clyde, his mother, Cummie, had been writing hardship letters to the governor to get him released as she needed him to help out at home, and at last, although too late for Clyde's toes, she got her results. By early 1932, Clyde, on crutches, was on the loose again.

Determined never to be separated from her man again, Bonnie threw herself into Clyde's criminal activities as much as she could, though he only involved her to a point. He and his band of marauders, including Ray Hamilton and Eastham buddy Ralph Fults, began hitting more small-time businesses. On April 30, 1932, one of these robberies went horribly awry—a gun went off and killed the owner of the grocery store they were knocking over. Now the law was on their tail not only for robbery, but for murder.

Bonnie wasn't there that night, but she would be with Clyde from then on, until the day they died in the spring of 1934.

There has been speculation about exactly how much involvement Bonnie had in Clyde's crimes, and whether or not she always just served as the driver of the getaway car. Whatever her role, Bonnie was pleased as punch to be on the run with her man. The two had a passionate relationship that was equally fun. It would not seem that any of Clyde's alleged sexual problems were an issue. They traveled with a camera and took pictures of each other, and sometimes left these behind when they fled. When the press got their hands on the shots, they had a field day. In a twisted way, Bonnie and Clyde were American heroes. They thumbed their noses at the Great Depression that was demoralizing the nation and took what they felt like taking—money and lives.

As happy as Bonnie was to be with Clyde all the time, she was attached to her mama and missed her deeply. So Clyde devised a scheme with his own mother whereby the families could get together on the sly, without alerting the police. When Cummie Barrow called Emma Parker and invited her to a dinner of red beans, it meant that the kids were coming home for a visit. Dutifully, they always brought money for their mamas. Somehow, they never got caught during these visits. Later, however, both Emma and Cummie would serve short sentences for harboring fugitives.

In late 1932, Bonnie and Clyde and the gang left the small-time jobs behind and moved to where the real money was: banks.

Many of Bonnie and Clyde's heists were pulled off without a hitch, but Clyde's careless driving would land Bonnie in a life-or-death situation. One night, he was driving so fast and distractedly, that he drove the car off a washed-out bridge. He escaped without injury. Bonnie, however, was not so lucky. She became trapped in the car, and was in such agony that she begged Clyde to kill her. That wasn't going to happen. He was eventually able to get her out of the car, but Bonnie had suffered horrible second- and third-degree burns on her legs. She needed medical attention and fast.

Clyde managed to bring her to a farm-house, where he coerced the owners into giving Bonnie a bed and looking after her. It is reported that Clyde never left her side while she healed.

Back on the run, it was only a matter of time before Bonnie and Clyde would be dead.

On November 21, 1933, Bonnie and Clyde headed back home to celebrate Cummie's birthday. The deputy sheriff of the town, Ted Hinton, knew it was Cummie's birthday and suspected Bonnie and Clyde might meet up with Mrs. Barrow during the day at a designated rendezvous point. Hinton knew both families, but he knew Bonnie better than he knew anyone else. He had always liked Bonnie, from his days as a young cop who patronized the diner where Bonnie worked. So it wasn't entirely easy for him to plot her downfall.

Hinton watched the Barrow residence the entire day, and when Cummie and her brood started loading the car with picnic baskets, he knew the time had come. When Bonnie and Clyde pulled up to the picnic spot, the sheriff ordered them to surrender. That gave them just enough time to race back to the car and hightail it out of there.

On May 23, 1934, the end came for Bonnie and Clyde. Hinton had gotten a lead about where they were staying from a former member of the Barrow gang. He knew they would be heading out of town early in the morning, and he and his men were ready for the car as it passed.

As Bonnie and Clyde drove past the checkpoint where the cops were waiting, they were ambushed. Bonnie watched in horror as a bullet chunked off part of her Clyde's skull—before she absorbed more bullets than her little 23-year-old body could handle, that is. It's reported that as soon as the car came to a stop, Hinton bolted over to the passenger side of the car and lifted Bonnie's fragile and failing body out, and rested her head in his lap as she died.

The bodies of Bonnie and Clyde were put on display for a few days before they were buried. Clyde was buried next to his brother. Bonnie was laid to rest in a family plot, with a simple inscription on her tombstone: "As the flowers are all made sweeter by the sunshine and the dew, so this old world is made brighter by the lives of folks like you." The inscription revealed just how sweet and loving Bonnie Parker was, and how much people cared about her—which makes her quite an enigma among women criminals.

Pauline Parker *(see Heavenly Creatures)*

Nancy Ling Perry *(see Symbionese Liberation Army Women)*

Katherine Ann Power
(1949–) a.k.a. Alice Metzinger

MANSLAUGHTER, BANK ROBBERY

The late 1960s and early 1970s were a time of great unrest for young, politically minded Americans. The outrage over the situation in Vietnam, as well as other social injustices, made criminals out of kids who cared too much to just stand by while bad stuff happened. In its most sincere incarnation, the Berkeley-based Symbionese Liberation Army (SLA; page 185) was envisioned as a way to band together and fight these injustices. And if violence is what it took to make the country stand up and take notice, then violence was what the SLA was prepared to instigate.

But an angry young man or woman didn't have to live in California to make a statement. At Brandeis University in Boston, Massachusetts, smaller factions were developing. One of these small groups was composed of a mere five members: Stanley Ray Bond, an ex-con who was taking classes; his associates, William "Lefty" Gilday and Robert Valeri; and a couple of female students, Susan Saxe and her roommate Kathy Power.

Katherine Power was as unlikely a candidate to get involved in criminal actions as one can imagine. She grew up the second of seven kids in a middle-class Denver, Colorado, suburb. She attended Catholic schools, and won scholarships for her academic performance. She threw herself wholeheartedly into everything she did, whether astounding the school by scoring ninth on a national achievement test or winning the Betty Crocker Homemaker Award for her original recipes. At graduation, she was valedictorian.

Kathy entered the heated Brandeis environment in 1967 as a sociology major. As she became more and more involved in her studies, she became more active in political groups around the campus. It was through these groups that she and her roommate Susan Saxe became friends with Stanley Rae Bond.

By 1970, the moral outrage felt about Vietnam had reached fever pitch for Kathy and her friends, and at Stanley's prompting, it was time to take matters into their own hands. But it was almost over before it

began. For their first statement, the group planned to hold up the State Street Bank and Trust, in Brighton, Massachusetts, and pour the proceeds into groups like the Black Panthers. On September 23, the group was ready, but their plan backfired horribly when a police officer, Walter Schroeder, not only highly decorated, but the father of nine children, got shot. He died the next day.

All of the perps successfully fled the scene. Within days, the three men, no doubt because of previous records, were taken into custody. Susan and Kathy managed to get away, leaving their lives, their families, and their educations behind; freedom was more important. The two stuck together for a while, some reports suggesting they were lovers during their time on the lam. They decided to part ways in 1975; Susan was captured shortly thereafter; Kathy managed to evade the law until she turned herself in more than 20 years later.

In her fugitive years, Kathy changed her name to Alice Metzinger, had a child, got married, worked as a chef, and toward the end even owned half interest in a successful Oregon-based restaurant. But as happy as the life could have made her, the demons were wriggling free, growing ever more stronger by the day. The guilt she felt over Officer Schroeder's death had pushed her to the breaking point, so, in 1993, Alice

Metzinger came clean to her then-teen-age son about her past (her husband, Ron Duncan, had known her secret for years). She threw a dinner party for close friends, and outed herself to them as well. Then she turned herself in.

Kathy had not seen or spoken to her parents since she went on the run, so at least one good thing about turning herself in was that she was able to see them; that they were still alive was a blessing. But of course, the most significant thing about coming clean was that she finally felt that she could live with herself again.

Katherine Power's trial took place at the end of 1993. She was sentenced to 8 to 12 years in prison, with a 20-year probation period—and an interesting twist. The judge ruled that if Power was to accept a film or book deal to tell her story to the general public, the sentence would automatically become a life sentence.

An exemplary prisoner, Power was released and allowed to go back to Oregon in October 1999—hardly six years into her sentence. She is not allowed to leave Oregon without permission, but she has gone back to her life there, living it as normally as possible. She is also now a grandmother.

Dorothea Puente (1929–) a.k.a. "The Killer Grandma"

MURDER, EMBEZZLEMENT, PROSTITUTION

In the great tradition of serial-killing grannies, started with Mary Ann Cotton (page 54) in the 1800s, and lovingly carried on by Nannie Doss (page 64) in the early to mid-twentieth century, Dorothea Puente killed for the payoff—not to collect on the life insurance policies of her family members, but so that she could make her living pilfering the Social Security benefits of the elderly, handicapped, disabled, invalid, or infirm boarders to whom she had opened her home. And like Belle Gunness (page 94), Puente buried her victims in her yard, which came to be known as the "Bone Garden."

Does Dorothea fit the serial killer profile? Pretty much. Dorothea Helen Gray grew up as a penniless orphan in California during the Great Depression. Both her parents had drunk themselves to death by the time young Dorothea was six. Before they died, however, they each abused their daughter regularly.

Dorothea was eventually rescued from the system by relatives who took her in to live with them in Fresno. But she didn't stay long. By the time she was 17, she became a wife for the first time; within two years, she became a widow. Desperate for cash, Dorothea began her criminal career at this point, forging checks as a means to get by. She wasn't very good at it and soon got busted, serving six months of a one-year jail term. Once released, she managed to get herself knocked up, but gave the baby girl up for adoption. This would be the only child she would have.

In the 1950s, Dorothea married Axel Johanson, but he didn't turn out to be an ideal mate. He was controlling and abusive, and by the early 1960s, Dorothea was essentially living on the streets, fending for herself, and finding more and more trouble for herself to get into: (1) She was arrested for being in a brothel and spent 90 days in jail; (2) she returned to her life of check forgery; (3) she committed several other small-time crimes as a means for getting by. In 1966 she finally divorced Johanson, became a nurse's aid, and generally cleaned up her act. She married yet again, this time to Robert Puente, a man 19 years her junior, and another man not worth the weight of his wedding band. Lord knows how she pulled this one off in the first place, but after two years of philandering by Robert, Dorothea was single again.

Dorothea finally found direction in the late 1960s when she got interested in running boardinghouses. By the mid-1970s,

when she married her fourth husband, Pedro Montalvo, she was running a pretty successful boardinghouse, but it didn't take her long to see what a mistake marrying Montalvo had been. He was a drunk and abusive, and before a year was up, Dorothea was on her own again. Not liking her own company that much, however, Dorothea spent a lot of time in bars and picking up worthless men for brief affairs. Around the same time, Dorothea started stealing her tenants' benefits checks. In 1982, she was arrested for fraud, but was released on bail and continued her activities until she was sentenced to five years in prison in August of that year.

While in prison, Dorothea made a pen pal, a man named Everson Gillmouth, with whom she fell in love—or at least he fell in love with her. She moved in with Gillmouth in September 1985, when she was sprung from prison. He wanted to marry her, but alas, this never came to pass. Once she had him join up all his finances with her own, she murdered him, put his corpse in a wooden box, and had the box tossed in the river.

Now Dorothea had the means to run a boardinghouse the way she saw fit. With her background as a nurse's aid, she was able to convince various social workers to refer their patients to her boardinghouse, where they could find affordable rent and the bonus of a landlady with a medical background.

Over the next three years, dozens of Mrs. Puente's tenants disappeared. In 1988, one of the social workers who had referred her so many clients, Peggy Nickerson, stopped by the house to visit with some of her old patients whom she hadn't seen in a while. Dorothea explained that they had—all of them—moved away, and none had left a forwarding address. Suspicious, Nickerson stopped referring her patients to Puente. It would take a visit from a second social worker, Judy Moise, to get the police over there. When Puente told Moise that her client, Bert Montoya, had moved to Mexico, she didn't buy it and filed a missing person's report.

Within a couple of days, the cops were all over Puente's property, having obtained a search warrant. They came at first on November 7. By November 11, they uncovered the first body in the "Bone Garden." And many more followed, each corpse with hands, feet, and head removed so as to prevent identification.

And somehow amidst all this madness, Dorothea managed to escape.

She wound up in Los Angeles, where she assumed the name Donna Johanson. She was able to avoid police for several days by holing up in a hotel room and laying low.

But then she got restless and headed to a bar to seek out spirits and male companionship. She found that companionship in one Charles Willgues, who liked her just fine at first, but when she started talking to him about how to defraud the government with his disability benefits and then invited herself to move in with him and make Thanksgiving dinner, he got a wee bit freaked out.

He made arrangements to see her the next day, but fatefully got an eyeful on TV later that night when he saw that Donna was actually Dorothea, psycho landlady from hell.

Instead of calling the police, he called a television network. So instead of being confronted by a SWAT team at her hotel door, she was greeted by a gaggle of reporters. The shock was enough for her to admit her real name.

Puente's hearings commenced in April 1990; by June, it was decided that Dorothea would go on trial for murder. The trial started in February 1993; it wasn't until July 15 that the jury went out for deliberations; it wasn't until August 26, 1993, that the jury reached a verdict. Dorothea was found guilty of murder, but was spared the death penalty. She was sentenced to life in prison without possibility of parole on December 11, 1993.

Mary Read (c. 1680–1721)

PIRACY

Because posing as a boy was something Mary Read had been used to doing almost from birth, she had no problem pulling off the disguise of a male pirate. She was so convincing that some legends state that Anne Bonny (page 33) herself fell for Mary, whom she thought was actually "Mark" Read. Of course, there are others that state the two women were indeed lovers, even knowing each other's true sex. Whatever the case may be, both left their decidedly feminine mark on the typically male-dominated world of high seas barbarism.

Far different from Bonny, who was hell-bent on causing trouble even as a child, Mary Read was a reluctant rogue at best. For all intents and purposes, she was swept up in the pirate's lifestyle by mere coincidence. She had tried her hand at the straight-and-narrow lifestyle, but circumstances would ultimately lead her down that rocky path. It has been said, however, that Mary put her heart and soul into her pirate's life, much as she had thrown herself into most pursuits, love or otherwise, in her life.

Before she was born, Mary's parents had lived in London, England, with their baby son. Mary's mother's husband was a doting father and husband, providing for his small family with the living he made at sea. One fateful day, he took off to sea on a voyage and never returned. Whether he ran off or disappeared due to circumstances beyond his control is not made clear in any of the literature.

What is clear, however, is that eventually Mary's mother ended up pregnant, and not by her missing-in-action husband. The young woman panicked that her husband's family would no longer help provide for her and her son, so she moved to Devon with her son to start a new life. Her plan was to stay with friends until she could figure out how to explain the new addition to the family. Sadly, the infant got sick and died; shortly after, Mary was born. No one ever knew who Mary's real father was.

Mary's mother had figured she might be able to return to London and pass the new baby off as her dead son, thereby ensuring some financial support from her long-lost husband's mother. That the new baby was a girl put a slight kink in her plans. As the mother of a soon-to-be pirate, Mary's mother was nothing if not cunning and decided that she would dress her little girl—and raise her—as a boy.

Surprisingly, she was able to pull off this charade until Mary was about 13 years old and the unmistakable signs of womanhood began to reveal themselves. Mary's grand-mother had already passed away by that point and Mary's mother found a new way to get money: she put her daughter to work as servant. Still posing as a boy, Mary soon grew restless of her job. As she still did a pretty good job passing herself off as a boy, she decided to run away and join the British Navy. When that got boring, she bailed on the British and fought with the French.

Eventually Mary met a man to whom she was undeniably drawn. He was a soldier in the same regiment as Mary. She soon became his constant "male" companion, his buddy, but when she realized she loved him, she knew she had to reveal her true identity to him. Inheriting the cunning that her mother used to scam her grandmother, she had to find a way after her revelation to become his wife. She simply would not set-tle for merely being his concubine. He was at first surprised, but then delighted that he was lucky enough to have a woman at his beck and call to satiate his lusty intentions. But she had other plans. Fighting against her own passion, she thwarted all his advances until he gave in and made her his wife.

They were soon married and gave up the traveling and fighting life to settle near the Castle of Breda. They opened a restaurant together, Three Horse-Shoes, where all their soldier friends came to eat. But it was not to last. Mary's husband soon died, and Mary had to reinvent herself. There was nothing left for her in this small-town life she creat-ed with her husband, and her wanderlust struck again.

Mary "transformed" herself back into a man and joined the crew of a ship heading to the West Indies. This would be the voy-age that changed her from soldier to pirate. Mary's ship was taken over by the infamous pirate, "Calico" Jack Rackam, and his gang. Mary decided to sign on with the *Revenge* crew, even though she despised pirates and everything they stood for.

On board, and also dressed as a man, was Anne Bonny, who was having an affair with Calico Jack. Anne fell almost immediately in love with the new crewman, and despite her ongoing relationship with Calico Jack, she advanced upon the young "lad" and revealed to "him" her womanhood. Natur-ally, Mary had no choice but to reveal hers. While stories have circulated about the women being lovers, this may be little more than a convenient convolution of the facts. It may have been little more than a misun-derstanding that both women were attract-ed to the men each posed to be. Whatever the situation, the women became fast friends.

Soon enough, Mary fell madly in love again, this time with one of Jack's pirates.

He was a strapping and sexy young lad, at least in her eyes, but not as fierce a warrior as Mary herself. She had always suspected as much, as he and she talked often about how much they hated the pirate's life and dreamed of doing something better with their lives. (It was the strength of their growing bond that caused her one day to impulsively "flash" her upper assets to him, making him the only other person aboard the *Revenge*, aside from Anne Bonny, who knew she was a woman.) But it was also these talks that made Mary realize he would not be able to defend himself if the need arose, and when it did, she took matters into her own hands.

One day, Mary's beloved got into an argument with one of his shipmates, and it was decided that the quarrel would be settled with a fight in the next port. Mary knew her love would lose the fight and probably end up dead, so she started a quarrel of her own with the shipmate and arranged to fight him two hours before the battle between the man and her lover. With the same intensity Mary threw into everything she did, she took the other pirate on and killed him almost immediately, saving her man from certain death.

The consummation of this great act of bravery would ultimately result in the sparing of Mary's life. As the story goes, shortly after the incident where she risked her life

to spare the life of her lover, the *Revenge* was taken over by the authorities. The attack was an ambush that caught the menfolk, who were at the time inebriated, by complete surprise. They were completely unable to fight. But two of the crewmembers were in perfect form: Mary Read and Anne Bonny. They took on the attackers with a vengeance.

The result of the capture was execution for all involved—with the exception of the two femme fatales on board. They escaped their fate with one simple phrase: "We plead our bellies." Both Mary and Anne were pregnant, and thus their lives were spared. However, that didn't mean that punishment of some sort was not in order. Read and Bonny were both sentenced to jail. While no one knows what became of Anne Bonny, Mary Read died in jail of a horrible fever long before her child was born.

Martha Rendall
(c. 1875–1909)

MURDER

If ever there was a wicked stepmother, it was the Australian Martha Rendall. And she wasn't even legally a stepmother—just a woman who happened to shack up with an unwitting father of five. Either way, within three years, she managed to make the hapless carpenter Thomas Morris father to just two. If neighbors hadn't interfered, he might have been father to none.

As soon as she moved in in 1906, she dominated the family. She ran a strict and severe household, and punished, abused, and even publicly humiliated her live-in lover's children. Most people who knew her were shocked by her parenting methods, but they generally turned their heads and minded their own business.

In 1907 and 1908, three of the Morris children came down with sore throats, and their doctor prescribed throat drops to heal their condition. As Martha was their "mother," it was her job to administer the medication. Within months, three of the children were dead. Autopsies revealed diphtheria as the cause of death in all three cases.

When young George Morris came down with a sore throat in 1909, he took no chances and ran like the wind away from the house of horrors. He was smart enough to know that foul play was afoot: Finally, authorities started to sense the same thing. Rendall's neighbors confirmed their suspicions.

The bodies of the three dead Morris children were exhumed, and it was at last discovered that Martha hadn't been treating them with the prescribed medication at all. In fact, what she was using, which would explain the cries of anguish from the house during medication time, was hydrochloric acid.

Martha and Thomas were both arrested. Thomas was acquitted of all charges; Martha was sentenced to death. On October 6, 1909, Martha became the last woman to be hanged in Australia.

Ethel Rosenberg
(1915–1953)

ESPIONAGE

Was she a treasonous, villainous spy who helped her husband give away the United States' secrets for the atomic bomb? Or was she a hapless-yet-aware pawn, dragged into her husband's spy indictment by the federal government in an attempt to make Julius crack? Or was Ethel Rosenberg an innocent? A fool for love, who went willingly to the electric chair to remain loyal and devoted to her husband, till death they do part? Up until the late 1990s, all of these possibilities were speculated. It could even have been speculated that both Ethel and Julius took the fall for Communist friends and the cause. But documentation found in the late 1990s proves, without a doubt, Julius's involvement in the spy ring that attempted to penetrate the Manhattan Project. Ethel's involvement, however, has not been definitively proven.

Born Ethel Greenglass on September 28, 1915, in New York City, Ethel Rosenberg was a sickly child, who suffered from spinal curvature and low blood pressure. Her father was in the sewing-machine business, and Ethel's parents had little money to give Ethel and her younger brother, David Greenglass, the finer things in life. Ethel had her dreams however, even if she was forever being squashed by her mother, Tessie—who unashamedly favored David. Ethel was passionate about music and wanted nothing more from life than to become a singer. This was not to be, however, both because of her many ailments and a lack of self-esteem ingrained in her through her mother's treatment.

Looking for a new passion to glom onto, Ethel developed a taste for politics as a teenager. After graduating high school, she worked for a shipping company and became involved in the labor movement. Though her union participation eventually got her fired, Ethel's ideologies did not waver, and soon afterward she became a member of the American Communist Party.

In 1939, the same year she joined the Communist Party, Ethel met a young City College student named Julius Rosenberg. Julius was majoring in electrical engineering, and like Ethel, was active in the communist movement. Julius was several years younger than Ethel, but it was reported to

be love at first sight. Neither Julius nor Ethel had dated very much before meeting each other, and less than a year later, when Ethel was nearly 24 and Julius just 21, they were married.

In the fall of 1940, Julius found a civilian job for the United States Army Signal Corps. He was later promoted to supervisor, but ended up losing his job in 1945, when the government found out about his Communist affiliation.

By the early 1950s, tensions between the United States and Russia were escalating over the development of nuclear technology. America was gripped by Cold War paranoia. It reached a fevered pitch during the Alger Hiss case, the ensuing arrest of Klaus Fuchs for passing classified government information to the Soviets, and the rise of Senator Joseph McCarthy and his virulent Communist witch-hunts.

It was through the Fuchs case that the FBI found another suspect, a soldier stationed at Los Alamos, where Fuchs was a physicist engaged in nuclear research on the Manhattan Project. The soldier, who later admitted to selling secrets to the Communists, was David Greenglass, Ethel Rosenberg's brother. During his confession, David implicated his brother-in-law Julius as being part of a spy web that stole classified atomic knowledge from Los Alamos and passed it to Russian agents. He sang like a canary, pointing the finger at his wife Ruth and his own sister, Ethel Rosenberg. With that information at hand, the FBI arrested Julius Rosenberg in front of his two young sons on July 17, 1950.

Ethel, with barely any evidence against her, was arrested less than a month later, on August 11, 1950, after testifying before a Grand Jury. The FBI's initial plan was to use Ethel's arrest as means to make her husband talk, but that tactic failed. On March 6, 1951, Julius and Ethel Rosenberg, along with Morton Sobell (an old college acquaintance of Julius' who was also implicated), were charged with conspiracy to commit espionage.

Though there was enough evidence to convict Julius of spying, the case against Ethel was hardly substantial. The only evidence provided was that Ethel sporadically helped type notes her brother David sent to Julius. But the prosecution, lead by U.S. Attorney Irving Saypol (who also prosecuted Alger Hiss) was relentless, and Ethel's demeanor while being cross-examined was vague at best. She constantly pleaded the Fifth Amendment, which to the jurors made her come off as haughty and secretive. On March 29, 1951, all three defendants were found guilty. Sobell received 30 years in prison for his role; the Rosenbergs were sentenced to death on April 5, 1951.

Though there was overwhelming international support for the Rosenbergs, especially Ethel (even the Pope asked for clemency), appeals were ultimately rejected. Protestors gathered in front of the prison, marching and chanting to set the Rosenbergs free. Even the Rosenbergs' two young sons, Robert and Michael, held signs reading "Don't Kill My Mommy and Daddy" in bold lettering. The Rosenbergs were eventually able to get the support of four Supreme Court justices; unfortunately, they needed five out of nine votes for a successful stay of execution.

President Eisenhower had no sympathy. Said he: "When democracy's enemies have been judged guilty of a crime as horrible as that of which the Rosenbergs were convicted, when in their most solemn judgment the tribunals of the United States have adjudged them guilty and the sentence just, I will not intervene in this matter."

The Rosenbergs' fate was firmly decided: They would die.

Throughout the ordeal, Ethel and Julius remained devoted to each other. The authorities, easily picking up on the bond between them, initially detained them in separate prisons, hoping the desperation of being apart would cause one or both to provide more information leading to other members of the perceived spy ring. It did not.

Ethel and Julius were both finally moved to Sing Sing, where they were separated by a concrete corridor and were permitted to see each other only on Wednesdays. Ethel comforted her husband by singing in her cell; he could barely hear her through the concrete. The Rosenbergs were also allowed to see their children once a month.

On June 19, 1953, the Rosenbergs were sent to the electric chair. Ethel was described as stoic as she kissed one of the prison matrons on the cheek and took her place upon the death throne. She was not killed by the first shocks that raced through her body and had to be electrocuted a second time. She was 37 years old.

Darlie Lynn Routier *(1970–)*

FILICIDE

A malicious, materialistic Medea? A maligned, misjudged mama? What is the real story behind the woman who at the time of this writing still sits on Texas's death row for the murder of her two sons? Her husband Darin and a handful of well-wishers believe that Darlie Lynn Routier has been unfairly indicted for the murders of her sons. But a slew of others, including the police on the murder scene, the majority of the media, and even many close friends, believe that Darlie, in order to maintain the lifestyle to which she and her husband had

grown accustomed, slaughtered her two young boys with a butcher's knife in an effort to cut extraneous expenses and collect the insurance bounty that rested on their tiny heads. While it is nearly inconceivable that a mother could so brutally butcher her own flesh and blood, the evidence paints an entirely probable picture.

Darlie Lynn Peck was born on January 4, 1970, the daughter of Darlie and Larry Peck, in Altoona, Pennsylvania. Her early life was great, but everything crumbled in 1977, when Darlie's parents divorced. A year later, the elder Darlie married Dennis Stahl, and the mother and her daughters relocated to Lubbock, Texas. Within a few years, this marriage was over as well.

It was Darlie's mother who first introduced her daughter to Darin Routier, a student who worked with Darlie Sr., at the local Sizzler. She saw him as a young man with a lot of potential, and her oldest daughter agreed. Darlie and Darin were married in August of 1988, right after Darlie graduated from high school. Within a year, Devon was born. Just over a year later came Damon. They were a happy young family, and they were on their way up the social ladder.

Indeed, the Routiers seemed to have it all. By the mid-1990s, they were a good-looking, upper-middle-class couple who lived in a miniature Georgian mansion with their three beautiful sons and their feisty Pomeranian, Domain. Shortly after their marriage, they started a company that they initially ran from home, but it became so successful that they had to purchase an office building to accommodate the operation. They enjoyed all of life's comforts. But their spending started to exceed their income. They began having marital problems, with all the trappings: public fighting and alleged adultery on both sides. The birth of their third child in 1995 made it seem like they would be able to pull it all back together, but ironically, it took the deaths of their two oldest sons to bring them back to the closeness they had enjoyed in their early years.

In the middle of the night of June 6, 1996, Darlie was awakened by one of her young sons calling out to her. She, along with her two oldest boys, was sleeping in the family room that night to seek some relief from the oppressive Texas summer heat. When she opened her eyes, she saw both boys on the floor, covered in their own blood, their little chests cut open like butchered cattle. Darlie claims that she saw a man in her house, and when he saw that she was awake he ran. She ran after him, but he was able to escape through a hole in a screen in the garage that he had cut, Darlie suspects, to enter the house in the first place. It was only then that Darlie

looked down and saw that her own neck had been slashed by the intruder, and that she was bleeding pretty heavily.

Darlie immediately screamed for her husband and then called 911. When the paramedics arrived, they thought Darlie was in a state of shock. She seemed emotionless, even though her bloody sons were lying at her feet. One had already bled to death; the other was still hanging on for dear life. The poor little thing died in the ambulance on the way to the hospital. Darlie was also taken to the hospital to have her wounds tended to. Even so, all she could think about and tell the police was that they had to find the intruder, whose description she kept feeding them even as her children fought for their dear sweet lives. She also kept making it a point to explain how her fingerprints had ended up on the murder weapon, one of the Routier family's own knives. The mother was suspect, and it was more than a few random fingerprints that led police to suspect her.

First, there was the family dog. When the detectives came to the scene, the feisty little fluffball barked and attacked like its very life depended on it. The housekeeper said this was the way the little dog acted when anyone not of the family was in the house. As everyone was fast asleep when Darlie's kids were hacked, it was hard to imagine why the vicious little Pomeranian didn't wake the parents, let alone the entire neighborhood, if an intruder was in the house and about to harm the family.

Second, the police were suspicious of the "neatness" of the scene. One of the detectives decided to do a test on the crime scene by spraying Luminol, a chemical that can detect the copper component of blood, even when the blood's been washed away. He found that blood had been cleaned from some areas, but not from others. There was also a now-cleaned bloodstain on the carpet, underneath a carefully placed vacuum cleaner.

But perhaps what tipped police off the most was the mother herself, and her complete nonreaction to the deaths of her children. One nurse recalls that when they wheeled Darlie into the emergency room, she was taken past her dead son. Any other mother would have burst out in tears. Darlie regarded the corpse with a blank stare. At the boys' funeral, Darlie didn't cry a single tear, and in fact, all she could concern herself with was consoling the other guests and noting who sent which flowers so that she wouldn't forget to send thank-you cards to anyone. A week after the deaths, the family visited the grave for a morbid birthday celebration, at which they sprayed Silly String over the burial site.

On January 18, 1997, the police finally felt they had enough on Darlie, and she was taken into custody. On June 29, she was officially indicted for the murders, and by October of that year, the case went to trial, which lasted almost an entire month.

On February 1, 1998, Darlie Lynn Routier was sentenced to death for the murder of her sons.

There are many who believe that Darlie is innocent and has been unjustly persecuted. In an article that Darin Routier wrote in his wife's defense, he said that he loves and supports his wife and that she is innocent. Why? "It's those eyes ..." he wrote, "that make me sure she didn't do it. After nine years of marriage, I know Darlie better than anyone. When I came running downstairs to find our living room a scene of carnage and my two boys bleeding to death on the carpet, I looked right into Darlie's eyes. When two soul mates look at each other, they don't have to speak. She was feeling the exact same thing I was feeling: shock. If she'd killed our children, she wouldn't have been able to look me in the eyes. I know that." It's amazing what it takes sometimes to pull a marriage back together.

Myra Maybelle Shirley
(1848–1889)
a.k.a. "Belle Starr"

ROBBERY

Was she the glamorous and notorious "bandit queen" she's been depicted as in Hollywood Westerns? Richard D. Arnott, in "Bandit Queen Belle Star," an article that appeared in *Wild West* magazine in 1997, says that "Although she was a companion to known thieves and felons and stole a horse or two, Myra Maybelle Shirley was neither a belle nor the star of any outlaw band … still she remains a legendary wild woman of the Old West."

On February 5, 1848, Belle became the second of three children born to John Shirley, a farmer, and his third wife, Eliza Pennington, a member of the infamous Hattfield clan. The family enjoyed a prosperous and proper Southern lifestyle in Missouri; that is, until the Civil War came along and wiped the South out. Myra's older brother, John Allison, affectionately known as "Bud," enlisted and was killed. A few years later, Myra's younger brother, Edward, was shot for allegedly stealing horses.

Shortly after the war ended, the Shirley family went bankrupt and moved to Texas to start a new life. Myra was 16 at the time. Before the war, she was a typical Southern

Belle, educated in the finest schools. After the War, it all went downhill. The once-prosperous family struggled even to eat and pay rent. It was at this time that Myra met up again with Jim Reed, a man she had fallen in love with when she lived back in Missouri. By this time, Reed had become an outlaw. They married on November 1, 1866, and moved back to Missouri; the next September, their daughter, Rosie Lee, whom they nicknamed "Pearl," was born.

Jim's illegal activities were starting to catch up with him, so in 1869, he moved his family to California. There, Myra gave birth to their son, James Edwin, in February 1871. The Reeds didn't remain in California for very long. Soon enough, Jim found himself in a whole heap of trouble, and they moved back to Texas to flee the law.

By 1873, Myra had had enough of her husband's criminal behavior—not to mention his extramarital affairs—and so she left him and moved back in with her parents. The couple never got back together, but Reed's enemies at least saw to it that she wouldn't need to go through the trouble of a divorce. In 1874, Reed was shot and killed.

What happened to Belle over the course of the next six years is anyone's guess. Some speculate that she turned to a life of crime because she was a poor and destitute single mother of two. Others say that she moved in with, and possibly married, Bruce Younger, the uncle of one of Jim Reed's "associates." According to Arnot's article, the next documented record of Belle was in 1880, when she married the much-younger-than-she, three-quarter Cherokee Sam Starr. It is only after her marriage to Starr that there is any record of Belle having been in trouble with the law; but the list grew quickly.

A horse-theft conviction in 1882 bought Belle and her new husband each a year in jail, for which both only served nine months. In 1884, they harbored a fugitive, John Middleton. In 1885, they were suspected of robbing the treasuries of the Seminole and Creek Indians. In 1886, Belle purchased a stolen horse and faced charges. Also that year, she was arrested for being part of a gang of bandits that robbed a few farms, and to this charge, she pled not guilty. Somehow, she managed to slip out of all convictions, but that didn't mean it turned out to be a good year. In December, Sam was shot and killed, and Belle once again became a widow. But she didn't stay that way for long. In order to keep her land, which had been Sam's because of his Cherokee status, she needed to marry a Cherokee, so within months, she wedded Sam's step-brother, July.

By this time, Belle had managed to become estranged from both her children, but especially from Pearl. In fact, Pearl came to hate her mother for Belle's interference in her romantic life. Belle didn't like the young man who was the object of Pearl's affection, so she sent Pearl away and told the boy that Pearl had run off and gotten married. Heartbroken, the dejected boy took a wife. And Pearl never forgave her mother. To make matters worse between mother and unmarried daughter, Pearl made Belle a grandma in 1887.

Mother and daughter's animosity meant that when Belle was gunned down from her horse and killed in 1889, Pearl was a prime suspect. But so was Belle's son, Eddie, who never forgave his mother her marriage to July Starr, who was also suspect. Edgar Watson, who wasn't related to Belle, was also a suspect due to a broken lease. But he was acquitted due to the evidence being circumstantial. Belle's murder remains unsolved to this day.

Belle Starr *(see Myra Maybelle Shirley)*

Symbionese Liberation Army Women

TERRORISM, ROBBERY, KIDNAPPING

The Symbionese Liberation Army (SLA)

The Symbionese Liberation Army (SLA) was a group started in 1971 in San Francisco by college student Robyn Sue Steiner, a woman who grew up in middle-class Miami, and who had briefly attended the University of Florida. The group was soon taken over, however, by a more violent wing it had produced, led by Donald DeFreeze, an ex-convict who threatened to kill Steiner if she didn't step down. She responded by fleeing to England. DeFreeze took over as the leader of the group, and the violent tone that would define the SLA for the next few years was established.

Essentially, the members of the SLA were angry about the war in Vietnam and fed up with social injustice in general. While the group was initially composed of educated, rebellious, middle-class California youths, the intent was to spread the word across the country and involve people of all ages and races and both genders. They chose as their symbol a seven-headed cobra, which symbolized their commitment to represent the interests of every walk of life, every race, and every religion. Anyone who stood for the same values were welcome to join the Symbionese Liberation Army—whence derived the name. Taken from the term *symbiosis,* a word that means the living together of dissimilar organisms for mutual benefit, the term *Symbionese* was meant to imply a group of different people coming together for mutual benefit. For the SLA, the mutually benefited were to be the SLA

itself and the poor and oppressed they would be assisting with their radical concepts and violent actions.

Their violent acts would be their trademark: They are what made the SLA stand out among radical groups preaching the same message at the time. But violence is also what led to the downfall of the group. While their actions certainly got them a lot of attention, their methods were more than frowned upon by lawmakers and shunned by pacifist groups who might have banded with them, but who chose to get their message across through other, nonviolent means.

The SLA robbed banks, bombed cars, and even committed a murder. On November 8, 1973, two members of the group shot Marcus Jones, superintendent of the wealthy Oakland, California, school system, with eight cyanide bullets, killing him.

One of the most famous of the SLA's crimes was the kidnapping of newspaper heiress Patricia Hearst in 1974. The 19-year-old was abducted from her Berkeley, California, apartment and held captive for more than three months. The ransom request: The SLA wanted Randolph Hearst to finance and distribute $2 million worth of food to the needy. During the time spent with her captors, Hearst claims to have been brainwashed into joining the group.

The SLA was a viable terrorist group until a shoot-out with police on May 22, 1974. Initially a raid to rescue the young heiress from her captors, the shootout claimed the lives of six SLA members. Hearst stayed on with the surviving members of the group, long enough to see a couple more members join, including Kathleen Soliah. By 1975, Hearst and a couple of the remaining original members were arrested, effectively putting an end to the group. Soliah was indicted in 1976 for conspiracy to commit murder and possession of explosives, but managed to evade authorities for 23 years until June of 1999.

Members of the group changed their white, "bourgeois," Christian names to more ethnic-sounding names to demonstrate their devotion to include anyone in the movement, provided they shared the SLA values. The group was made up of men and women, but for the purposes of this book, here are the women.

Angela Atwood ("Gelina") (1949–1974)

A one-time prom queen, Angela DeAngelis was born and raised in the suburbs of New Jersey. She was popular and perky, a good student, and a generally conservative soul. After finishing high school, Angela headed to Indiana University, where she was known as "Angel." There, through her involvement in the drama department, she met future SLA cohorts Bill and Emily Harris, and the man who would become her husband, Gary Atwood, a strong radical on the campus. From there, her politics completely changed and she was sucked into a world of LSD and demonstrations.

Gary and Angel moved to Berkley in 1972 to continue their politics. It was here that Angel met and befriended Kathleen Soliah, another future member of the SLA, but this would be long after Angel got involved in the group in 1973.

The Atwoods' marriage began to deteriorate and they went their separate ways, but Angela soon reconnected with the Harrises, who also moved to Berkley in 1972.

Angela assumed the name "Gelina" and fought with the SLA until she was slain by authorities in the famous 1974 massacre.

Camille Hall ("Gabi") (1945–1974)

Older than the other women in the group by at least a couple of years, Camille Hall, known as "Candy" to friends and family growing up, did not have the qualities one would expect in a terrorist. She was a pacifist working in Minnesota until her lesbianism betrayed her otherwise unassuming lifestyle. The time was ripe to make a change, so Camille headed first to Los Angeles in 1968, then to Berkeley in 1972, where her erotic tendencies would not only be tolerated, but embraced.

It was in Berkeley where she met and fell in love with her neighbor, Patricia Soltysik. The two women carried on a brief affair that ended when Patricia fell in love with another woman. Camilla left for Europe to start anew, but returned after only a couple of months and rekindled her fling with Patricia.

Once again the affair did not last, though they maintained a casual relationship for the remainder of their short lives. At Patricia's prompting, Camilla changed her name to Gabi and joined the SLA, in which Patricia was already heavily involved. Her love for Patricia ultimately led to her death as Camilla was one of the members of the SLA to be gunned down in the 1974 shootout, when she stormed from a crawl hole in the building, pistol in hand, and began firing at the SWAT team. Her lifeless body was pulled back in, but whether this was done by Patricia in a final act of devotion will never be known.

Emily Harris ("Yolanda")
(1947-)

A native of Baltimore, Maryland, Emily Harris, nee Schwartz, grew up in Chicago and attended Indiana University, where she was a member of the Chi Omega sorority, and nearly completely oblivious of the evils

of her bourgeois lifestyle. That is, until she met Bill Harris, who would become her husband.

Bill Harris had grown up in much the same bourgeois fog as Emily, but he had served in Vietnam, which had completely changed his political orientation to radical activist. Emily was in love with Bill, which made his politics all the more appealing to her. The couple moved to San Francisco in 1972, shortly after their friends, Gary and Angela Atwood, and were married soon after.

Along with Angela, Bill and Emily Harris joined the SLA in 1973. Emily fell in love with the group's leader, Donald DeFreeze, and divided her time—and body—between him and Bill. The Harrises, along with Patricia Hearst, were among the only survivors of the 1974 battle that left six core members of the group dead.

Patricia Hearst ("Tania")
(1954-)

Patty Hearst, who prefers to be called "Patricia," lives a subdued Connecticut suburban life in a Tudor house with her husband of more than 20 years and former bodyguard, Bernard Shaw, and their two children. But the image of the rifle-brandishing "poor little rich girl" who was first captured by and then joined the SLA in 1974 remains the image called to mind by most people who remember the antics of that group in the mid-1970s.

Patricia's involvement in the SLA came as quite a surprise, both to herself and to the nation. At the time of her abduction, she was living a fairly unassuming life (for an heiress) with her then-fiancé, Steven Weed, taking courses at Berkeley. He was 26 and a former tutor of hers; she was a whisper from turning 20. On February 4, 1974, her entire life would change.

The SLA targeted Hearst for kidnapping in an effort to force her father, Randolph Hearst, to finance and distribute over $2 million worth of food to the needy. On that fateful evening, members of the SLA broke into the apartment Patricia shared with Weed, beat him, and abducted her.

The SLA held Patricia for months, even after her father made good on the ransom. For most of the first 57 days of her capture, she was blindfolded and kept in a closet. Then came the image that shocked the world: Patty, dressed in fatigues, toting a submachine gun. By May of 1974, Patty became a full-fledged member of the SLA, and named herself Tania after a Bolivian woman who had been the companion of Che Guevara.

How did this proper, upper-class girl, who made good enough grades in high school to graduate a year early, end up on the side of

those who had kidnapped and tormented her? She had never been in trouble before. In fact, possibly the worst thing the Catholic-school girl had done was to tell a nun having a screaming fit to go to hell.

In an interview with *Ladies Home Journal* in 1996, Patricia matter-of-factly explained that she was brainwashed. And while she was still angry at the group that brainwashed her, she was especially angry at the government for prosecuting her for her involvement in the SLA. "They were so nasty," she told reporter Anne Taylor Fleming. "They never again prosecuted someone who'd been kidnapped, for what they'd done. It just wouldn't happen today. We've had so many more hostage situations since then. We know what happens to people when they're captured. We don't take what people say when they're in captivity seriously."

Hearst was involved in several attacks with the SLA, most notably the siege that wiped out most of the group in the shootout and fire in May 1974. She managed to escape with Emily and Bill Harris, and continued to work with the SLA, even as new members like Kathleen Soliah joined in the months that followed. She and the Harrises were finally brought to justice on September 18, 1975. In March 1976, more than two years after the night of her abduction,

Hearst was tried and convicted for bank robbery and felonious use of arms. Her sentence was commuted by President Carter in 1979, and she was eventually pardoned by President Clinton.

Nancy Ling Perry ("Fahizah") (1947–1974)

A one-time Republican and conservative, Nancy Ling Perry's life would change forever when she transferred from Whittier to Berkeley in her second year of college. The move would be more than a physical one, and would eventually lead Perry to become second-in-command in the SLA.

But that didn't happen right away. Nancy's conservative politics began to deteriorate gradually. In 1968, she married a black jazz musician named Gilbert Perry. It was a stormy marriage that eventually ended in the early 1970s.

After the breakup, Nancy tried to complete school and made money working various odd jobs. Nothing in school held her interest, however, and she ended up dropping out of every program she enrolled in. One thing that did hold particular interest for her were prison programs she become involved in. Through these programs, she met Patricia Soltysik and Donald DeFreeze, who turned her on to the SLA in 1973.

Changing her name to Fahizah, Nancy fought with the SLA until her death in 1974. She was the first to emerge from the crawl hole in the building where fellow SLA members were holed up. She was dressed in army fatigues with a hunting knife attached to her belt, shouting and shooting, and was the first to go down in the torrent of bullets from the guns of the SWAT team.

Kathleen Soliah (1947–) a.k.a. Sara Jane Olson

Kathleen Soliah joined the SLA late in the game. In fact, it wasn't until after her best friend and acting buddy Angela Atwood was killed in Los Angeles during the SLA-SWAT team showdown that she took the cause seriously. But when she did, she swooped in with a vengeance, angry at the death of her friend. Her anger caused her to make an impassioned speech at Berkeley's Ho Chi Minh Park, which condemned the police and made her a very visible target for the FBI. But despite her high profile in the organization, she was able to evade authorities for nearly 25 years.

Like most members of the SLA, Kathleen had a decidedly middle-class background. She grew up in the small town of Barnesville, Minnesota. In 1956, Soliah's father moved his family to Lompoc, California, where he held a position as an English teacher and athletic coach.

Kathleen attended the University of California at Santa Barbara and moved to Berkeley shortly after her graduation as a theater major.

In Berkeley, she met Angela Atwood when the two waitressed together and acted in various plays. Angela joined the SLA in 1973, but at the time, Kathleen was content to live her life without the group's radical politics. All that changed when Angela was killed in 1974.

Kathleen took part in several of the now-small group's activities, the most famous of which was to plant pipe bombs under two police cars. The bombs were packed with about 100 heavy-duty construction nails that were to be unleashed upon explosion. The bombs failed to go off, but from this point in August of 1975, Kathleen was officially on the run.

She first went back to Minnesota and changed her name to Sara Jane Olson. She married Gerald Peterson, a doctor, and the couple moved to Zimbabwe for several years. They came back to the States, settling in St. Paul, and started a family in a quiet suburb of the city.

Sara Jane was an exemplary member of the community, raising three daughters and becoming something of a celebrity in the local theater community. It was when her celebrity went national that it was time to worry. America's Most Wanted did a segment on her in 1999 that ultimately led the FBI to find her.

In 2001, Olson pled guilty to the terrorism charge. Her fate has not yet been determined at the time of this writing.

Patricia Soltysik ("Mizmoon") (1950–1974)

Another onetime-conservative-turned-radical, Patricia Soltysik grew up in a fairly normal middle-class family, the third of seven children and the oldest of five daughters. Her father supported his family as a pharmacist.

Patricia was a gifted student who graduated in the top ten percent of her class and was even the treasurer of her senior class. Next to Patricia Hearst, she was the youngest member of the SLA.

Soltysik attended Berkeley on a scholarship, and soon became deeply enmeshed in the nonacademic aspects of campus life. For a while, she lived with a boyfriend, who, by 1970, got a job with IBM and hightailed it away from the Berkeley scene and his relationship with Patricia.

Patricia spent the next couple of years experimenting with lesbianism and bisexuality, and eventually fell in love with her neighbor, Camilla Hall, one of the oldest members of the SLA. She and Camilla parted ways in 1972 when Patricia took up with another woman and Camilla headed to Europe. Camilla was back in just a couple of months, however, and the two resumed their affair, if only for a short time.

In Camilla's absence, Patricia became involved in prison movements, where she met Donald DeFreeze and Nancy Ling Perry. Patricia changed her name to Mizmoon and joined the SLA. It was only a matter of time before she convinced her on-again-off-again lover Camilla to sign up as well.

Patricia's young life was ended in the May 1974 massacre that claimed the lives of five other SLA members—the two who brought her in and the one she had recruited among them.

Pamela Smart *(1967–)*

CONSPIRACY TO COMMIT MURDER

In 1991, future Academy Award– and Emmy Award–winning actress Helen Hunt played the role of Pamela Smart in a made-for-TV-movie called *Death in New Hampshire*. In 1995, Australian actress Nicole Kidman gave a powerful and colorful performance as Pamela Smart in the Gus Van Sant–directed *To Die For*, in a role that

established her as more than a pretty leading lady, but as a talented actress. The film was based on a novel of the same title by Joyce Maynard; both films and the novel were based on the real-life story of Pamela Smart, the New Hampshire media specialist accused of seducing her teenaged lover into murdering her husband.

The Smart trial was the first of its kind, in terms of media attention and cameras in the courtroom. Supporters of Pam Smart believe that the media had so much power in her case that she was not given a fair trial. They believed that everyone—judge, jury, Hollywood, the world—had already decided before her trial that she was guilty of seducing a young boy into killing her husband.

Smart, who's serving a life sentence, says she's innocent. She claims that her lover, William Flynn, became angry when she tried to break off their affair and so killed her husband out of pure jealousy and malice. She says that he manipulated her into having an affair with him in the first place. That she was vulnerable, and that he just swooped down on her.

When Pam Smart met William, she was a highly successful, confident young woman, advanced beyond her years. When most people are still trying to get through college, Pam was a media director for various schools, married, and owned her own home. She was a woman of the world and a woman with her own mind. That she would even suggest that a 15-year-old boy, who lost his virginity to this sophisticated woman, was in control of *her* mind, is an insult to herself and her accomplishments. No one will ever know what really happened except for Pam and William Flynn; however, these are the facts that unfolded during the trial. At this point, neither is changing their story.

Pamela Anne Wojas, or Pame (pronounced *Pam-ee*), as she liked to call herself, grew up in an upper-middle-class family in a New Hampshire suburb. Her parents, John and Linda, provided their three children with a comfortable lifestyle. No alcoholism. No abuse. Pame glided through high school like a tequila shot rolling down a block of ice at a frat party. In school, she was a class officer, a cheerleader, and an honors student. She was confident and determined, even completing her college education at Florida State University in only three years.

Pame aspired to be "the next Barbara Walters," and dreamed of living a glamorous life. It might have been that she came to realize that her husband, Gregg Smart, didn't fit into her picture of the future as well as she would have hoped.

Gregg met Pamela when they were both still in high school, and they attended the same college. He had "sexy," shoulder-length hair. She had a college radio show for which she adopted the moniker "Maiden of Metal." They were a match, with their his-and-hers mullets, bonding over heavy metal music and a passion for parties. They married shortly after graduation and moved back to New Hampshire to be closer to their families.

The marriage started on a high note, but perhaps because Gregg and Pame were so young, they hit a trouble patch within a few months. Gregg admitted to having a one-night-stand, which crushed his young wife. She retaliated by having an affair with one of the students she worked with as a director of media for a number of different schools. And it is at this point that the story forks off: one path for those who believe that Pame was innocent; one for those who don't.

Choose your own adventure here: For those who believe in her innocence, such as her parents and various followers of the story, including Jennifer Furio, author of *Letters from Prison: Voices of Women Murderers,* Pame was at a point of unbelievably low self-esteem due to her husband's infidelity. William Flynn, the 16-year-old student who would later stand trial for pulling the trigger and ending Gregg Smart's life, had an obvious crush on Mrs. Smart and began to pursue her. She relented at first, but then tried to end the affair because she loved her husband and wished desperately to reconcile with him. On May 1, 1990, a jealous Flynn broke into the Smarts' condo with a couple of buddies, and killed Gregg Smart, his rival, in cold blood.

For those who believe that a grown woman will undoubtedly have more influence on a virginal 15-year-old boy than he could ever exert on her, Smart sought William out. She immediately picked up on his attraction to her, and she used it to her advantage. She seduced him in a way that a young boy can only fantasize about, acting out scenes from *9¹/₂ Weeks,* and dancing suggestively to music like Van Halen's "Black and Blue." Once she had him hooked, she convinced him to kill her husband, saying that if he really loved her, he would do it, because the only way they could be together is if he killed Gregg. Later, in the trial, Flynn whimpered that Pamela told him that Gregg was abusive to her and that he would never give her a divorce. That murder really was the only way out for Pame.

Faced with not ever having sex with this woman again, Flynn knew what he had to do. Pame planned the details of the crime, telling him exactly when and how to kill her husband, and advising him to make sure it looked like a botched robbery attempt.

Perhaps the sickest detail of the case: Pame allegedly told Flynn to make sure that her beloved pooch, a Shih Tsu named Haley, was locked in the basement at the time so he wouldn't be traumatized by the murder.

So Flynn enlisted a couple of friends, telling them that Pame would pay them $500 each, and on the night of May 1, Flynn, along with longtime friends Vance "J. R." Lattime, and Patrick "Pete" Randall, headed to the Smart condo. Randall and Lattime later testified that they didn't go for the money; they went to protect their friend form getting caught.

Twenty-four-year-old insurance agent Gregg Smart had no idea what he was going home to that night. Lattime waited outside as "lookout" while Flynn and Randall ransacked the house, then waited in the dark for Gregg. When he entered, Randall grabbed him from behind, put a knife to his throat, and demanded he turn over his wallet and wedding ring. Gregg released the wallet, but not the ring. "My wife would kill me," said he. Ahem.

Flynn pointed the gun he had obtained at Gregg, begged "God, forgive me," and pulled the trigger.

When Pame got home, she put on quite a show, screaming and crying and running through the streets, waking all the neighbors.

Of course, both sides of the story about the events that lead up to Gregg Smart's death are utterly surreal, which is essentially why the case was devoured by the media—and why it translated so well into publishing and film. But before the media got their grubby paws on the story, the police were already suspicious of Pame. She seemed too calm. When they came to question her, even days after the crime scene was investigated and finished, a large stain of blood remained on the carpet. Pame unconsciously walked right over it several times. Finally, her mother had presence of mind to cover it with a towel, but Pame still did not regard the spot where her husband breathed his last breath with any special reverence.

On August 1, 1990, Derry police tracked down Pamela at work and told her that they had at last found her husband's killer: It was her.

During her trial, she who claimed to hate the media attention, played up to it. And then, Pame Smart did something pretty stupid, throwing off the investigation as well as shooting her own self in the foot: She ignored the police who begged her not to speak with the press, and gave an extensive television interview to reporter Bill Spencer. The die was cast: Neither prosecution nor defense would be able to clearly represent their case, because the general public would already be biased.

The Smart murder case was the first time television cameras were allowed in a courtroom. The country was riveted. In the days before Court TV, major networks preempted their soaps to broadcast the trial in the afternoon.

The trial was a circus. The boys plea bargained for lesser charges. Pame testified in her own defense, and thought she had it all under control. Until the prosecution played their wildcard that is. There was another child involved in the gang, a girl who had taken a strong liking to Pame and who regarded her as a mentor: Cecelia Pierce. Cecelia agreed to wear a wire in her talks when she visited Pame. And in those talks, Pame wrote her own ticket to the slammer. Cecelia baited Pame; her glib and expletive responses showed her involvement in the murder. On March 21, 1991, Pame Smart learned her fate: life in prison without possibility of parole. Randall and Flynn will be eligible for parole in 2018; due to his cooperation, Lattime will be up for parole in 2005.

Since her incarceration, Pamela has been moved to Bedford Hills Correctional Facility in Westchester County, New York, far away from her family. In prison, she has spent her time tutoring fellow inmates to get their

GEDs, and working on her own Master's degree. But this hasn't always ensured her popularity. Instead, because of her celebrity status, she is usually tormented by inmates and guards alike. In 1997, she was so brutally beaten by a few inmates that she needed reconstructive surgery. Despite several attempts at appeal, Pamela is still, at the time of this writing, looking at life in prison without possibility of parole.

Madeline Smith
(1835–1928)

MURDER

Could a man love a woman so much that he would kill himself and frame her for the murder so that no other man could or would have her? That's what the defense wanted the jury to believe when Madeline Smith's lover, Emile L'Angelier, died from arsenic poisoning in Glasgow, Scotland, in 1857. The eerie part of it all was that, in fact, it was entirely feasible that this was the truth. After all, Madeleine Smith was the granddaughter of the famed architect David Hamilton, designer of the Royal Exchange, among other important structures. And she was a 21-year-old proper Victorian lady. A lady simply did not do that kind of thing. And then there was him: a constant depressive who often fantasized about suicide—and who had developed an obsession for

arsenic. Certainly, stranger things have been known to happen.

Madeleine Smith was the daughter of Janet Hamilton and John Smith, an aspiring young architect who had made the acquaintance of his future father-in-law at the opening of the Royal Exchange in 1829. Hamilton took on the role of mentor to the 23-year-old Smith, and soon he was invited to the Hamilton home for parties and dinners, which is how he came to fall in love with Frank's daughter, Janet. They were married a few years later and in 1835 welcomed their first child, a daughter, originally named Magdalene for her grandmother, but later changed to Madeleine.

Madeleine's childhood started out fortunate, but hard times hit the Smiths in the 1840s. First off was the death of Madeleine's grandfather, David Hamilton, in 1843. He seemed to take the family's good luck and prosperity to the other side with him, because that year, Madeleine's parents filed for bankruptcy. It wouldn't be until the early 1850s that the family was once again fortunate and part of Glasgow's elite. Madeleine was able to attend a proper finishing school in London, and upon her return at age 18, it was time for her to begin her search for a husband. All would have been proper and smooth had she not made the unexpected acquaintance of one Emile L'Angelier later that year.

Emile, a Frenchman, ended up in Glasgow after taking part in the Revolution of 1848. He had a reputation for being morose and intense. He was an adventurer. A dreamer. And not a proper match for a Victorian lady of Madeleine's pedigree. It mattered not to him. He wanted the finer things in life and was determined to land himself a wife of proper station. When the 34-year-old Frenchman laid eyes on the pretty black-haired, gray-eyed, porcelain-skinned Madeleine, he made it his calling in life to marry her.

In those days of Victorian propriety, there was not an appropriate way for Emile to meet Madeleine, so he somehow staged a casual meeting on the street. At the time, Madeleine was quasi-betrothed to a man of her father's choosing, a very boring, but proper, Victorian gentleman. When she met the disheveled and intense Emile, the 18-year-old girl was intrigued. He was everything her sheltered life was not, not to mention the excitement of running around with someone of whom her stern and repressed family would never approve.

Emile and Madeleine began a love affair almost immediately. In true Victorian tradition, they hardly saw each other, but communicated through letters that became evermore passionate as the years went on. When they did see each other, she gave him

her virtue. Even after that, the correspondence continued and she and Emile were determined to marry, with or without her parents' consent.

Or at least this is what she had led him to believe.

Madeleine was a young girl living a fantasy. It was highly unlikely that she would give up the life of privilege she had grown into. In a way, she was playing a game with the older Emile, intentional or not. This became painfully obvious to Emile when Madeleine started to lose interest in her little game when she was 21 years old. She had talked herself into falling in love with her father's choice of husband, and wrote a cold and callous note to Emile to tell him that it was over. Emile did not react well to the news, and threatening to tell her father that she had lost her virginity, and would prove it by showing him the letters she had sent over the years.

Madeleine was naturally terrified at this prospect, and pleaded with Emile not to expose her, not to sully the memory of the beautiful love they had shared by ruining her life. She begged him to meet with her and hand her letters back. He was not having any of it.

And here's where the story gets weird. Did Madeleine begin poisoning Emile at clandestine meetings the two would have after this point, or had Emile begun to poison himself, as part of his strategy to ruin Madeleine's life for setting her up to look like his murderer?

People who had known Emile for years had always known him to be fascinated with the effects of arsenic, and had known him to use it in small doses for its varied affects. They also knew that he was chronically on the verge of suicide, especially when it came to lost love. As an old acquaintance recalled, years before Emile met Madeleine: "One morning [Emile and I] had walked to Leith Pier and he said he had a great mind to throw himself over because he was quite tired of his existence. I have seen him reading newspaper accounts of suicide, and I have heard him say that there was a person who had the courage that he should have had, that he wished the same courage, or something to that effect."

So it is possible that he had intended to kill himself, and was using Madeleine in his plan. This becomes more apparent in his diary, in which he makes it a point to even fabricate meetings with Madeleine, after which he always subtly references feeling ill.

Before Emile was found dead by his landlady on the morning of March 23, 1957, he had made it a point to mention the words "Madeleine" and "arsenic" and "I'm not feeling that well" and "I hope I have not been poisoned" to as many people as he could talk with. Madeleine Smith, pretty 21-year-old socialite, emerged the prime suspect in Emile's murder. She was taken into custody on March 31.

Madeleine's trial lasted nine days, and her lawyer, John Inglis, was able to show reasonable doubt by somehow convincing the jury that Emile had been planning his own death for years, and that he dragged Madeleine's name into it only to get revenge on her. The jury came back with a verdict of "not proven"; in other words, they were not altogether convinced that Madeleine was innocent, but that it was entirely feasible that Emile, the lovesick nutjob, had actually set her up.

If he had in fact set her up, Emile had succeeded in at least well distancing Madeleine from Glasgow society. Soon after her acquittal, she changed her name to Lena Smith and moved to London. There, she married designer George Wardle, and lived in Bloomsbury until her husband's death. Afterward, she moved to the United States with her son, and soon met and married William A. Sheehy, who was nearly 30 years her junior. Madeleine died in 1928, and is buried in Mount Hope Cemetery in New York under the name Lena Wardle Sheehy.

Susan Smith *(1971–)*

FILICIDE

The missing Smith children had a country living in fear in late October 1994. That a man could carjack a woman with two small children, and then tell the woman there wasn't time for her to un-strap her boys from their car seats, that he had to take off right away, leaving Susan Smith deserted and destitute. And that the crime had been perpetrated by a black man just fueled old and long-forgotten fires. Of course, that was until the real horror surfaced. That Susan Smith had not been carjacked at all. That she, in fact, had murdered her own children in the hopes of rekindling a love affair. That was the real horror.

She was born Susan Leigh Vaughan on September 26, 1971. Her mother, Linda, was a homemaker; her father, Harry, who she cherished over all else in the world, was a former firefighter. Harry and Linda should never have gotten married. They married because Linda was 17 and pregnant with son Michael—and 21-year-old Harry was not the father. No matter. He was crazy, almost certifiably so, over Linda, which would eventually lead to the collapse of their marriage and his emotional collapse and suicide.

Harry and Linda had two more children together, Scotty and Susan. That the marriage was built on this precarious foundation meant there wasn't a lot of happiness in the Vaughan home. Harry drank and accused Linda of having affairs. The kids lived with constant stress.

Linda divorced Harry at the end of 1977; on January 15, 1978, a terminally distraught Harry killed himself. The light of Susan's life had been snuffed out.

Before Harry's body was in the ground, Linda remarried. Her new husband, Beverly, or Bev as he was called, Russell, was a successful businessman. Finally, Linda would have the life she believed she had deserved. Linda was determined to hold on to her man, and her lifestyle, and when daughter Susan confided in her mother that Bev had molested her, Linda turned a stiff, dead ear to her daughter's gripes. Bev calmed down for a while, but when Susan was an adult, the relationship would again become sexual, albeit this time consensual.

Susan did well in school. She was sure she'd be heading to college after her high school graduation in 1989. But sometimes life throws us a curve ball.

After her junior year, Susan took a job at the Winn-Dixie, a local Union, South Carolina, grocery store. There, she was sleeping with one of the managers and at least one of the other employees. She was in severe emotional trouble, and in 1988, she tried to kill herself with an overdose of aspirin and Tylenol. One "good" thing that came out of her job at Winn-Dixie, however, is that it was here that she met and started seeing David Smith. He was dating someone else at the same time, but when Susan became pregnant, he did the noble thing by breaking up with his girlfriend and marrying Susan.

In October 1991, when most people her age were cramming for midterms in their sophomore year of college, Susan gave birth to her first son, Michael Daniel Smith. Susan was doing her best to keep up, taking college courses when she wasn't working or nursing. Even before the baby was born, it became glaringly obvious that Susan and David had made a grave error by marrying. The next year, they would separate and reconcile as often as they'd change their underwear. They were both having affairs, and it didn't help matters at all that they still worked together—and that David was Susan's boss at the Winn-Dixie.

In 1992, the young couple decided to try to make their marriage work. They bought a new house, and, in the summer of 1993, their second child, Alexander Tyler, was born. Soon the only thing keeping them together was the kids. They had both sought romance in the arms of others. Susan got a new job so she wouldn't have to be exposed to David's new love interest daily

at the store. This should have been a good thing; it was not. While Susan excelled at her job and got several promotions in just a matter of months, Conso Products would be the place where she met 27-year-old Tom Findlay, who, when she began seeing him romantically, became the love of her life. In 1994, that would be over, too.

And in 1994, David and Susan would make one last go of salvaging their marriage, but in September, the divorce was finalized.

Also in 1994, Alexander and Michael Smith would be murdered by their own mother.

After the divorce, Susan was completely worn down. In the past months, she had been keeping up sexual relationships with David, with Tom Findlay, and, grossly so, her stepfather, Bev. All this on top of working full-time and raising her kids as a single mom. Tom had decided that he no longer wanted to see her, among other reasons because he was not really willing to raise and support another man's children.

Snapping time was imminent. Susan was drinking heavily and was deeply depressed. On October 25, 1994, Susan decided to take her own life. She would do this by driving her car into a nearby lake. And, she would take her children with her in an act of altruistic filicide, because she could not imagine how unbearable their little lives would be without having a mother around.

She aimed her red Mazda at the lake, put the car in neutral, and began to slide. But just as the car was inches from the lake, she chickened out and pulled the emergency break. She stepped out of the car. Then, without thinking a second about it, she leaned back in the car, released the brake, and watched the Mazda roll into the lake, with her two little boys strapped into their car seats in the back seat. Once she saw the last of the car sink, she raced to the nearest house with her cockamamie story.

The whole town, lo, the whole nation, was up in arms about this horrible crime that had occurred. But police were paying pretty close attention. Soon, Susan's story started to become more and more inconsistent with each telling. Within a week, they no longer believed her. On November 3, 1994, Union County sheriff Wells got Susan to break down and confess her crime.

If the carjacking story caused such a stir, imagine what the truth did. Susan Smith was known as the biggest monster who ever lived. The thing that baffled David the most: Susan had known exactly where the car ended up in the lake. She stayed around to watch her babies submerge into the murky depths.

Susan's case went to trial on July 19, 1995. All the while, she was held in police custody, without bail. Among those called to testify were Tom Findlay, who talked about his relationship with Susan, and

Susan's stepfather, Bev, who admitted to his sexual relationship with Susan and who wished to shoulder some of the blame. The trial lasted only until the twenty-second, when, after only two and a half hours of deliberation, the jury came back with their verdict: Susan Smith was guilty.

The prosecution was going for a death penalty verdict, but they were not given it. Susan Smith had proven to be pathetic enough to evade it; and besides, it would be a greater torture for her to live and spend every day for the rest of her life thinking about what she had done to those boys.

Susan was sentenced to 30 years to life in prison and isn't eligible for parole until 2025.

Kathleen Soliah *(see Symbionese Liberation Army Women)*

Patricia Soltysik *(see Symbionese Liberation Army Women)*

Edith Thompson
(1893–1923)

MURDER

Edith Thompson may well have been a woman who was persecuted more for her lifestyle than for her crimes. In fact, it was not even fully proven that Edith had actually committed a crime before she was sent to the scaffold. In post-Victorian London, Edith seemed to do everything that a woman of those times ought not to have done. She committed adultery, she held down a job, which paid more than her husband's job, and she even had an abortion. Oh, and she had a lover who was eight years younger than she was, and he gave her the sexual pleasure that her husband did not. Perhaps she shouldn't have written to her lover about the ecstasy of the brilliant orgasm he had given her one sunny afternoon in a very public park. But who knew at the time that those letters would follow her to court?

If Edith Thompson ever did anything conventional, it was to marry young. Edith was barely 20 when she married Percy Thompson. And as she grew up, she realized what a horrible mistake she had made. It wasn't that Percy was a bad man. There's no evidence that he was a nasty drunk or a wife beater or anything along those lines. He was simply, well, a bore. Edith, or Edie, as she liked to be called, was a voracious reader of romantic fiction; each and every year, Percy proved himself to be less the man her romance novels idealized. She liked to go out and drink champagne and, scandalously, smoke in public. Hubby was something of a homebody, and if he wanted to go out, it would be to attend a civilized affair like an opera or a play. She was a bubbling personality starved for excitement.

Enter Fred Bywaters.

Edie met Fred while she was taking a weekend vacation in the country. He was her sister Avis's beau and considerably younger than she was. This didn't stop the electric current that sizzled between them, however. By the end of the weekend, they were lovers. Their affair would last a nearly a year and a half.

They weren't in physical contact all this time, however. To make his living, Fred worked as a ship's laundryman and was often away at sea. They continued their infatuation through letters, which were sweet and, at times, quite explicit. She called Fred "Darlint," and wrote about how much she missed her little boy toy. "If only I had you here to put my head on your shoulder and just sleep and dream and forget" and "You are going to love me always, aren't you? Even when you are cross with me, and when you are, I'll ruffle your hair lots of times until you have to melt—and smile at me—then you'll take me in your arms and hold me so tight I can't breathe, and kiss me all over until I have to say 'Stop, stop at once.'"

These letters would come back to haunt Edie at her trial, when they were used against her. It wasn't just the romantic nature of the letters that implicated Edie, it was that some of them actually spelled out Edie's unhappiness in her marriage and how she fantasized about killing her husband. In one letter, she griped about how unfair it was that a woman she knew had "lost three husbands in eleven years and some people I know can't lose one." But the letters that really sealed her fate were the ones in which she "plotted" with Fred to kill her husband. In one she wrote of poisoning Percy; in another, of crushing glass into Percy's meals. An autopsy revealed no traces of either arsenic or glass in Percy's stomach, but the intent, so believed the jury, was there.

Fred became increasingly consumed with Edie, and he was more and more frustrated by her husband's lack of appreciation for her. One day, he decided to take matters into his own hands.

So on October 3, 1922, as Edie and Percy were walking home from one of their respectable outings, Fred lunged out of the bushes and stabbed Percy to death. Edith was horrified—at first screaming for help because her husband was "ill"—not "bleeding"—and needed medical attention. Her damners took this as a sure sign that she was protecting Fred and trying to cover up.

What followed was a whirlwind of moral outrage, with everything unraveling at breakneck speed. Percy was killed early in October. By December, Edith and Fred were both in custody and on trial for the murder. There were no letters from Edie that encouraged Fred to take the action he took

on that fateful night. But judge and jury firmly believed that because of Edie's sophistication, she controlled Fred; if he killed her husband, it surely must have been at Edie's behest. They both appealed and were both denied appeal on December 21. On January 9, 1923, Edith and Fred were strung up on scaffolds on opposite sides of London.

No one believed that Edie was going to hang—least of all Edie. The morning of her execution, she nonchalantly munched a light breakfast, and it wasn't until the matron came to dress her and take her to the scaffold that she freaked out. Edie was beside herself, screaming and carrying on. By the time she made it to the noose, she was unconscious. After she was killed, she began to bleed from between her legs. Many have speculated that perhaps she was pregnant at the time of her death, and that the force of the hanging caused a spontaneous miscarriage. The severe moralists believed it had everything to do with the abortion she had administered to herself a few years back, that had completely ripped apart her uterus. But the question remains, even all these years after her death: Did Edith Thompson really play a role in the murder of her husband? No one will ever know. Fred went to his last breath proclaiming Edith's innocence. And most people who believed so changed their minds over the years; Edith's executioner was compelled to take his own life several years after the fact. What is known is that walking to the beat of her own drummer had more than a little something to do with her death.

Tokyo Rose *(see Iva Toguri D'Aquino)*

Jane Toppan *(1854–1938)*

MURDER

"That is my ambition, to have killed more people—more helpless people—than any man or woman who has ever lived."

These were the words of Jane Toppan, a nurse accused of killing more than 30 patients and patients' families, at her trial when she was called to testify in her own defense. One would think that an execution might be the proper punishment for a woman who felt so little remorse for her crimes, but Jane was found to be certifiably insane. She lived out the remainder of her days in a Massachusetts asylum, where she was reputed to try to get some of the nurses to help her poison some of the other patients. But was she really insane, or just plain evil?

It's easy to believe that she wasn't playing with a full deck. For one thing, insanity ran in her family. When she was an infant, her mother died, causing her father to snap. Jane was born Nora Kelly in the middle of the nineteenth century in Boston. Her father was a tailor, and he had a really tough time keeping his lid screwed on after his wife's unexpected death. One day while he was working in his shop he even attempted to sew his eyelids shut with a needle and thread. That was enough for social services to relocate Nora and her three sisters to an orphanage.

Nora was adopted by the Toppans when she was five years old. They renamed her "Jane," and moved her to Lowell, Massachusetts, where she had a fairly normal childhood and adolescence. She exhibited no abnormal behavior, nothing that would indicate that she would end up like her father (and like another one of her sisters who had also, by the time Jane was a young adult, been committed to an asylum). It looked like the Kelly madness was a latent variety that needed something to trigger it, however. Jane's natural father had found his trigger in the death of his wife; Jane found it in the aftermath of being jilted by a fiancé. After she was dumped she was never the same.

But life went on for poor, single Jane, and in her mid-20s, she realized it was time to start a career. She enrolled in courses to become a nurse. Her instructors were more than a little concerned about Jane's obsession with autopsies, but she made good grades so they were able to look the other way. Jane was dropped from the program, however, when two of her patients died from mysterious causes. Jane didn't let a little thing like a degree stand in her way of becoming a nurse, so she "doctored" up a certificate and began to rent herself out as a personal nurse.

For the next 20 years, Jane brought her talents to several families throughout the New England area. And hence, a serial killer was born. Jane enjoyed her killing spree until a surviving member of a family she had all but entirely wiped out became suspicious and went to police. She was finally arrested in Amherst on October 29, 1901, for the deaths of more than 30 former patients, as well as her own foster sister. It later came out that the death toll may have been as high as a 100.

Insane or evil, Jane lived out the rest of her days in an asylum, where she lived a quiet existence until her natural death at age 84.

Karla Faye Tucker
(1959–1998)

MURDER

On June 13, 1983, a 23-year-old Karla Faye Tucker broke into the home of the man who was not being a good husband to her best friend. She was there, with her boyfriend,

Danny Garrett, to play a prank on Jerry Lynn Dean. They were going to steal his motorcycle—no big deal. But then Dean woke up and foiled their plan. And then Satan must have come into the house, because before she knew it, Danny had grabbed a hammer and had stolen off into the bedroom. She followed closely behind. Danny started bashing Dean's skull in with the hammer. And Karla was wickedly turned on.

Not wanting to miss out on the fun, Karla darted out into the living room and grabbed the first tool she could find: a pick axe. Back into the bedroom she scampered, and to her utter delight, she discovered Dean had been in bed with another woman. It was her turn. Karla lifted the ax and came down on the woman, time after time, until she had chopped poor Deborah Thorton to a pulpy soup. Then, she finished Dean off. Later, Karla would admit that she had climaxed three times while she chopped away at Deborah. This is the same woman who years later, in prison, would find God, and even have the Pope beg a pardon for her life.

What the hell was going on in their minds that night? A lot of drugs is one thing. The couple had left a party hosted by Karla's sister, Kari. Or, more like it, a drug and sex orgy. Karla's best friend and Dean's wife, Shawn, was at the party, and she was black and blue from her latest beating. No one would ever dispute that Karla Faye Tucker was a passionate woman. She cared very deeply for her friend and was tired of Dean, whom she had never liked; and he always hated her as well. So while everyone else at the party was sleeping off their various indulgences, Karla and Danny were plotting. Never in their wildest fantasies did either ever believe they would take things so far.

Who was Karla Faye Tucker?

Born in Harris County, Texas, on November 18, 1959, Karla Faye was the third of three daughters. Her childhood was normal enough. The family was happy for the most part. They took vacations. They had meals together. If there was anything odd about her childhood, it was that her parents married and divorced several times. Not really the stuff for making a murderer. Finally, the Tuckers decided to call it quits for good, and Dad got custody of the girls. They were totally out of control. He couldn't handle them. And during the divorce proceedings, Karla Faye learned what might have been the catalyst to bring her over to the dark side: her father, was not, in fact, her biological father. Whether this is valid or not, it was after coming by this knowledge that Karla started her slide.

By age 10, she was smoking pot. She went to parties with her older sisters, and before she had even crossed over into puberty, she was sexually active. By the time she was 14, she learned that she could parlay sex into money, and so she became a prostitute. By this time, she was living with her mother, who proved to be no help in teaching her daughter to walk the straight and narrow. In fact, one day, she walked in on her daughter rolling a joint, and scolded her. But not for rolling a joint—for rolling it incorrectly. And to ensure that all the ingredients of this tragic Karla Faye Tucker cocktail were mixed in, at the tender age of 16, she married a mechanic named Stephen Griffith. She would leave him in just a few short months.

Within months, Karla Faye was back in the drug scene, hanging out with her sisters and all their drug-addled friends. In 1983, she met Daniel Garrett, who was 14 years her senior, and she moved in with him only a few weeks later. By June, their romance would culminate in a foile a deux of the goriest kind.

Still high out of their minds when they returned to the party that bloody June night, Karla Faye and Danny bragged to all of their friends about what they had done. Within days, they were both arrested for the double murder.

In September, the pair was indicted. Karla's trial began on April 11 and lasted seven days. On April 19, 1984, Karla Faye

Tucker was found guilty: Her sentence, death. Garrett, who had been tried separately, was also found guilty, though he didn't live to be executed.

In prison, Karla, version 2.0, was born. Feeling utterly sorry for her predicament, a priest left Karla a copy of the Bible. Out of boredom more than anything else, she picked up the book. And it spoke to her. Stranded on death row and at last taking the time to think about her life, Karla Faye Tucker found God.

Karla Faye's lawyers fought for years for an appeal, or at least a commutation of her sentence to life. They argued that she had changed, and that her presence in the prison was uplifting to the other inmates. She had, indeed, become their spiritual center. Others also stepped in to champion her cause. The brother of Deborah Thorton, Ron Carlson, visited Karla daily and established a deep friendship with her. (Deborah's cuckholded husband, Richard Thorton, showed no such forgiveness, however.) Karla Faye even managed to get married while in prison, to a minister named Dana Brown.

Karla Faye did everything she could to save her life, even drafting an impassioned plea to then-Governor George W. Bush. But the law would have nothing of it. Karla Faye's fate remained intact, and her execution was scheduled for February 3, 1998.

The religious right didn't take Karla Faye's fate lying down. She had become their Saul, their Mary Magdeline, their very own modern-day example of the redeemed sinner. Even Pat Robertson and Newt Gingrich jumped on the "save Karla Faye" bandwagon. Sister Helen Prejean, who wrote *Dead Man Walking,* befriended Karla Faye and fought for her cause. It was to no avail. The day before the execution, even the Vatican swooped in, as his Holiness himself, Pope John Paul II, wrote to the governor, begging him to spare Karla's life. Church did not win over state. Not in this battle.

On the evening of February 3, Karla Faye savored her last supper: a humble dinner that consisted of a banana, a peach, and a salad. By 6:30 P.M., she was executed by lethal injection, the first woman to be executed in Texas since the Civil War.

Leslie Van Houton *(see Manson Women)*

Ella Watson (c. 1861–1889) a.k.a. "Cattle Kate"

PROSTITUTION

Was Ella Watson really a criminal? Or was she simply the victim of a brutal and undeserved lynching? The Old West certainly had its own laws and its own way of administering justice, but it's interesting to note that Ella wasn't strung up for her known criminal activity—namely prostitution—but for something entirely political in nature. Whatever the reason, she has gone down in history as the first woman ever hanged by vigilantes in the Old West.

Ella Watson was the daughter of a wealthy farmer in Smith County, Kansas. When she was 18 years old, she married and, in the spirit of the day, headed west with her new husband to start a life together. The marriage was short-lived; whether this was because of the strain of Ella's leaving everyone she loved behind or because her husband was a jerk—or perhaps a combination of both—is not known. What is known, however, is that Ella was stuck in West Nowhere, Wyoming, with no means to support herself and no idea how she was going to get by.

Prostitution was a natural for women who found themselves in such a situation in those days, so Ella embraced her new profession, working chiefly in Cheyenne and Rawlings. It was through her work that she came to know her second husband, Jim Averil. He was a cattle rancher based on the Sweetwater River.

Jim and Ella were soon married, but Ella continued to work. Some say that he acted as her pimp, but there's nothing to substantiate this claim. In addition to their ranching activities, Ella and Jim ran a saloon in Sweetwater, where Ella conducted her business as usual (perhaps why people get the idea that Jim acted as her pimp).

The cattle-raising game was as political as anything else in the late nineteenth century. Generally, most of the land and the cattle were owned by a few elite cattle barons. They allowed their cattle to roam free, which meant they were known to lose a few here and there. Many small ranchers started their businesses with what became known as these "maverick" cattle. When business was good, the cattle barons looked the other way. But the winter of 1886–1887 was so unbearable that many ranchers—big and small—lost a fair amount of their herds to the elements.

Ella Watson had, before this winter, been helping her husband to acquire a herd through the acquisition of maverick cattle. How? By accepting livestock as payment for services rendered, of course. But as it became harder and harder to acquire cattle, Jim Averil became more and more vocal about the injustices of the cattle barons. It was his big mouth that led to the lynching.

How powerful were the cattle barons? On July 20, 1889, Ella and Jim were forcibly taken from their home and hanged, without going to trial. No one was ever tried for their murders.

Kate Webster *(1849–1879)*

MURDER, PROSTITUTION, ROBBERY

Times were tough for the lower classes in Victorian England. As Dickens detailed in his novels, many folks peddled wares on the streets to feed their families. They sold apples, matchbooks, flowers—whatever they could scrape up to try and make a shilling here and a sixpence there. Kate Webster was not well-to-do. She had no family, but she still peddled what she could. In her case, it was "drippings." These drippings were not from pork or beef or mutton, however; they were, well, from humans. After Webster murdered her employer, she hacked the body to pieces and then boiled the dismembered remains in an attempt to get rid of the body. And the ever-resourceful Webster even found a way to turn a profit on her loss—of employer, that is.

Kate Webster, maniacal maid, was born in Killane, County Wexford, Ireland, in 1849. Her family was piss poor, but her parents were good people, well liked and well respected in the community. Although she was born to the Websters, Kate was an anomaly. Her behavior even early on made most wonder where she really came from. Even as a young child, she stole, she lied, she swindled the other children. When she was a teenager, she managed to steal a large sum of money, source unknown, and left Ireland behind.

Kate headed to Liverpool where she stole some more, scammed, bamboozled, bilked, duped, and schmoozed to make ends meet. She spent a lot of time in pubs, and soon she decided there was at least one thing she could sell. Before long, she fell into prostitution. She got knocked up, gave birth to a son (no one knows what happened to him) then started to rob boardinghouses, because that's where she could make the serious cash. She was in and out of prison in the mid-to late 1870s, and then found another way by which to make ends meet. She became a domestic.

In 1879, she took a job as a maid to a wealthy woman named Julia Thomas. It wasn't long before Mrs. Thomas saw Kate's true colors and regretted hiring her. Kate would hardly show up for work, and when she did, she was usually drunk. Julia had had enough and fired Kate in May 1879, five months after she hired the woman. This turned out to be Mrs. Thomas's final regret.

A couple of days after her dismissal, Kate showed up at the Thomas house, drunk and vengeful. She lay in wait while the old woman was at church, and when Mrs. Thomas returned, Kate pounced on her and bashed her about the head. In an attempt to get away from her attacker, Mrs. Thomas ended up falling over the second-floor railing to her death. Not convinced that the body was yet lifeless, Kate took an axe and began bashing the corpse. Next, she dragged the corpse to the kitchen and chopped it to bits. And if that isn't gruesome enough, she then proceeded to fill a few pots with water, boiled the water on the stove, and tossed in the various body parts.

While Mrs. Thomas simmered, Kate cleaned up the gore. Then, she delicately scraped the film of, um, "juices" that had congealed on the surface of the brew. These she set aside to sell as drippings on the street. After she removed the "meat," which had melted away from the bone, from the pots, she put the "meal" in burlap bags and put the bags in a crate. Then, she tossed the bones in the fireplace.

Kate talked a neighborhood boy into helping her bring the crate to the river, and while he walked away, she tossed the crate into the water. She was able to make six shillings pawning off the old woman's gold bridgework. And then she had another flash of entrepreneurial genius: She assumed Julia Thomas's identity in an effort to sell off her belongings and make even more coin off her crime.

Her plan didn't yield the dividends she had hoped for, however. She only made £68 on the entire haul. And then everything started to unravel.

In a couple of days, a few unwitting fisherman netted the crate containing what was left of Julia Thomas. Almost around the same time, neighbors started to become concerned that they hadn't seen Mrs. Thomas in a while. The pieces came together, and Kate Webster was the prime suspect in the murder of Julia Thomas. (Lord knows what kind of number this did on the unknowing folks who purchased Kate's "drippings" for their culinary endeavors.) Kate evaded her captors and managed to get back to Ireland, but she was soon picked up and dragged back to England.

Her trial lasted seven days. She swore to her innocence, even trying to pit the blame on the men who bought the contents of Mrs. Thomas's house, but judge and jury would have none of it. Kate Webster met her fate in the form of a noose on July 29, 1879.

Rosemary West *(1953-)*

MURDER, FILICIDE

Several women have made it into this ghoulish collection for falling in with the wrong men and their sexual perversions, and many have made the cut for killing their own children; but can one, without breaking down and vomiting, read the tale of a woman who brutally sexually assaulted and raped her own 16-year-old daughter—with her husband, the child's father—before killing her? Pause. Shudder. Bolt. Mommie Dearest, indeed!

Not since the 1960s and the Moors Murders perpetrated by Myra Hindley (page 113) and Ian Brady had Great Britain seen such a horrible display of mindless, senseless molesting and butchering by a couple. And at least Myra and Ian never reproduced.

Rosemary West was born Rosemary Pauline Letts in Northam, North Devon, England, on November 29, 1953. Certainly her childhood was not ideal, but it was child's play compared to the hell she would later inflict on her own brood. Rosemary's mother, Daisy, was a depressive; her father, Bill, a schizophrenic. The family moved around a lot.

Rosemary's sexual appetite was insatiable, and she had eked out quite a reputation for herself. When her nuclear family fell apart, Rosemary lived with her mother's sister, Glenys, and her husband. By 1969, Rosemary left her uncle and aunt (and they were not sorry to see her go) to live with her father.

In 1969, Rosemary, or "Dozie Rosy" as she was called, met Fred West, a fellow cracker. He came replete with his own set of childhood traumas, having learned early on,

the, um, pleasures, of incest, when he was seduced by his own mother before his voice had even changed. Fred was not the sharpest tool in the shed, and he left school altogether by age 15. By the time he was 16, he had his first "significant" relationship with a girl, which lasted for years. He and Catherine "Rena" Costello were on and off, but she was pregnant with someone else's spawn when they decided to get married. He never forgave Rena for bearing someone else's child, as was evidenced by his treatment of Charmaine Carol Mary once she was born. The kid never had a chance. In just a few years, she would become one of Fred and Rosemary's many victims. Rena and Fred had another child together, Anne Marie, whom Fred doted on. But despite this compensation, the marriage didn't last.

Enter Rosemary, all of 15 years old and about to embark on the ride of her life.

The romance was slow to start. Fred was in the process of committing various petty crimes and serving sporadic jail terms. In February of 1970, Rosemary found herself pregnant with daughter, and eventual victim, Heather. At this point, she was officially disowned by her father. She moved in with Fred and his two children, and soon found herself raising all the children when Fred was incarcerated yet again. Fred finally got divorced from Rena and married Rosemary in 1972. But by this point,

Charmaine was already missing. The depraved crimes of the Wests had begun.

In the coming years, Rosemary and Fred would lure several young girls back to their home. Each would take turns sexually abusing the girls, who would ultimately "disappear." By this time, the couple had turned their residence into a boardinghouse. Some of their victims had been lured back to the house as "nannies"; others were boarders; and still others simply befriended the couple.

By 1972, Rosemary and Fred had taken to sexually abusing Anne Marie, Fred's second child, and the one that he had sired with Rena. By the time the child was eight years old, she was repeatedly taken into the basement by her "parents," who performed all kinds of sadistic sex acts on the child. In the meantime, Rosemary was picking up some extra cash turning tricks, and eventually the couple had enough money to buy the home where they performed all their heinous acts.

Anne Marie finally ran away from home in 1980. This was fine with her parents, as, in part due to Rosemary's "career," several more mouths to feed had popped up in the West household. But there was only one that was "old" enough to partake in Mum and Dad's sexual deviancies: their firstborn, Heather. In 1987, after enduring years of

sexual abuse, Heather tried to get away from her parents by applying for a job as a camp counselor. She didn't get the position, but Rosemary and Fred pretended she did. Because that summer, Heather "disappeared"—that is, until her body was dug up years later, after her parents were caught.

In 1992, the gig was up. A girl who had escaped the Wests reported them to the police. In August of that year, Fred and Rosemary were arrested. Somehow they managed to get off. But their freedom was not to last. In February 1994, a search warrant was granted, and the property around the West home was excavated. What the police found was enough to turn a stomach or two.

By the end of the month, Fred completely broke and told authorities exactly where they should be digging. Ten bodies were found.

In 1995, before Fred went to trial, he hung himself in his jail cell, leaving Rosemary to face all the charges on her own. After her 8-week trial, she was convicted for all 10 counts of murder, and in October 1995, Rosemary West was handed 10 life sentences for the crimes she and Fred had committed. At the time of this writing, she is still fighting for an appeal.

Catherine May Wood *(see Lethal Nurses)*

Aileen Wuornos *(1956–)*
a.k.a. Lori Grady
a.k.a. Lee Blahovec
a.k.a. Cammie Marsh Greene

MURDER

She has been touted "the first female serial killer"; that, of course, is not true—even considering the other women who are included in this book. What makes people believe that she is, however, was her methodology: She selected a specific target to kill, and always killed in the same way. In 2001, Aileen Wuornos gave up appealing her sentence. She admitted her guilt, and has accepted her fate.

Born in Rochester, Michigan, on February 29, 1956 into the perfect setup for dysfunction (Aileen's parents were both teenagers when she was born, completely ill-equipped to handle the responsibility of raising Aileen and her younger brother, Keith), from an early age there seemed to be nowhere for the young girl to go but down a straight path to hell. Aileen's father, Leo Dale Pittman, may have been responsible for the unstable relationship Aileen had with sanity. Before her birth, her mother, Diane Wuornos, had already divorced Leo. Within a few years, he was in prison on charges of child molestation. In 1969, he was strangled by fellow inmates; not a surprise, for the fate of child molesters on

the inside is always a bleak one. Her mother abandoned Aileen and Keith with a baby-sitter when Aileen was barely three years old.

The children were eventually taken in by their maternal grandparents, who could not offer much in terms of a stable life for the young children. Their grandfather, Lauri Wuornos, was an insatiable drunk; their grandmother, Britta, an enabler. It wasn't until Aileen was 12 years old that she learned that Britta and Lauri weren't her real parents, and what had happened with Leo and Diane.

Aileen had hardly been what one would consider a "normal" child before that point. She and Keith got into more trouble than the average siblings. When she was six, Keith and Aileen experimented with lighter fluid and matches, leaving Aileen's face horribly burned and scarred for life. There was also a rumor—started by Aileen—that she and Keith had been lovers. This has never been confirmed.

In 1971, when Aileen was just 14 years old, she got pregnant and gave birth to a boy, but she never disclosed who the father was. This was March. The rest of the year, lo, the decade, would not improve. On July 7, Aileen's grandmother, Britta, died. The cause was cited as liver failure, but Diane suspected it was Lauri who did Britta in. This may have been true: Within a few years, Lauri committed suicide. Aileen and Keith went to live in foster homes instead of enduring the fate of being raised by the mother who had abandoned them. Then, in 1976, Keith died of throat cancer. As far as Aileen was concerned, from that point, she had no one.

Even before receiving the $10,000 she inherited from her brother's life insurance policy, Aileen headed out on her own. As a young girl with no education, beauty, or charm of any kind to fall back on, she delved into prostitution. And from the time she left her grandparents' home and jumped around in foster care, she was officially a drifter.

Aileen tried her hand at marriage in the mid-1970s. Lewis Fell was a fossil with one foot in the grave. Why she married him is not known. Perhaps she was seeking out a father figure. Perhaps it was because he was a man she wasn't threatened by. He could never beat or rape her; she was physically stronger than he was. For whatever the reason, it didn't last. Fell was granted an annulment on the grounds that Aileen routinely beat him with his own cane when she didn't get her way.

Instead of setting up a home of her own with the money she inherited from her brother, she chose to squander the cash on a new car and other such frivolities. She wrecked the car only a few months after she

purchased it. The next 10 years included a string of arrests, prison time, bad relationships with inappropriate men, more drifting, more prostitution, more petty crimes, more arrests, and more jail time.

In 1986, Aileen changed her sexual orientation when she met Tyria Moore, a 24-year-old lesbian, in Daytona, Florida.

Tyria was a maid at a local motel, but soon quit her job to be supported exclusively by Aileen through the various johns she was able to seduce for a buck here and there. They were both, admittedly, madly in love, at least for a short while. Even after the fireworks were snuffed out, the pair remained inseparable for the next four years, Tyria becoming a willing accomplice in Aileen's criminally charged schemes. Aileen's murders, however, would not be part of Tyria's involvement in the crimes.

All the years they were together, they drifted like land-bound flotsam and jetsam. Their crimes, by the standards that Aileen would soon set, were minor at best. A mugging here, an assault there, and a little vandalism thrown in for good measure. They went around under aliases: Aileen switching off from Susan Blahovec and Cammie Marsh Greene; Tyria sticking mainly with Tina Moore. Throughout Aileen's arrest record, one personality trait remains consistent: poor attitude. Even when she was on trial and facing death, Aileen never lost this aspect of her personality.

By the end of 1989, Aileen upped the ante in the crimes she committed. All of a sudden, middle-aged men, most of them truckers, began to disappear in Florida. Eventually their bodies would turn up naked and shot to death. It seemed just as soon as one was found and an investigation was underway, another dead trucker would pop up.

Later, during Aileen's trial, Tyria would admit that she knew what Aileen was up to, and while she tried to look the other way, she eventually had no choice but to leave her longtime consort and sometimes cohort.

How did police link the killings to the drifting, seemingly inconsequential prostitute Aileen Wuornos? It wasn't easy. Aileen was like the wind. She had no permanent address, no roots to dig up. When it looked like there was a pattern among the men who had been butchered, police realized they were after one suspect. Putting their feelers out, they were able to track the exploits of a pair of criminally charged lesbians. They eventually put the pieces together and, sifting through all the various aliases, they were able to pin the two women down as Tyria Moore and Aileen Wuornos. Tyria was easy to find. After leaving Aileen, she retreated home to

Pennsylvania to live with her sister. She agreed to help the police find Aileen.

The search began in 1989; it wasn't until 1991 that police finally found Aileen. Or more like it, until she turned herself in. Of course, this only happened after a well-orchestrated sting operation by police. Two undercover officers, posing as locals, met up with Aileen in a Florida bar called The Last Resort. They spent a night drinking with her, buying her beers. The next night, they busted her.

Perhaps Aileen already knew what she was in for. Maybe she had already been tipped off by Tyria, who still, at least at that point, retained some semblance of loyalty to her one-time love. Perhaps Aileen was following the case through the newspapers and got tired of running. In any case, on January 16, 1991, Aileen confessed. Well, kind of.

She told police that she had, in fact, killed those men. But her killings were done in self-defense. "I shot 'em cause to me it felt like a self-defending thing," she told police. "... I felt like if I didn't shoot 'em and I didn't kill 'em ... if they survived, my ass would be gettin' in trouble for attempted murder, so I'm up shit's creek anyway ... I mean, I had to kill 'em ... or it's like retaliation, too. It's like, 'you bastards, you were going to hurt me.'" She told police that they were (all) going to brutally rape her, and she had to protect herself and her own life. This is the story she stuck with all through her trial, and even throughout most of the time she served behind bars. Until she gave up, that is.

After Aileen's arrest, she finally found "family." A born-again Christian woman named Arlene Pralle had been following Aileen's case. Arlene took it upon herself to befriend the lost soul known as Aileen Wuornos and bring her some kind of "salvation." After countless letters and regular visits, Arlene decided to legally adopt Aileen. This was weird on one hand, because Aileen was about to be convicted for countless murders; on the other hand, Aileen was already 34 years old—it was kind of late to be adopted. Whatever. It mattered not to Arlene. As she told Aileen in the beginning: "You're going to think me crazy, but Jesus told me to write to you." To the press, of her dubious decision, she said, "It's as though a part of me is trapped in jail with her" and "If the world could know the real Aileen Wuornos, there's not a jury that would convict her."

Apparently, the world never knew the real Aileen. In a trial that began on January 14, 1992, Aileen was tried for the murder of her first victim, Richard Mallory. On January 27, the jury came back with their verdict: guilty. Aileen subsequently went on trial for a couple of the other murders, and just pled guilty to some of the others.

None of this did anything to preclude the attitude that the law in all of its forms had come to detest over the years, however. After the verdict was read, and Aileen was sentenced to the electric chair on January 31, she lashed out at the jury: "I hope your wife and children get raped in the ass." And then, after some colorful gesticulation, she let out a mumbled "Motherfucker."

Many rushed to make a quick buck to tell the story: A few police officers even tried to make book deals before the case went to trial. Aside from her "mother," Arlene, she had no friends. No allies. Even her beloved Tyria had turned against her in the end in an effort to save her own behind.

In the meantime, several books have been written about Aileen's life and crimes. In June 2001, an opera, *Wuornos,* opened in San Francisco. No one ever understood Aileen, but she was a subject of constant intrigue nonetheless.

During all the time she served, Aileen always proclaimed that she killed in self-defense. And her attorneys continued to appeal her case. That is, until July of 2001. By that time, she gave up. She told her accusers that she was guilty as charged. There was no self-defense involved. And she was literally begging to be executed. At the time of this writing, that poor lost soul still lives among us.

Dr. Alice Wynekoop
(1870–1951)

MURDER

The Oedipus Complex gone terribly awry… Or at least that's how psychiatrists have been trying to explain this odd case of murder by a mama who tried to alleviate her beloved son of his wifely burden.

Not since the Great Fire had Chicago seen such a senseless waste of life as it had when, in 1933, the young wife of ne'er-do-well Earle Wynekoop was found dead in her mother-in-law's basement-slash-operating room, naked and face-down on the operating table with a bullet in her back.

Dr. Alice Lindsay Wynekoop moved to Chicago with her husband and her young children in 1901. Frank and Alice were both respected physicians. Alice, especially, had made great strides. As a female professional at the turn of the twentieth century, she had long since shattered the low-hanging glass ceiling of the times. She was a well-respected promoter of women's rights and a suffragette. And when her husband died shortly after the move, she raised her children on her own, running her practice from the basement of the family home.

Of the Wynekoop children, one, Mary Louise, would die before reaching adulthood. The other daughter, Catherine Wynekoop, would follow in her parents' footsteps, growing up to become a respected physician. Frank and Alice's only son, however, would prove to be a disappointment—he was a shameless underachiever and ne'er do well, although Mommy always loved and favored him above the other children. In 1930, Earle finally made a go at being respectable, and the 27-year-old mama's boy married a cute, redheaded, 18-year-old, well-to-do heiress violinist from Indianapolis named Rheta Gardner. But marriage proved to be as challenging as any other aspect of adulthood to this perpetual Peter Pan. Within a few months of the nuptials, Earle was back on the prowl, bedding any pretty, or not-so-pretty—it mattered not—young thing that would have him. The lascivious cad was in the habit of leaving his young wife home alone with his mother (yes, they lived at the Wynekoop residence) for days at a time to go about a-philandering. It was during one of these forays that his marital problems were ended for him—and by his own mother, Alice.

Rheta and her mother-in-law had a tepid-to-cool relationship, and when her husband left for days at a time on his various extramarital forays, Rheta kept herself occupied by staying in her room, playing her violin. As Alice told it, one day Rheta was complaining of some unusual pains, and asked her mother-in-law if she wouldn't mind examining her. Also as Alice told it, she was glad to do anything to make her daughter-in-law more comfortable. Alice said that she had asked Rheta to give herself some chloroform so that she would be more comfortable during the exam. The violinist didn't know what the proper amount should be, and thus, overdosed. How did that explain the bullet wound? Terrified for her reputation, the good doctor admitted shooting the girl in the back to make it look like robbers or better yet, drug addicts, had broken in and killed the girl.

The police were utterly confused. Not only could they not make sense of such a senseless death, they could not make sense of Dr. Alice. She had been running around telling people that her daughter-in-law succumbed to tuberculosis. On top of that, a collection of varied individuals had come to the doctor's defense, vehemently exclaiming her innocence—but the doctor had not yet been suspected in the death.

Earle received the news of his wife's death and his mother's possible involvement when he was heading to the Grand Canyon on a train with his trollop du juor. And he actually cut his trip short.

When Earle arrived in Chicago, he told police that he had been home all the while, and that he was the one who killed his wife, not his mama. But Alice would not let her

son take the fall. She swore up and down that she was the killer and was ready to pay the price.

The relationship, that is, the nature of the relationship, between Alice and Earle, has always caused much speculation. While she may have just been an overly doting mother, love letters between the two eventually surfaced, which suggested a much more complicated attachment. Was Rheta's murder an act of vengeance? Did Alice imagine she was killing a rival, and not a daughter? As Alice and her son are both long dead, no one will ever really know the answer to this troubling question.

Alice's case went to trial, and within six months, she was found guilty of murder. She was sentenced to 25 years behind bars, of which she only served 16. She died a couple of years after she was released from prison, a ruined woman who would never enjoy the reinstatement of the reputation she had worked so many years to establish.

Andrea Yates (1965–)

FILICIDE

Never had there ever been such an outpouring of sympathy for a self-confessed murderess before Andrea Yates. And one who murdered all of her children in one tub of bathwater for that matter. Andrea Yates, the woman who was hailed a monster when she called the cops on herself in June 2001, has in the months since become a martyr, a poster child for depressives everywhere.

When the news broke in the quiet suburban neighborhood of Clear Lake, Texas, neighbors and friends of the Yateses were simply baffled. No one had ever heard Andrea Yates so much as raise her voice to her children, let alone anyone else. And there was never a question of whether the kids were abused. They most certainly were not. And, as many have noted, they were quite possibly the best-behaved kids in the neighborhood. So what happened?

Andrea Yates was born Andrea Pia Kennedy in 1965, to Jutta and Andrew Kennedy. She was quiet but studious in school, graduating second in her class at Milby High School. She was also captain of the swim team. She was a chronic overachiever who took a lot of pride in her accomplishments.

After high school, Andrea went on to nursing school, where she also excelled. She received her Bachelor's degree in nursing in 1986.

Nursing was a great fit for Andrea's personality. She was the ultimate caregiver, always putting herself behind whomever needed to be tended to at the time. She loved working, and stayed with it until her first child was born. From that point on, she was exclusively a mother, and had very little identity apart from that. Russell did not want her to work; he wanted her to stay home with the kids, and he wanted them to continue to have kids, as many as possible. It was also because of Russell that the family was Methodist (Andrea was born and raised Catholic) and that the home was filled with religious artifacts.

Russell had too much control.

Andrea Kennedy met Russell Yates in 1989; in April 1993, they married. Their first child was born 10 months later. The Yateses had five children: Noah, seven, John, five, Paul, three, Luke, two, and Mary, six months. And if that isn't enough for one person to handle around the clock, all of Andrea's children were home schooled, which meant Mom didn't get a break even for a couple of hours during the day.

On top of that, Andrea was also taking care of her 80-plus-year-old father, who was suffering from Alzheimer's. She had spread herself too thin. It was too much. When Andrea's father, Andrew Kennedy, died on March 12, it triggered the postpartum psychosis she had been experiencing on and off for a few years.

Andrea had been thinking about killing her children for a while: On the Morning of June 20, 2001, enough was enough. She finally snapped. She kissed her husband good-bye as he left for work. She knew her mother-in-law would be around in a couple of hours to help her out with the kids, so she had to act fast.

Andrea went to the bathroom and filled the tub with water. When it was filled, she summoned her children, one by one, placed them in the tub, and drowned them. While she was drowning the baby, little Mary, her oldest son, seven-year-old Noah came in and innocently asked his mama what she was doing. Before she could answer, he figured it out, and bolted. Andrea chased him down and dragged him to the tub, where she drowned him next to his already-dead baby sister. All of the children except Noah were found on the bed, lying under a sheet. Noah was still in the tub.

Certainly it is easy to feel sympathy for Andrea Yates and her mental condition when she committed these murders; but it's much more difficult to feel anything but horror and sympathy for all those children, especially Noah who was old enough to know what was going on, and to make of it that Mommy was the bad guy and that he needed to run for his life. What was going through that poor child's mind as his mother chased him down and drowned him?

Andrea Yates had emotional problems, and depression ran in her family. She was suffering from postpartum psychosis, a rare condition which is far more severe than the typical postpartum blues or more serious postpartum depression many new mothers feel. Andrea had her first bout with this affliction two years prior, right after her son Luke was born. During her illness, she tried to commit suicide. It was at this point that Andrea was put on serious meds, which she went off for a while. The reasons for this have not been made clear.

Andrea was on a daily antipsychosis cocktail of four different drugs: Haldol, Effexor, Remeran, and Wellbutrin. The Haldol, which was the cornerstone of her medications, was prescribed, as it generally is, to suppress psychotic hallucinations and visions. When Andrea murdered her children, she had, for some reason, been off the Haldol for about two weeks.

Additionally, Andrea had been hospitalized for another suicide attempt just weeks before she murdered her children. Hello! Cry for help, anyone? Why couldn't a nanny or baby-sitter be hired to help this woman—at least to change diapers or clean bathrooms or make dinner or something?

Yates was arrested on June 20. She was transferred to a psychiatric unit on July 24, and has been on constant suicide watch since her arrest. On September 12, it was decided that she was competent to stand trial.

The jury is still out on whether or not Andrea will be executed for her crimes (quite literally; at the time of this writing, all that is known is that a trial date has been set for January 7, 2002), but the district attorney is fighting for the death penalty. At the time of this writing, there are 55 women on death row in the United States; 9 for killing their children. Only Yates is putting up an insanity defense.

Bibliography

BOOKS

Bugliosi, Vincent, with Curt Gentry. *Helter Skelter: The True Story of the Manson Murders.* New York: Bantam Books, 1974.

Edmonds, Andy. *Bugsy's Baby: The Secret Life of Mob Queen Virginia Hill.* New York: Carol Publishing Group, 1993.

Furio, Jennifer. *Letters from Prison: Voices of Women Murderers.* New York: Algora Publishing, 2001.

Glut, Donald F. *The Dracula Book.* New Jersey: The Scarecrow Press, Inc., 1975.

Jones, Ann. *Women Who Kill.* Boston: Beacon Press, 1996.

Klock, Frank. *Predators: Tales of Infamous Women.* New York: Drake Publishers, Inc., 1974.

Moon, Tom. *Loyal and Lethal Ladies of Espionage.* Lincoln, NE: iUniverse.com, Inc., 2000.

Nelson, Bill. *Manson: Behind the Scenes.* Costa Mesa, CA: Pen Power Publications, 1997.

Newton, Michael. *Bad Girls Do It!: An Encyclopedia of Female Murderers.* Port Townsend, WA: Loompanics Unlimited, 1993.

Rafter, Nicole Hahn. *Encyclopedia of Women and Crime.* Phoenix: Oryx Press, 2000.

Schechter, Harold, and David Everitt. *The A to Z Encyclopedia of Serial Killers.* New York: Pocket Books, 1996.

Scott, Gini Graham. *Homicide: 100 Years of Murder in America.* Lincolnwood, IL: Roxbury Park, 1998.

PERIODICALS

Arnott, Richard D. "Bandit Queen Belle Starr." *Wild West.* August 1997, p. 34(8).

Atkinson, Jim. "Death and the Matrons." *Texas Monthly.* October 1996, p. 128.

"Bambi's Song—Inside and Out." *Maclean's.* April 27, 1992, p. 52.

"Behind the House of Horror." *U.S. News & World Report.* November 28, 1988, p. 12.

Berlins, Marcel. "Presumed Guilty." *The Guardian.* June 15, 2001.

Bickley, Claire. "A Head for Details." *Toronto Sun.* October 7, 2000.

"Black Widow Killer Executed." *The Washington Post.* March 31, 1998, p. A03.

"The Black Widow of Hamilton." *Maclean's.* September 10, 2001, p. 61.

Brady, Diane. "Heidi and the Mighty: Will the Alleged Movieland Madam Tell All?" *Maclean's*. August 23, 1993, p. 42.

Brower, Montgomery. "Unmasking a Murderous Mother, Crime Writer Ann Rule Closes the Book on Another Psychopath." *People Weekly*. September 14, 1987, p. 125.

Brown, Steven. "Serial Killer Aileen Wuornos the Subject of Opera Premiering Friday." *Knight-Ridder/Tribune News Service*. June 21, 2001.

"Burgert, Philip. "Former Trade Group Secretary Called Spy." *American Metal Market*. September 14, 1999, p. 2.

"But Who Would Want Her?" *Maclean's*. January 15, 2001, p. 19.

"Buttafinished: After Mary Jo's Shooting, Two Jail Terms for Joey and a Life in Scandal's Shadow, the Buttafuocos Break Up." *People Weekly*. July 3, 2000, p. 128.

"'California Dreamin': Fearing Extradition, Killer Kenneth Kimes Confesses to Irene Silverman's Murder." *People Weekly*. December 4, 2000, p. 87.

Carney, Thomas. "The Fugitive." *Los Angeles Magazine*. January 2000, p. 112.

Cartwright, Gary. "The Whole Shootin' Match." *Texas Monthly*. February 2001, p. 74.

Cohen, Jacob. "The Romance of Revolutionary Violence: The Kathy Power Case." *National Review*. December 13, 1993, p. 28(6).

Colloff, Pamela. "Bandits of the Century." *Texas Monthly*. December 1999, p. 157.

Cone, Tracie. "Convicted Murderer's Daughter Makes a Tearful Surprise Appearance." *Knight-Ridder/ Tribune News Service*. September 22, 1993.

————. "Landlady Found Guilty of Murdering 3 Tenants." *Knight-Ridder/Tribune News Service*. August 27, 1993.

"Cover Story: The Girl Who Almost Killed Ford." *Time*. September 11, 1995, p. 35.

Crittenden, Yvonne. "Keeler Reveals the Truth." *Toronto Sun*.

Curtis, Gregory. "Karla Faye Tucker: Because of Her, the Whole World Took a Second Look at the Death Penalty." *Texas Monthly*. September 1998, p. 134.

"Damsel of Death." *Time*. February 10, 1992, p. 31.

Daniels, Anthony. "In Darkest England." *National Review*. November 6, 1995, p. 30.

Davis, Alisha. "Lolita at Large." *Newsweek*. May 17, 1999, p. 92.

Davis, Don. "'I've Lost My Children, Please Don't Take My Life.'" *Cosmopolitan*. March 1998, p. 182.

———. "'Please Listen: I'm on Death Row and I'm Innocent.'" *Cosmopolitan*. February 1998, p. 196.

Dawson, Jill. "The End of Innocence?" *Marie Claire*. May 2001.

De La Cruz, Donna. "Attorneys for Mother and Son Proclaim Their Innocence." *Associated Press*. July 14, 1998.

Denson, Bryan. "Katherine Ann Power Turns Up in Oregon, Plans to Stay." *The Oregonian*. October 28, 1999.

Dingus, Anne. "Bonnie and Clyde." *Texas Monthly*. January 1997, p. 224.

Dolgoff, Stephanie, and Darlie Routier. "Life on Death Row." *Cosmopolitan*. March 1998, p. 186.

Draper, Roger. "A Tragedy Without a Hero." *The New Leader*. May 20, 1991, p. 3.

Duggan, Paul. "Texas Board Won't Spare Condemned Woman." *The Washington Post*. February 23, 2000.

———. "Texas-Sized Case of Injustice?: Defense Lawyer's Lapses Stir Doubts on Fairness Toward a Woman Facing Execution." *The Washington Post*. February 22, 2000.

Eftimiades, Maria. "Joey Gets His: The Amy Fisher Story Ends With a Jail Sentence." *People Weekly*. November 29, 1993, p. 48.

"End of the Line: Guilty of Murder, a Mother-and-Son Team of Grifters Faces Life in Prison—or Worse." *People Weekly*. June 5, 2000, p. 78.

Evans, Michael. "Duke Agreed to Visit Soviet Bastards." *UK Times*. April 28, 2000.

"Executing Tucker." *Maclean's*. February 16, 1998, p. 35.

"'Face-to-Face with Jesus': After a Long and Passionate Debate, Karla Faye Tucker Goes to Her Death." *People Weekly*. February 16, 1998, p. 157.

Fleming, Anne Taylor. "The Heiress." *Ladies Home Journal*. September 1996, p. 124.

Flowers, R. Barri. "The Sex-Slave Murders." *Cosmopolitan*. January 1997, p. 186.

"Forsaking All Others: The Real Betty Broderick Story Including Prison Interviews." *Publishers Weekly*. March 8, 1993, p. 60.

"Freedom Now: Jailed Seven Years for Shooting Mary Jo Buttafuoco, Amy Fisher Gets Forgiveness—and a Reduced Sentence." *People Weekly.* May 17, 1999, p. 80.

Fried, Joseph P. "She Goes by Madam, in Print and in Spirit." *The New York Times.* October 28, 2001.

"Fugitive Is Arrested in Bomb Plot; In '75, Woman Led FBI to Patty Hearst." *The Washington Post.* June 17, 1999, p. A16.

Gertz, Bill. "Early Cold War Spies Exposed." *Insight on the News.* August 7, 1995, p. 35.

Gleick, Elizabeth. "The Hard Case of Mary Bell." *Time International.* May 11, 1998, p. 38.

Goff, Liz. "The Dirty 30: The Borough's Most Notorious." *Queens Tribune.*

"Grandma's Last Roundup." *Time.* November 26, 1990, p. 39.

Green, Michelle. "The Faded Flower of a Great British Scandal: Christine Keeler Heeds a Last Call to the Limelight." *People Weekly.* April 24, 1989, p. 76.

Hancock, Lee. "Medical Records Outline Andrea Yates' Mental Decline." *Knight-Ridder/Tribune News Service.* September 4, 2001.

Hart, Jordana. "Inmate's Introspection: Longtime Fugitive Katherine Ann Power Talks of Her Life and Her Crime." *Knight-Ridder/Tribune News Service.* July 5, 1994.

"He Said 'No.': After Kent Walker Rejected His Mother Sante Kimes's Criminal Ways, She Made His Brother Kenny a Killer." *People Weekly.* May 7, 2001, p. 105.

"Hiding in Plain Sight: Kathleen Soliah and Her Terrorist Past Evaded the Law for Nearly 25 Years. Now Comes the Reckoning." *Time.* June 28, 1999, p. 44+.

Hill, Amelia. "Manson Disciple Pleads for Forgiveness After 32 Years." *The Observer.* June 24, 2001.

"Hola to You." *The Economist (US).* September 18, 1999, p. 62.

Hollandsworth, Skip. "Her Dark Places." *Texas Monthly.* August 2001, p. 114.

"Homolka Denied Early Release." *Maclean's.* March 19, 2001, p. 17.

"How a Hollywood Sting Operation Hooked Heidi." *People Weekly.* August 23, 1993, p. 56.

Hymowitz, Kay S. "Cries Unheard—Why Children Kill: The Story of Mary Bell." *Commentary.* September 1999, p. 68.

"Inn Cold Blood: Lizzy Borden Bed and Breakfast Museum in Fall River." *People Weekly.* August 5, 1996, p. 65.

"Justice for Sale: The Rosemary West Trial." *The Economist.* November 25, 1995, p. 53.

Kaihla, Paul. "Bambi's Story." *Maclean's.* September 23, 1991, p. 18.

"Katherine Ann Power." *People Weekly.* December 27, 1993, p. 88.

Kennedy, Dana. "Indecent Exposure." *Entertainment Weekly.* August 20, 1993, p. 8.

"Killing Her Way to Fame." *Time.* February 18, 1991, p. 45.

King, Florence. "Misanthrope's Corner." *National Review.* October 23, 2000.

Koltnow, Barry. "Heidi Fleiss Wanted Power, Fame and Fortune, but Ended Up with Notoriety Instead." *Knight-Ridder/Tribune News Service.* February 28, 1996.

Koury, Renee. "Alleged Member of '70s Radical Group Arrested in Minnesota." *Knight-Ridder/Tribune News Service*, June 17, 1999.

Kunen, James S. "Florida Cops Say Seven Men Met Death on the Highway When They Picked Up Accused Serial Killer Aileen Wuornos." *People Weekly.* February 25, 1991, p. 44.

"The Lady Vanishes." *People Weekly.* July 27, 1998, p. 58.

Lambert, Pam. "Alice Doesn't Live Here Anymore." *People Weekly.* October 4, 1993, p. 61.

————. "Heidi's High Life: Movietown Marriages Shake and Careers Quake as Hard-Partying High School Dropout Stands Accused of Being the 'Madam to the Stars.'" *People Weekly.* August 23, 1993, p. 50.

Lane, Christopher. "The Delirium of Interpretation: Rewriting the Papin Affair." *Differences: A Journal of Feminist Culture Studies.* Summer 1993, p. 24.

Lelis, Ludmilla. "Florida Judge Rules Female Serial Killer May End Appeals." *Knight-Ridder/Tribune News Service.* July 20, 2001.

Mackenzie, Hilary. "A Downhill Road." *Maclean's.* September 23, 1991, p. 24.

Many, Christine. "Follow-Up: A Second Chance." *Ladies Home Journal.* March 2000, p. 31.

Martin, Doug. "Buenoano Dies in Florida's Electric Chair." *The Gainsville Sun.*

Maull, Samuel. "Sante Kimes Allowed to Use Public Funds for Appeal." *The Associated Press.* November 1, 2000.

McCombs, Phil. "A Wanted Woman; The FBI Says It's Found 1970s Terrorist Kathleen Soliah. For Her Family and Friends, the Searching Has Just Begun." *The Washington Post.* July 1, 1999, p. C1.

McGraw, Dan. "Convert Convict Put to Death." *U.S. News & World Report.* February 16, 1998, p. 42.

Milkovits, Amanda. "The Pam Smart Case—10 Years Later." *Foster's Daily Democrat.*

Miller, Michael. "Manson's Legacy of Fear Lives on 30 Years Later." *Reuters.* August 9, 1999.

"Missing Banker May Have Had Links with Alleged Scam Artists." *India in New York Chronicle.* July 17, 1998.

Moore, Robert F., and Amy Mayron. "Fugitive Believed to be from Symbionese Liberation Army Arrested." *Knight-Ridder/Tribune News Service.* June 17, 1999.

"'Mommy and Clyde' Blaze Trail of Deceit, Death, and Lies Leads to Murder." *The Observer.* May 14, 2000.

"A Mother No More: A Woman Tells Police She Drowned Her Five Children. What Could Have Led Her to This Act of Madness?" *Time.* July 2, 2001, p. 30.

"Motherhood and Murder: Andrea Yates Was the Ultimate Caregiver—Until Depression and the Strains of Raising Five Children Drove Her to an Unspeakable Crime. Her Descent Into Darkness." *Newsweek.* July 2, 2001, p. 20.

"Myra Hindley: Mob Justice." *The Economist (US).* October 24, 1998, p. 2.

Neumeyer, Kathleen. "With No Remorse: The Continuing Story of Betty Broderick." *Ladies Home Journal.* March 1997, p. 128.

O'Meara, Kelly Patricia. "Did Drugs Distort Mother's Nature?" *Insight on the News.* August 13, 2001, p. 14.

Pattison, Kermit and Amy Mayron. "Friends Say 'Sara' Anything but a Terrorist." *Knight-Ridder/Tribune News Service.* June 18, 1999.

"Pauline Parker Found." *London Daily Mail.* January 6, 1997, p. 17.

Pearson, Patricia. "Behind Every Successful Psychopath." *Saturday Night.* October 1995, p. 50.

"A Pilgrim's Progress." *People Weekly.* August 5, 1985, p. 100.

Plummer, William. "Grieving Spouse or Black Widow? Police Say Pamela Smart Had Her 16-Year-Old Lover Murder Her Husband." *People Weekly.* February 4, 1991, p. 105.

Radish, Kris. "Absence of Trust: Bembenek Talks About Life in Prison." *Maclean's*. September 23, 1991, p. 22.

Radosh, Ronald. "Final Verdict: The KGB Convicts the Rosenbergs." *The New Republic*. April 7, 1997, p. 12.

———. "Socialist Heroes: Proof the Rosenbergs Spied." *The New Republic*. October 22, 1990, p. 12.

———. "The Venona Files." *The New Republic*. August 7, 1995, p. 25.

Ragan, David. "Stars Who Use the P Word." *Cosmopolitan*. February 1997, p. 157.

Rasmussen, Cecilia. "The Painful Ordeal of Tokyo Rose." *Los Angeles Times*.

Rosario, Ruben. "SLA Has Violent History of Domestic Terrorism." *Knight-Ridder/Tribune News Service*. June 17, 1999.

Roth, Edwin. "British Media Hampered by Strict Contempt Law." *Editor and Publisher*. September 17, 1994, p. 14.

Rudenko, Alexandra. "Hartwick Students Create Exhibit on Eva Coo." *The Daily Star*.

Rufford, Nicholas. "M15 Lifts Veil on Mata Hari's Luckless Lovers." *The Sunday Times*. January 24, 1999.

"Sante Kimes Appears in California Court After Extradition from New York." *The Associated Press*. June 20, 2001.

Sawicki, Stephen. "School Aide Pam Smart Coaxed Her Student Lover to Kill Her Husband—Only to Receive a Lesson in Justice." *People Weekly*. April 8, 1991, p. 93.

Schneir, Walter, and Miriam Schneir. "Cryptic Answers." *The Nation*. August 14, 1995, p. 152.

"78-Year-Old Faye Copeland's Death Penalty Overturned." *The Associated Press*. August 9, 1999.

Smolowe, Jill. "Hidden in Plain Sight: To Evade the Law During Her 23 Years as a Fugitive, Radical Kathleen Soliah Reinvented Herself as the Mom Next Door." *People Weekly*. July 26, 1999, p. 88+.

Stanley, Alessandra. "Case of the Classy Madam: A Blueblood's Bordello is Busted." *Time*. October 29, 1984, p. 39.

Sterngold, James. "'70s Radical Pleads Guilty in Bomb Plot." *The New York Times,* November 1, 2001.

———. "'70s Radical Reaffirms Guilty Plea." *The New York Times,* November 7, 2001.

———. "Comments by '70s Radical Cast Doubt on Plea Deal." *The New York Times,* November 2, 2001.

Surovell, Hariette. "Queenpins of the Cali Cartel." *Exquisite Corpse: A Journal of Letters and Life.* April/May 2000.

"Sweet Spinster Who Is One of the World's Lost Killers." *The Express.* January 6, 1997.

"Texas Mother's Murder Trial Set for Jan. 7." *The Washington Post.* October 4, 2001.

"Time Trek." *Current Events.* December 1, 2000, p. 2.

"Time Trip." *Current Events.* March 23, 2001, p. 2.

"The Trunk Murderess: Winnie Ruth Judd." *Publishers Weekly.* September 7, 1992, p. 86.

"The Twisted Saga of Karla Homolka." *Maclean's.* May 8, 2000, p. 23.

Walker, Kent, with Mark Schone. "My Mother and Brother Are Murderous Grifters. I Escaped Their Evil. Barely." *Talk.* May 2001, p. 77.

Waller, J. Michael, and Jamie Dettmer. "Cold War Spies Unmasked by Insight May Face Prosecution." *Insight on the News.* November 22, 1999, p. 6.

"Wife Held After Husband Found Dismembered." *The Detroit News.* April 17, 1996.

Yelin, Jessica. "Madam Ex: Is Heidi Fleiss Going Down for the Last Time?" *Los Angeles Magazine.* December 1995, p. 104.

WORLD WIDE WEB

Ackerman, Todd. "Postpartum Depression's Role Doubted." HoustonChronicle.com. June 25, 2001.

———. "Yates Had Taken Anti-Psychotic Drug." HoustonChronicle.com. June 25, 2001.

"Amy Fisher." The Official Amy Fisher Organization website.

Aiuto, Russel. "Lizzie Borden." The Crime Library website.

———. "The Rosenbergs: A Case of Love, Espionage, Deceit and Betrayal." The Crime Library website.

———. "The Borgias." Dark Horse Multimedia, The Crime Library website.

Banta, Shauna. "18th Century Women Pirates: Anne Bonny and Mary Read."

Bardsley, Marilyn. "Charles Starkweather and Caril Fugate." The Crime Library website.

———. "Paul Bernardo and Karla Homolka." The Crime Library website.

Bardwell, S. K., Mike Glenn, and Ruth Rendon. "Investigator: Mother Described Methodical Drowning of 5 Kids." HoustonChronicle.com. June 27, 2001.

"Barker, Ma." Britannica website.

Bernstein, Alan. "Mom Depicted as Private, Caring, Burdened." HoustonChronicle.com. June 27, 2001.

Bexte, Martina. "Who Was Mata Hari?" pagewise.com.

"Case for Appeal: Judy A. Buenoano." Emory University Law School website.

"Charles Manson." The Crime Library website.

Cobbey, Nan. "Jean Harris: A New Life After 12 Years' Prison Education." Episcopal Life website.

"Coffman, Cynthia Lynn." California Department of Corrections website.

"Countess Bathory." nocturnalsouls. virtualave.net.

"Debra Jean Milke's Story." debbiemilke.com.

Deutsch, Linda. "Soliah to Return Home for Now: Minnesota Mother and Former Fugitive Will Have Limited Freedom Until Trial." abcnews.com.

Doherty, Kieran, and Reuters. "Spy Scandal Rocks Britain." abcnews.com.

"Dorothea Puente: Killing for Profit." The Crime Library website.

dyarstraights.com. "Sayonara, 'Tokyo Rose' ... Hello Again, 'Orphan Ann'!" "Orphan Ann" Home Page.

"Elizabeth Bathory—the Blood Countess." BBC Online.

Erenreich, Barbara. "Susan Smith: Corrupted by Love?" Time.com. August 7, 1995.

"Exotic Performer and Notorious Spy Mata Hari." Women's Stories website.

"Famous Vampires: Elizabeth Bathory." darkness.org.

Federal Bureau of Investigation. "Barker-Karpis Gang Summary." FBI website.

Feldman, Claudia. "Yates' Mother Mystified by Children's Drownings." HoustonChronicle.com. July 5, 2001.

"First Woman on 'Top Ten' Caught." gotcha.com.

"Florida's Black Widow Executed." CNN.com.

Gado, Mark. "The Last Stop: Women in the Electric Chair." The Crime Library website.

"George 'Machine Gun' Kelly." alcatrazhistory.com.

"George 'Machine Gun' Kelly." fbi.gov.

Geringer, Joseph. "Betty Broderick: Divorce … Desperation … Death." The Crime Library website.

———. "Bonnie and Clyde: Romeo and Juliet in a Getaway Car." The Crime Library website.

———. "Darlie Routier: Doting Mother/ Deadly Mother." The Crime Library website.

———. "Diane Downs: Her Children Got in the Way of Her Love." The Crime Library website.

———. "Karla Faye Tucker: Texas' Controversial Murderess." The Crime Library website.

———. "Nannie Doss: Lonely Hearts Lady Loved Her Men to Death." The Crime Library website.

———. "Winnie Ruth Judd: 'The Trunk Murderess' In Perspective." The Crime Library website.

Glenn, Mike and Miriam Garcia. "5 Kids Found Slain in Clear Lake." HoustonChronicle.com. June 25, 2001.

"Grand Jury Indicts Mother Accused of Drowning Children." ABC News Online. July 30, 2001.

"Grandmother: I Was Right to Spy." The BBC News website, September 20, 1999.

"The Greenlease Kidnapping." FBI website.

Goldman, Teraisa J. "What Happened to Caril Ann Fugate of the Starkweather Murders?" True Crime Fanatic website.

Harper, Roy. "The Lynette 'Squeaky' Fromme Interview. Outershell.com.

Hasselbach, Ingo. "Death in the Desert: The Deborah Milke Story." truthinjustice.org.

"How They Found the Spy of the Century." The BBC News website, September 21, 1999.

Howard, Clark. "The True Story of Barbara Graham." The Crime Library website.

"In the News: This Week November 16, 1975." pophistorynow.com.

"Interview: Betty Broderick I 1997." Lexxicon website.

Johnson, Captain Charles. "A General History of the Pyrates." arthurransome.org.

Jones, Thomas L. "Ruth Ellis: The Last to Hang." The Crime Library website.

"Judge Overturns Faye Copeland's Death Sentence." Jefferson City News Tribune Online Edition. August 10, 1999.

Kaelin, James Charles. "Orphan Ann" ('Tokyo Rose')." earthstation1.com.

Kephart, Beth. "The Bad Seed." Salon.com. April 14, 1999.

"KGB Deep Background: Biographies." pbs.org.

Kidd, Paul B. "The Birnies: Australia House of Horrors." The Crime Library website.

"Konon Molody." CNN.com.

Kudish, Richard. "Alvin Karpis: Pursuit of the Last Public Enemy." The Crime Library website.

"Leslie van Houten Parole Hearing." Court TV Online.

Leveritt, Mara. "Two Girls' Roads Diverged." arktimes.com. March 24, 2000.

Levey, Curt A. "States Rights Are Also Civil Rights." *The National Law Journal.* December 4, 2000. The Center for Individual Rights website.

Linder, Doug. "The Rosenbergs Trial: An Account." University of Missouri—Kansas City Law School website.

"Lizzie Borden: The Trial of the Century, 1893." University of Missouri-Kansas City School of Law website.

"Lizzie Borden's Hatchet of Death and Stuff." roadsideamerica.com.

Locy, Toni. "For Jailed Kingpins, A Cocaine Kinship." washingtonpost.com, August 19, 1996, p. A01.

"M15 Watched Mata Hari." BBC News website, January 26, 1999.

MacGowan, Douglas. "Mary Ann Cotton." The Crime Library website.

MacLeod, Marlee. "Aileen Wuornos: Killer Who Preyed on Truck Drivers." The Crime Library website.

————. "Gerald and Charlene Gallego." The Crime Library website.

————. "Judith Ann Neelly: Death Row at 18." The Crime Library website.

————. "Marie Hilley: Inscrutable Black Widow." The Crime Library website.

"The Madeline Smith Story." fix.lawfirm.co.uk

Maloney, J. J. "The Greenlease Kidnapping." Crime Magazine website.

————. "Sharon Kinne: *La Pistolera.*" Crime Magazine Online.

Martin, John. "Hearst Saga Lives On: Reporter Remembers 1974 Kidnapping." abcnews.com.

May, Allan. "George 'Machine Gun' Kelly: Bank Robbing and Kidnapping Desperado." The Crime Library website.

McGraw, Seamus. "Judge Sends Gluzman to Prison for Life." northjersey.com. May 1, 1997.

McIntosh, Jim. "The Husband-Killer Who Shocked the Nation." apbnews.com. April 28, 2000.

"Melita Norwood: A Secret Life." The BBC News website, September 11, 1999.

"Mother, Son Convicted of Murdering New York Millionaire." CNN.com. May 19, 2000.

"Mother-Son Murderers Appear in L.A. Court." Channel 2000 website. June 28, 2001.

Nemo, John. "Leading a Double Life?: No Bail Yet for Alleged SLA Member." abcnews.com.

"Newspapers Tell How Mother Allegedly Killed Kids." CNN.com. June 23, 2001.

Noe, Denise. "Elizabeth Bathory: The Blood Countess." The Crime Library website.

———. "The Alice Crimmins Case." The Crime Library website.

———. "The Jean Harris Case." The Crime Library website.

———. "The Torturing Death of Sylvia Marie Likens." The Crime Library website.

O'Brien, Keith. "They Call Her Tokyo Rose." weeklywire.com. January 20, 1998.

"Olson Admits She's Kathleen Soliah." channel4000.com.

Olsen, Gregg. "Starvation Heights." starvationheights.com.

"Pamela Smart Accusing Fellow Inmates of Assault." NewStandard website, November 10, 1997.

"The Parker-Hulme Murder Case." library. christchurch.org.nz.

"The Patricia Campbell Hearst Page." patty-hearst.com.

Pavlik, Rick. "Cattle Kate Wilson: First Woman Hanged by Vigilantes." wondersofthewest.com.

Pergament, Rachel. "Susan Smith: Child Murderer or Victim?" The Crime Library website.

"Picture of the Day: Mata Hari." The HistoryNet website, October 15, 2000.

"Polly Adler's Brothel." dorothyparkernyc.com.

"Q&A: A Spy Revealed." The BBC News website, September 11, 1999.

"Q&A: Spy Scandal Under Scrutiny." The BBC News website, September 14, 1999.

Ramsland, Katherine. "Angles of Death: The Nurses." The Crime Library website.

———. "Bambi Bembenek." The Crime Library website.

"Ruth Ellis." BTopenworld website.

"Ruth Ellis." Divas—the Site website.

Ryan, Gail. "Wanted—Symbionese Liberation Army Suspects." Los Angeles Political Historical Society website.

"The Sara Jane Olson Case." patty-hearst.com.

Schiffmann, William. "An Heiress Abducted: Patty Hearst, 25 Years After Her Kidnapping." abcnews.com.

Scott, Shirly Lynn. "Mary Bell: Portrait of a Killer as a Young Girl." The Crime Library website.

Sealey, Geraldine. "'Black Widow' Executed." ABC News Online. February 25, 2000.

"'70s Fugitive in Court Today." cnn.com, June 17, 1999.

"Sex-Slave Murder Accomplice Released." *Las Vegas Review-Journal* website, July 18, 1997.

"Shayler: Why Norwood Will Be Spared." The BBC News website, December 20, 1999.

"SLA Member Biographies." patty-hearst.com.

"Starr, Myra Maybelle Shirley." The Handbook of Texas Online.

Steel, Fiona. "Addicted to Love: The Sunset Strip Murders." The Crime Library website.

———. "Murder on the Moors: The Ian Brady and Myra Hindley Story." The Crime Library website.

Taylor, Troy. "The House of 'Weird Death': The Mysterious Events at the Wynekoop Mansion." prairieghosts.com.

Teachey, Lisa. "DA Will Seek to Put Yates on Death Row." HoustonChronicle.com. August 9, 2001.

———. "Death Penalty Sought for Mom Accused of Drowning Kids." HoustonChronicle.com. August 8, 2001.

———. "Expert Details Yates' Psychosis." HoustonChronicle.com. September 19, 2001.

———. "Mom Charged in Drownings Moved to Psychiatric Unit." HoustonChronicle.com. July 24, 2001.

———. "Several Groups Rally Behind Drive to Assist Yates." HoustonChronicle.com. August 28, 2001.

"Texas Executes Betty Lou Beets for Husband's Murder." CNN.com. February 24, 2000.

"Texas Executes Betty Lou Beets." CBS News Online.

"Texas vs. Karla Faye Tucker: A Question of Mercy." Court TV Online.

Tolson, Mike. "Researchers Say 'Filicide' Not Rare." HoustonChronicle.com. June 25, 2001.

———. "What Now for Andrea Yates?" HoustonChronicle.com. July 1, 2001.

Transcripts of the Amy Fisher Trial, Hard Copy: "Amy Fisher Tape She Sent to Paul Makely While in Prison," September 27, 1992; "Statement Rose and Elliot Fisher Read After Amy's Sentencing," December 2, 1992; "Statement Read by Mary Jo Buttafuoco at Amy's Sentencing," December 2, 1992; "Lolita's Last Stand," June 6, 1997." The Official Amy Fisher Fan Club website.

Vallee, Brian. "Evelyn Dick—in a New Light." The Hamilton Spectator website.

Warren, Audrey. "Andrea Yates' Siblings: Depression Runs in Family." HoustonChronicle.com. June 28, 2001.

———. "Friends Say Yates They Knew Couldn't Hurt Anyone." HoustonChronicle.com. June 26, 2001.

White, Jerry. "Texas Executes 62-Year-Old Great Grandmother Betty Lou Beets." World Socialist website. February 26, 2000.

"WWII Broadcaster Tokyo Rose (1916–)." Women's Stories.

INDEX

About the Author

Francine Hornberger is the owner of Hornberger Publishing Services, a packaging, writing, and editorial firm based in New York City. She has profiled celebrities for *People* magazine online, and, as Maggie Marron, is the author of a dozen celebrity-profile books.

ALPHA

KNOWLEDGE FOR LIFE

TITLES BY ALPHA BOOKS

Al Qaeda
ISBN: 0-02-864352-6
Paul L. Williams
Price: $14.95

Bear-Proof Investing
ISBN: 0-02-864204-X
Kenneth E. Little
Price: $21.95

Blindsided
ISBN: 0-02-864309-7
Edie Milligan
Price: $12.95

Business is a Contact Sport
ISBN: 0-02-864163-9
Tom Richardson & Augusto Vidaurreta
Price: $24.95

Become a Recognized Authority
ISBN: 0-02-864283-X
Robert W. Bly
Price: $18.95

Everything I Learned About People, I learned from a Round of Golf
ISBN: 0-02-864342-9
John Andrisani
Price: $16.95

Life's Big Questions
ISBN: 0-02-864302-X
Pastor William R. Grimbol & Rabbi Jeffrey Astrachan
Price: $12.95

Mistresses of Mayhem
ISBN: 0-02-864260-0
Francine Hornberger
Price: $16.95

Save Energy, Save Money
ISBN: 0-02-864279-1
Alvin Ubell & George Merlis
Price: $14.95

Windfall
ISBN: 0-02-864205-8
Marla Brill
Price: $24.95

ALSO FROM ALPHA BOOKS